PRINCE2

CCTA
Central Computer and Telecommunications Agency

LONDON: THE STATIONERY OFFICE

First published1996
Revised edition 1998
Fourth impression (with amendments) 1999
Ninth impression 2001

ISBN 0 11 330855 8

Published by agreement with CCTA and the Controller of HMSO by:

    The Stationery Office Ltd
    St Crispins
    Duke Street
    NORWICH NR3 1PD

For further information regarding this publication and other CCTA products, please contact:

    Help Desk
    CCTA
    Rosebery Court
    St Andrews Business Park
    Norwich NR7 0HS
    Telephone (01603) 704567

Published by The Stationery Office and available from:

The Stationery Office
(mail, telephone and fax orders only)
PO Box 29, Norwich NR3 1GN
General enquiries/Telephone orders 0870 600 5522
Fax orders 0870 600 5533

www.thestationeryoffice.com

The Stationery Office Bookshops
123 Kingsway, London WC2B 6PQ
020 7242 6393 Fax 020 7242 6394
68-69 Bull Street, Birmingham B4 6AD
0121 236 9696 Fax 0121 236 9699
33 Wine Street, Bristol BS1 2BQ
0117 926 4306 Fax 0117 929 4515
9-21 Princess Street, Manchester M60 8AS
0161 834 7201 Fax 0161 833 0634
16 Arthur Street, Belfast BT1 4GD
028 9023 8451 Fax 028 9023 5401
The Stationery Office Oriel Bookshop
18-19 High Street, Cardiff CF1 2BZ
029 2039 5548 Fax 029 2038 4347
71 Lothian Road, Edinburgh EH3 9AZ
0870 606 5566 Fax 0870 606 5588

The Stationery Office's Accredited Agents
(see Yellow Pages)

and through good booksellers

Printed in the United Kingdom for The Stationery Office
TJ004006 04/01 C50 9385 14667

Acknowledgements

The consortium of Duhig Berry, WS Atkins and Penzer Allen, under contract to CCTA, is acknowledged for the design and development of PRINCE 2. Parity Consulting is acknowledged for assisting the consortium in the design and development of the PRINCE 2 Process Model.

Parity Consulting and Pearce Mayfield Associates, under contract to CCTA, are acknowledged for providing project assurance to the PRINCE 2 Project Board.

CCTA would also like to thank the following individuals and organisations for their contributions and support throughout the design and development of PRINCE 2.

Mike Allen	Department of Education and Employment
Rob Herson	Parity Consulting
Jeremy Cox	Parity Consulting
Patrick Mayfield	Pearce Mayfield Associates
Colin Bentley	Hampshire Training Consultants
Dick Bennett	Duhig Berry
Alan Berry	Duhig Berry

In particular, CCTA would like to express special thanks to all members – over 150 individuals and organisations – of the PRINCE 2 User Review Panel, and the large number of other contributors, who gave their time freely to input ideas and comments during the Quality Reviews.

Foreword

Nowadays, most organisations are experiencing unprecedented levels of change. Change has become a way of life for organisations that need to remain effective and competitive in order to thrive. It is essential to manage the inherent risk associated with change and innovation.

Projects bring together resources, skills, technology and ideas to deliver business benefits or to achieve business objectives. Good project management helps to ensure that these benefits or objectives are achieved within budget, within time and to the required quality.

PRINCE is a project management method designed to provide a framework covering the wide variety of disciplines and activities required within a project. The focus throughout PRINCE is on the business case, which describes the rationale and business justification for the project. The business case drives all the project management processes, from initial project set-up through to the finish of the project.

Many organisations are employing the skills and services of external suppliers, working alongside in-house resources, to enhance their ability to deliver successful projects. PRINCE provides a mechanism to harness these resources and enable the project team to work together effectively.

PRINCE embodies many years of good practice in project management and provides a flexible and adaptable approach to suit all projects.

I commend the PRINCE approach to you. May PRINCE help you to achieve successful outcomes to your projects!

Bob Assirati
Chief Executive, CCTA

Contents

Introduction

1   Introduction

PRINCE was established in 1989 by CCTA (the Central Computer and Telecommunications Agency). The method was originally based on PROMPT, a project management method created by Simpact Systems Ltd in 1975. PROMPT was adopted by CCTA in 1979 as the standard to be used for all Government information system projects. When PRINCE was launched in 1989, it effectively superseded PROMPT within Government projects. PRINCE remains in the public domain and copyright is retained by the Crown. PRINCE® is a registered trademark of CCTA.

Projects may exist in their own right, may have relationships with other projects, or may be part of a larger programme of work. PRINCE is applicable in all of these situations.

1.1   Why use a project management method?

Project failures are all too common – some make the headlines, but the vast majority are quickly forgotten. The reasons for failure are many and varied.
Some common causes are:

- lack of co-ordination of resources and activities

- lack of communication with interested parties, leading to products being delivered that are not what the customer wanted

- poor estimation of duration and costs, leading to projects taking more time and costing more money than expected

- insufficient measurables

- inadequate planning of resources, activities, and scheduling

- lack of control over progress, so that projects do not reveal their exact status until too late

- lack of quality control, resulting in the delivery of products that are unacceptable or unusable.

Without a project management method, those who commission a project, those who manage it and those who work on it will have different ideas about how things should be organised and when the different aspects of the project will be completed. Those involved will not be clear about how much responsibility, authority and accountability they have and, as a result, there will often be confusion surrounding the project. Without a project management method, projects are rarely completed on time and within acceptable cost – and this is especially true of large projects.

A good project management method will guide the project through a controlled, well managed, visible set of activities to achieve the desired results. PRINCE adopts the principles of good project management to avoid the problems identified above and so helps to achieve successful projects. These principles are:

- a project is a finite process with a definite start and end

- projects always need to be managed in order to be successful

- for genuine commitment to the project, all parties must be clear about why the project is needed, what it is intended to achieve, how the outcome is to be achieved, and what their responsibilities are in that achievement.

1.2   What is PRINCE?

PRINCE (**PR**ojects **IN** Controlled Environments) is a structured method for effective project management. It is a *de facto* standard used extensively by the UK

Government and is widely recognised and used in the private sector, both in the UK and internationally. PRINCE, the method, is in the public domain, offering non-proprietorial best-practice guidance on project management. PRINCE® is, however, a registered trademark of CCTA.

The key features of PRINCE are:

- its focus on business justification
- a defined organisation structure for the project management team
- its product-based planning approach
- its emphasis on dividing the project into manageable and controllable stages
- its flexibility to be applied at a level appropriate to the project.

1.3   Benefits of using PRINCE

PRINCE provides benefits to the managers and directors of a project and to an organisation, through the controllable use of resources and the ability to manage business and project risk more effectively.

PRINCE embodies established and proven best practice in project management. It is widely recognised and understood, providing a common language for all participants in a project. PRINCE encourages formal recognition of responsibilities within a project and focuses on what a project is to deliver, why, when and for whom.

PRINCE provides projects with:

- a controlled and organised start, middle and end
- regular reviews of progress against plan and against the business case
- flexible decision points
- automatic management control of any deviations from the plan
- the involvement of management and stakeholders at the right time and place during the project
- good communication channels between the project, project management, and the rest of the organisation.

Project Managers using PRINCE are able to:

- establish terms of reference as a pre-requisite to the start of a project
- use a defined structure for delegation, authority and communication
- divide the project into manageable stages for more accurate planning
- ensure resource commitment from management is part of any approval to proceed
- provide regular but brief management reports
- keep meetings with management and stakeholders to a minimum but at the vital points in the project.

Those who will be directly involved with using the results of a project are able to:

- participate in all the decision making on a project
- if desired, be fully involved in day-to-day progress
- participate in quality checks throughout the project
- ensure their requirements are being adequately satisfied.

For senior management PRINCE uses the 'management by exception' concept. Senior managers are kept fully informed of the project status without having to attend regular, time-consuming meetings.

There are many organisations providing training, consultancy and tools services for PRINCE, thus ensuring a competitive supply. In addition, there is an active user group dedicated to the support, promotion and strengthening of the method.

1.4   Structure of the manual

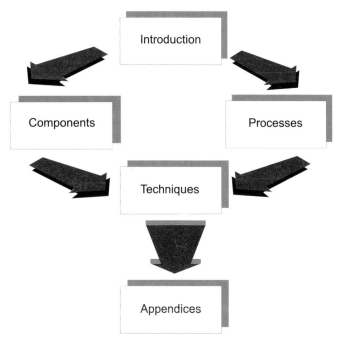

Figure I–1: Structure of the manual

There are five major parts to this manual, as shown in Figure I–1:

- *Introduction* presents the basic principles governing project management and how PRINCE addresses them; it also shows how PRINCE fits with related aspects such as programme management, quality management and the management of risk.

- *Components* explains and describes the major elements of project management, such as organisation and control, and how PRINCE incorporates them. These components represent the 'raw materials' of good project management, including quality management and the management of risk.

- *Processes* describes the PRINCE process model, explaining what has to be done to manage the project by bringing together and applying the 'raw materials' in a successful manner.

- *Techniques* explains the various techniques of project management that are unique to PRINCE.

- *Appendices* offers Product Description outlines for PRINCE management products, role descriptions, a series of 'healthcheck' questions for organisations to ask themselves when using PRINCE, and a comparison between the Quality Systems standard, ISO 9001, and PRINCE.

In addition, there is a full Glossary of terms.

1.5   Using the manual

This manual is aimed at people who will be playing a part in a PRINCE project, or who wish to understand how PRINCE contributes to the project management process; this would include senior managers responsible for the overall direction of a project, Project Managers, project auditors, quality assurance personnel and members of the project team. In addition, line managers of project personnel may find it useful to gain an appreciation of their staff's involvement in a project by reviewing the *Introduction*.

This manual has been designed to provide a complete reference to the PRINCE method. As such, the entire manual provides essential reading for all Project Managers. However, the following is offered as a focus for specific groups:

- for Project Managers coming to PRINCE for the first time
    - read and understand Section 2.3 *PRINCE in context* and Section 2.4 *Overview of PRINCE* of Chapter 2 *An introduction to PRINCE* to appreciate the overall approach PRINCE takes to creating and managing the project
    - read and understand the *Components* section (Chapters 3 to 11) in order to familiarise themselves with the interaction between the components and the processes
    - use the process model, described in Chapter 12 *Introduction to Processes*, as the basis for planning a project and deciding on resource requirements.

- for Project Managers already familiar with PRINCE
    - read and understand the process model, described in the *Processes* section, to appreciate the changes of emphasis and process-driven approach.

- senior managers who will be involved in the project at Project Board level should gain an appreciation of PRINCE and their roles within a project by studying the *Introduction* (Chapters 1 and 2), *Organisation* (Chapter 4), *Introduction to Processes* (Chapter 12), and the description of *Directing a Project (DP)* (Chapter 15) within the *Processes* section of the manual.

- Programme Managers with PRINCE projects in their programme should gain a clear understanding of the approach PRINCE takes to creating and managing a project.

1.6   PRINCE terminology

The following list of terms are the most important to understand with regard to PRINCE and are all included in the Glossary. Readers should familiarise themselves with them to prevent any possible confusion when using PRINCE.

Product, deliverable or **outcome** is used to describe everything that the project has to create or change, however physical or otherwise these may be. Results of projects can vary enormously from physical items, such as buildings and machinery, to intangible things such as culture change and public perception.

Customer is used to represent the person or group who has commissioned the work and will be benefiting from the end results.

User is defined as the person or group who will use or operate the final product. In some situations, the Customer and User may be the same group of people.

Supplier is used to mean the group that is providing specialist resources and skills to the project, or is providing goods and services, to create the project outcome required by the Customer and Users.

Business Case is used to define the information that justifies the setting up, continuation or termination of the project. It answers the question 'Why should this project be done?' It is updated at key points throughout the project.

Programme is a collection of projects that together achieve a beneficial change for an organisation.

2   An introduction to PRINCE

2.1   What is a project?

PRINCE defines a project as:

> *'a management environment that is created for the purpose of delivering one or more business products according to a specified business case'*

Another definition of a project might be

> *'a temporary organisation that is needed to produce a unique and pre-defined outcome or result at a pre-specified time using predetermined resources'*

PRINCE additionally supposes that those responsible for the project will not have experience of working together to produce a similar set of outcomes or results for the same Customer in the past; that co-ordination between those working on the project will need to be well organised; and that the responsibilities shared amongst those undertaking the work, those managing it and those sponsoring it will need to be clearly defined.

A PRINCE project, therefore, has the following characteristics:

- a finite and defined lifespan

- defined and measurable business products

- a corresponding set of activities to achieve the business products

- a defined amount of resources

- an organisation structure, with defined responsibilities, to manage the project.

Each project falls within a specific business context. A project may be stand-alone, it may be one in a sequence of related projects, or it may form part of a programme or corporate strategy.

A project, by its nature, is a temporary structure, created to achieve a specified business benefit or objective. When the work has been completed, the project is disbanded.

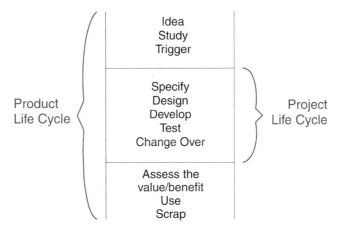

Figure 2–1: Product and project life cycles

A project has a life cycle, which is the path and sequence through the various activities to produce the final product. The term 'life cycle' is also used to describe the life of a product. The two should not be confused. Figure 2–1 shows how a **product** life cycle might start from the initial idea or conception, through to the operation of the product, finishing with the eventual scrapping of the product when it comes to the end of its usefulness. The project life cycle covers the tasks of specifying and designing a product, through to its testing and hand-over into operational use. PRINCE covers **the project life cycle** plus some pre-project preparation.

2.2   The scope of PRINCE

Figure 2–2 shows where PRINCE fits into a business and project environment. PRINCE is not intended to cover all subjects relevant to project management. The project management techniques and tools needed will vary according to the project type and the corporate environment. There are also certain aspects of project management that are well covered by existing and proven methods and are therefore excluded from PRINCE. Examples of these aspects are:

- people management techniques such as motivation, delegation and team leadership

- generic planning techniques such as Gantt Charts and Critical Path Analysis

- risk management techniques

- the creation and management of corporate quality management and quality assurance mechanisms

- business case management, budgetary control and earned value analysis.

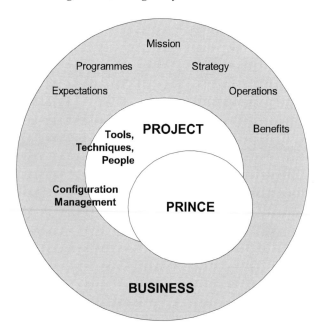

Figure 2–2: The PRINCE relationship with projects and business

PRINCE covers the management of the project, and the management of the resources involved in carrying out the activities of the project. It does not cover the specialist techniques involved in the creation of the products. This is the job of other methods, although PRINCE must interface with them to enable information on such areas as estimating, for example, to be provided for project management.

Although PRINCE is centred on the project, it begins before the project does by preparing the ground so that the project starts in an organised and controlled manner.

Another often critical project area is procurement. PRINCE assumes that the project is run within the context of a contract. The contracting process is not included within the method itself. Contracting and procurement are themselves technical activities (like software engineering) and can therefore be managed using the PRINCE method. If procurement or contracting is to be undertaken during the early stages of the project, changes may be needed to the Project Board and other parts of the Project Management Team once these stages have been completed. For example, it may be appropriate to have a senior representative of the contractor organisation as a member of the Project Board (in the role of Senior Supplier).

Contract and procurement issues will also increase the importance of a complete and accurate Project Initiation Document (PID) which will need to be kept in line with the text of the contract(s). Where PRINCE describes project roles, the conversion of these into formal job definitions for a particular project will also require careful attention, for example Project Assurance, the approval of Product Descriptions, and the allocation of risk 'ownership'.

2.3   PRINCE in context

PRINCE is designed to be used on any type of project in any environment. It contains a complete set of concepts and project management processes that are the minimum requirements for a properly run and managed project. However, the way PRINCE is applied to each project will vary considerably, and tailoring the method to suit the circumstances of a particular project is critical to its successful use.

PRINCE projects are always focused on delivering specified products to meet a specified Business Case. There will be many higher-level issues surrounding the project. These will need to be dealt with by other methods and approaches, such as programme management. PRINCE is aimed at the middle ground between these higher-level, more strategic, issues and the specialist production processes underneath project management.

Few projects can be completed entirely in isolation from other work. PRINCE projects may exist as part of a programme, contributing to the realisation of benefits of a larger organisational change. In a programme context, the outputs from one project may be used as input by another project. There may be other dependencies between projects, such as shared resources. PRINCE places strong emphasis on the products that the project is required to deliver and so provides a firm basis for defining the boundaries.

Within any project there are various groups of people with an interest in the project and its outcome, including:

- Customers, who have commissioned the work and will be benefiting from the end results.

- Users, who will use or operate the final product; the Customer and User may be the same group of people in some situations.

- Suppliers, who are providing specialist resources and/or skills to the project or are providing goods and services.

- sub-contractors, who provide products or services to the Supplier.

The Customer/Supplier environment assumes that there will be a Customer who will specify the desired outcome, make use of the final products and (in most cases) pay for the project, and a (prime) Supplier who will provide resources and skills to create that outcome. PRINCE is written from the standpoint that these two parties come from separately managed areas and typically from commercially separate organisations. Where, as will often be the case, both Customer and Supplier have a common management, this will influence the composition of the Project Management Team.

Whatever the team composition, the Customer should always participate (throughout the project) in the creation and verification of products.

2.4   Overview of PRINCE

PRINCE is a process-based approach to project management. The processes define the management activities to be carried out during the project. In addition, PRINCE describes a number of components that are applied within the appropriate activities. Figure 2–3 shows the components positioned around the central process model. Each component is described in further detail, in the *Components* section of this manual, showing how the particular subject affects project management and providing guidance on when and how to address the issues.

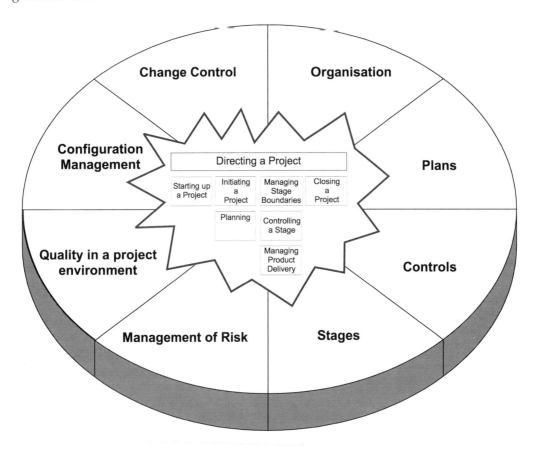

Figure 2–3: PRINCE processes and components

The PRINCE process model, shown in Figure 2–4, consists of eight distinctive management processes, covering the activities from setting the project off on the right track, through controlling and managing the project's progress, to the completion of the project. The common Planning process is used by many of the other processes.

Throughout the process model there are various project management products that are the inputs and outputs of each process. Planning in PRINCE is product-based. Each product is identified and defined, and its delivery is controlled. The responsibilities for the various activities, decision-making and support requirements are fully defined within the *Processes* section of this manual.

The product-based planning technique also enables the project to state the standard of quality to which each product must conform. In addition, quality testing mechanisms are specified in order to prove that the products are meeting their required quality standard. PRINCE describes a specific technique, Quality Review, that is particularly suitable for the quality testing of document-based products. There is a wide range of additional testing techniques that might be appropriate for the project. The Project Quality Plan and the Stage Quality Plans must state what these are, when and how they will be applied and by whom.

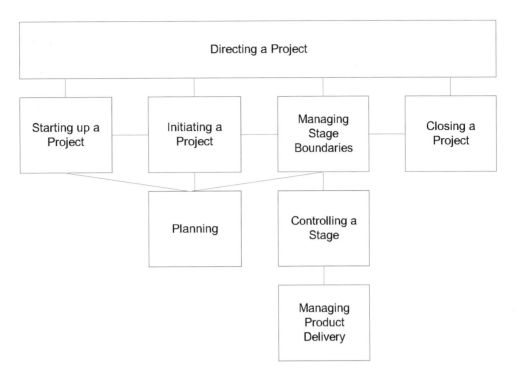

Figure 2–4: The PRINCE process model

The project, by its nature, is set up to deal with change, and the future is always less predictable than with routine work. In addition, projects can be large and complex, dealing with novel or unusual factors. Risk is therefore a major factor to consider during project management, and PRINCE incorporates the management of risk into its processes.

The process model provides the flexibility to establish a number of Stages, each forming a distinct unit for management purposes. Each Stage has a defined set of products or outcomes, activities, a finite lifespan, resources and an organisational structure. The completion of each Stage is determined by the satisfactory completion of the agreed products. Stage boundaries need to be appropriate to the particular project and may be chosen according to one or more of the following:

- the sequence of delivery of the products

- the grouping of products into self-consistent sets

- the natural decision points for feedback and review.

Whatever the nature or size of the project, PRINCE defines an Initiation Stage that covers the planning and definition of the project. The Initiation Stage enables a management review before making any commitment to later Stage(s) and their associated resources and costs.

In some situations, a study might be required to investigate the situation and determine options for the way ahead. Using PRINCE, the optimum approach would be to handle the study as a separate and distinct project, and then operate a second project to implement the results of the study.

Figure 2–5 shows the (relatively) simple life cycle for a study-type project. It has one Project Plan, Business Case and set of risks. The possible options may each vary enormously in their cost and timescales. Each option would have a different Project Plan, Business Case and set of risks. Having chosen the appropriate option, the second project would proceed with a straightforward set of project information.

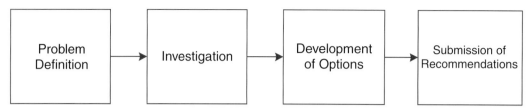

Figure 2–5: Life cycle of a study project

PRINCE enables the project to capture and retain the business benefits that are the driving force behind the project itself. The benefits are stated in the project's Business Case. Benefits can take many different forms:

- financial, in the form of additional profit or avoided costs

- strategic, by providing a platform to move towards one of the organisation's strategic aims

- legislative, by fulfilling some absolute requirement laid down by head office or a Government minister.

Throughout a PRINCE project, the Business Case is reviewed and progress is measured against any revised expectations of achieving defined benefits. During any project there are often opportunities to discover new benefits, which may enhance the project's outcome or indeed impact on another project. However, any deviations from the original Business Case must be controlled through the Project Board.

During the project, the specification of products will inevitably need to change. These changes need to be controlled because they can easily destroy the project's chance of success. Controlling changes is linked to version control, a topic that is covered within PRINCE under Configuration Management and Change Control (see Chapters 10, 11 and 22). Configuration Management is an essential part of project control as it is focused on controlling the products being delivered, knowing where they are at any point in time, what their status is, who is working on them, and which is the latest version.

Components

3   Introduction to the PRINCE components

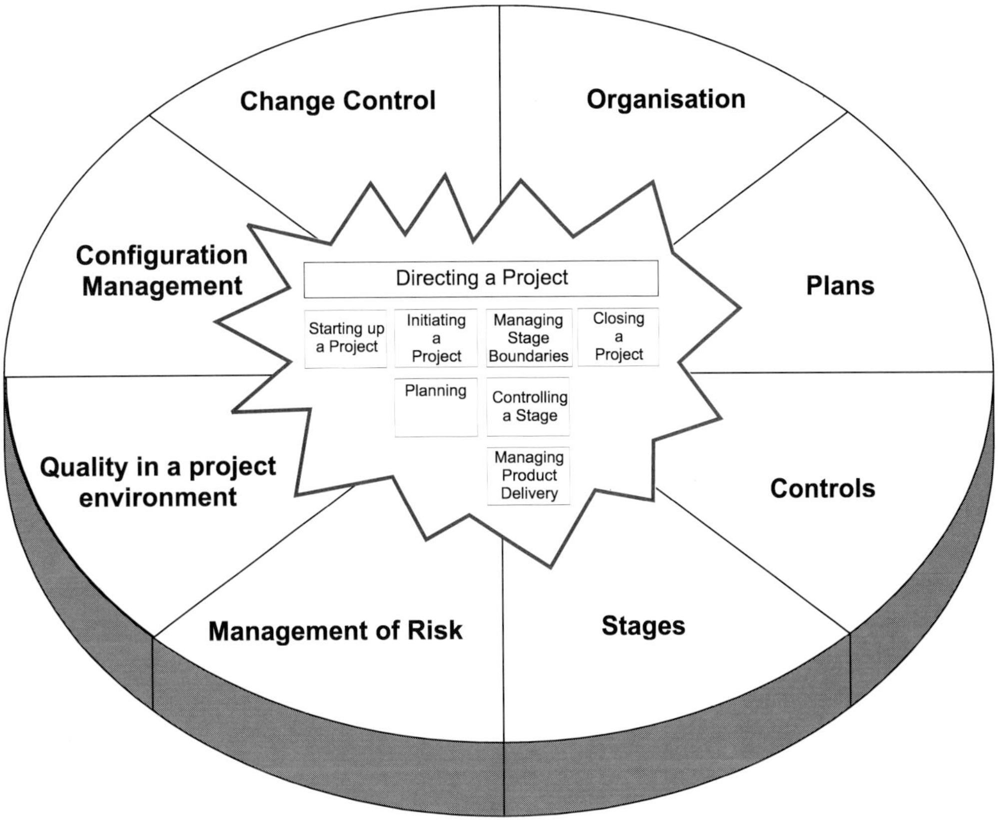

Figure 3–1: The PRINCE components

As shown in Figure 3–1, PRINCE has a number of components that are used by the processes:

- Organisation
- Plans
- Controls
- Stages
- Management of Risk
- Quality in a project environment
- Configuration Management
- Change Control.

The following chapters of the manual explain the philosophy of these components and how they should be used.

There are also *Hints and tips* on using and tailoring the components to suit various situations and types of project.

4   Organisation

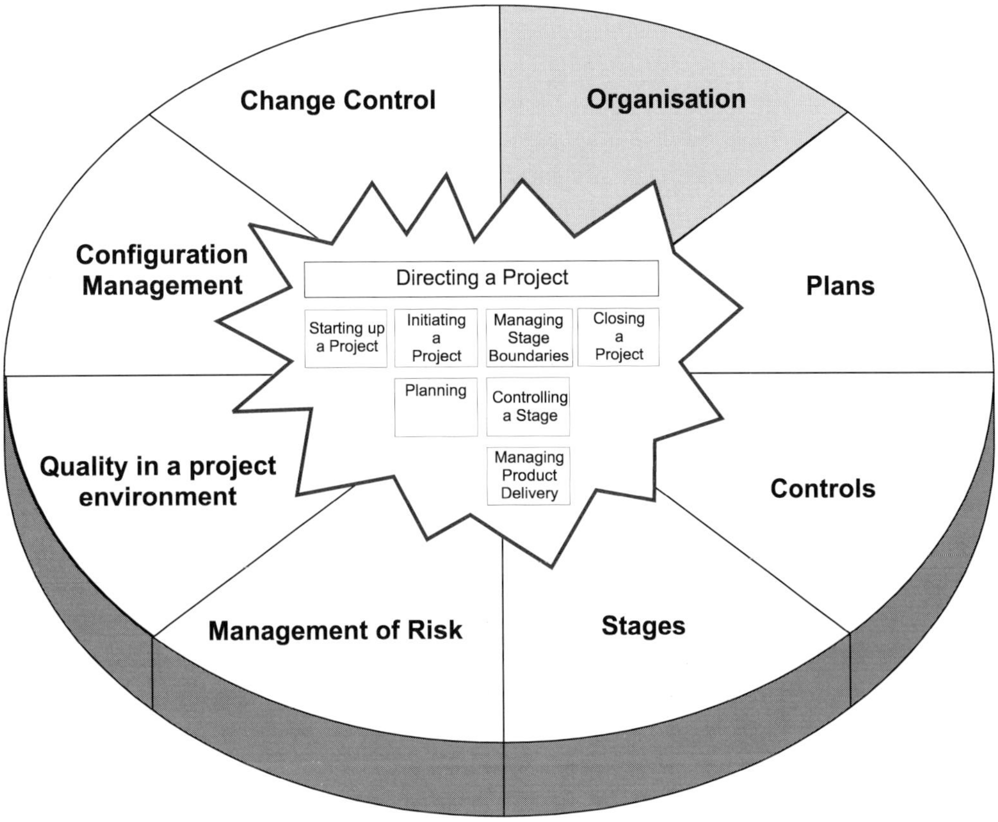

Figure 4–1: Organisation in the PRINCE template

4.1   Overview

The PRINCE project management structure is based on a Customer/Supplier environment. The structure assumes that there will be a Customer who will specify the desired outcome, make use of the outcome and probably pay for the project, and a (prime) Supplier who will provide the resources and skills to create that outcome. This assumption has a bearing on how the project is organised.

The Customer and Supplier may be part of the same corporate body or may be independent of one another.

Establishing an effective organisational structure for the project is crucial to its success. Every project has need for direction, management, control and communication. PRINCE offers an approach that provides these elements and is sufficiently flexible to be mapped to any environment.

A project needs a different organisational structure from line management. It needs to be more flexible and is likely to require a broad base of skills for a comparatively short period of time. The project is normally cross-functional, an involved partnership.

The project organisation combines people who may be working full time on the project with others who have to divide their time between the project and other duties. The Project Manager will have direct management control over some of the project staff, but may also have to direct staff who report to another management structure.

The management structure of those with a problem to be solved will very often be different from that of those providing the solution. They will have different priorities, different interests to protect, but in some way they must be united in the common aims of the project. The management level that will make the decisions and the commitments on behalf of their interests is too busy to be involved on a day-to-day basis with the project. But most projects need day-to-day management if they are to be successful.

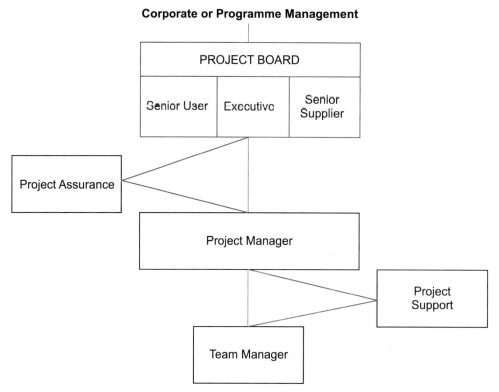

Figure 4–2: Project management structure

The PRINCE project management structure (Figure 4–2) consists of roles and responsibilities that bring together the various interests and skills involved in, and required by, the project.

Good project management practice requires the fulfilment of a number of generic, well defined roles. For the project to be successful, it is important to define these roles at the outset.

A project management structure is a temporary structure specifically designed to manage the project to its successful conclusion to meet the requirements defined in the Project Brief. The structure allows for channels of communication to decision-making forums and should be backed up by job definitions that specify the responsibilities, goals, limits of authority, relationships, skills, knowledge and experience required for all roles in the project organisation.

All the roles set out in Figure 4–2 need to be accommodated within job descriptions. In addition, the relationship between people's authority and responsibility within the project and their normal management responsibility and authority needs to be understood by those concerned and documented.

In order to be flexible and meet the needs of different environments and different project sizes, PRINCE does not define management *jobs* to be allocated on a one-to-one basis to people. PRINCE defines *roles*, which might be allocated, shared, divided or combined according to the project's needs. Associated with this is the concept that responsibilities for a role can be moved to another role or delegated, but they should not be dropped.

Some of the PRINCE roles cannot be shared or delegated if they are to be undertaken effectively. The Project Manager role cannot be shared, nor can the Project Manager or Project Board roles be delegated.

Corporate cultures differ, but PRINCE can be used no matter what corporate organisation structure exists.

4.1.1 Four layers

PRINCE separates the management of the project from the work required to develop the products, and concentrates on the former.

A fundamental principle is that the project organisation structure has four layers, which undertake:

- direction of the project
- day-to-day management of the project
- team management
- the work to create the products.

The first three are performed by the Project Management Team, the fourth by the project team itself.

4.1.2 The Project Manager and the project team

PRINCE provides for a single focus for day-to-day management of the project, namely the Project Manager, who has well-defined responsibilities and accountability. Figure 4–3 gives an idea of the many facets to the role of Project Manager. The Project Manager needs a project organisation structure that will take responsibility for some of these facets and provide support in performing some of the other facets.

Figure 4–3: The many facets of the Project Manager role

To meet these needs PRINCE provides a structure for a Project Management Team that supports:

- roles for decision makers
- management by exception for the decision makers
- full- or part-time project management
- controlled delegation of some day-to-day management responsibilities, where required, to Team Managers
- roles for the independent inspection of all aspects of project performance
- administrative support, as required, to the Project Manager and Team Managers

19

- agreement by all concerned on what the various roles and responsibilities are
- lines of communication between the Project Management Team members.

Hints and tips for Project Management organisation

Contractual and commercial arrangements will often interfere with the ideal project management organisation.

The project organisation structure should include links with the more permanent, functional or line management structures within both the Customer and Supplier communities.

4.1.3 Three project interests

PRINCE mandates the structure and composition of the Project Board as depicted in Figure 4–4. Three interests must be represented on the Project Board at all times.

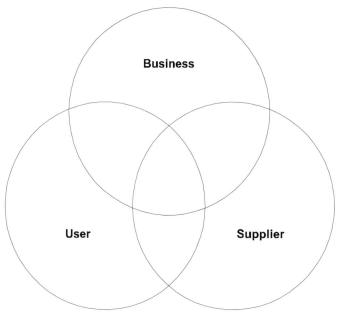

Figure 4–4: The Three project interests

Business

The product(s) of the project should meet a business need. The project should give value for money. There should, therefore, be representation from the business viewpoint to ensure that these two prerequisites exist before commitment to the project is made, and remain in existence throughout the project. PRINCE makes a distinction between the business and the requirements of those who will use the final product(s). The Executive role is defined to look after the business interests (representing the Customer).

User

There will be an individual, group or groups for whom some or all of the following will apply:

- they will use the final product
- the product will achieve an objective for them
- they will use the end result to deliver benefits
- they will be impacted by the outcome.

The User presence is needed to specify the desired outcome and ensure that the project delivers it. User management should therefore be represented on the Project Board.

Supplier

The creation of the end product (and possibly its subsequent operation) will need resources with certain skills. Representation is needed from the Supplier who will provide the necessary skills. The Supplier may need to use both in-house and external teams to construct the final outcome.

4.1.4 The Customer/Supplier environment

PRINCE is defined in terms of a Customer/Supplier environment. There are many combinations of Customer and Supplier that may affect the organisation and control of the project. Combinations worth considering are:

- a Customer with an in-house 'Supplier'. Even here they may have separate budgets and therefore need separate 'Business Cases'.

- projects sponsored by a single Customer versus those supporting multiple Customers

- those projects that are supplied by a single source versus those with multiple Suppliers

- situations that involve a consortium of equal Customers and/or Suppliers versus those that involve a 'legal' hierarchy of either:
  – projects supplied by an in-house source (part of the parent organisation)
  – those with a mixture of in-house and external Suppliers.

The project's direction set by the Project Board must reflect the agreements and decisions of the three interests defined in 4.1.3.

NOTE: Customer specialists may also be involved in setting the direction of the project, especially in cases where the project is part of a Programme.

The Project Board is the forum where senior management representatives of the Customer and Supplier come together to make decisions and commitments to the project. There may be times when the Customer management needs to meet without the Supplier to discuss confidential matters or prepare a joint approach, and vice versa. There may, therefore, be separate management groups as shown in Figure 4–5, but within PRINCE the Project Board is regarded as a joint forum.

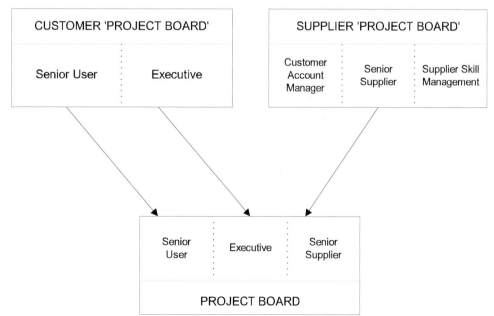

Figure 4–5: Example Customer/Supplier project management organisation

It may be difficult in certain business environments to contemplate having the Supplier represented on the Project Board, but there must be a common platform for decisions that affect all parties. The Senior Supplier role is needed if the Project Board is to enable full decision-making. It is therefore important that the Business, User and Supplier interests are adequately represented, because they all need to make commitments to the project, and those commitments need to be agreed.

At times there may be questions of confidentiality or conflicts of interest. The Customer representatives on the Project Board may not wish to discuss everything in front of the Supplier, and vice versa. There is nothing to prevent either party having private meetings to make internal decisions and/or discuss their position before meeting with the other party. The main objectives are full communication and agreed decisions, and the Project Board composition including the Senior Supplier is a powerful aid to achieving these.

If there are problems in identifying an external contractor who could take the role of Senior Supplier (for example, the project is a procurement one and the supplier has not yet been identified) the Customer's procurement manager or contracts manager could take on the role. Whoever is in the Senior Supplier role must have the appropriate authority to deploy Supplier resources.

In Customer/Supplier situations there will always be two Business Cases: the Customer's and the Supplier's. Unless otherwise stated, in this manual any references to the Business Case mean the Customer's Business Case.

In tailoring the Project Manager and Team Manager roles in a Customer/Supplier environment, consideration must be given to whether it is acceptable for Customer resources to be managed by a Supplier, or Supplier resources to be managed by the Customer representative. If such a situation is permitted, the division of management responsibilities for human resource management should be made clear – for example, appraisals, promotion and training.

4.2   The PRINCE Project Management Team

Below is a summary of the Project Management Team. A full description of each role is provided in *Appendix C: Project Management Team roles*.

4.2.1 Project Board

The Project Board represents at managerial level the Business, User and Supplier interests of the project. The Project Board members must have authority because they are the decision makers and responsible for the commitment of resources to the project, such as personnel, cash and equipment.

The level of manager required to fill the roles will depend on such factors as the budget and importance of the project. Their Project Board responsibilities will be in addition to their normal work, which makes it important that PRINCE offers them management by exception, keeping them regularly informed but only asking for joint decision making at key points in the project.

The Project Board consists of three roles:

- Executive
- Senior User
- Senior Supplier.

These roles should ideally be assigned to individuals who can stay with the project throughout its life.

The Project Board is appointed by corporate or programme management to provide overall direction and management of the project. The Project Board is accountable for the success of the project, and has responsibility and authority for the project within the remit (the Project Mandate) set by corporate or programme management.

The Project Board approves all major plans and authorises any major deviation from agreed Stage Plans. It is the authority that signs off the completion of each Stage as well as authorising the start of the next Stage. It ensures that required resources are committed and arbitrates on any conflicts within the project or negotiates a solution to any problems between the project and external bodies. In addition, it approves the appointment and responsibilities of the Project Manager.

The Project Board is responsible for assurance that the project remains on course to deliver products of the required quality to meet the Business Case defined in the Project Initiation Document. According to the size, complexity and risk of the project, the Project Board may decide to introduce specific additional resources to address some of its Project Assurance activities. Later in this chapter Project Assurance is discussed.

The Project Board is the project's 'voice' to the outside world and is responsible for any publicity or other dissemination of information about the project.

4.2.2 Executive

The Executive is ultimately accountable for the project, supported by the Senior User and Senior Supplier. The Executive has to ensure that the project gives value for money, ensuring a Business Case focused approach to the project, balancing the demands of business, User and Supplier.

Throughout the project the Executive 'owns' the Business Case.

The Executive is the link to corporate or Programme management.

4.2.3 Senior User

The Senior User is accountable for any products supplied by the Users, such as making sure that requirements have been clearly and completely defined, that what is produced is fit for its purpose and for monitoring that the solution will meet User needs within the constraints of the Business Case.

The role represents the interests of all those who will use the final product(s) of the project, those for whom the product will achieve an objective, those who will use the product to deliver benefits, or those who will be affected by the project. The Senior User role is responsible for:

- providing User resources
- ensuring that the project produces products and outcomes that meet User requirements
- ensuring that the products and outcomes provide the expected User benefits.

The Senior User is responsible for Project Assurance from a User perspective. Other resources may be assigned to undertake these assurance activities on behalf of (and reporting to) the Senior User.

The Senior User role may require more than one person to cover all the User interests. For the sake of effectiveness, the role should not be split between too many people. The *Hints and tips* section below gives guidance on solutions to the problem of too many contenders for the Senior User role.

4.2.4 Senior Supplier

The Senior Supplier needs to achieve the results required by the Senior User. The Senior Supplier is accountable for the quality of all products delivered by the Supplier(s). Part of this is to ensure that proposals for designing and developing the products are realistic. This means that they are likely to achieve the results required by the Senior User within the cost and time parameters for which the Executive is accountable. The role represents the interests of those designing, developing, facilitating, procuring, implementing (and also possibly those responsible for operating and maintaining) the supplied products. The Senior Supplier role must have the authority to commit or acquire the required Supplier resources. The Senior Supplier has responsibility for the Supplier's Business Case.

It should be noted that in some environments the Customer may share design authority or have a major say in it.

The involvement of multiple Suppliers may necessitate more than a single Senior Supplier representative on the Project Board.

Hints and tips for the Project Board

Project Board members are normally very busy outside the project. There is a danger in larger projects that if they don't delegate their assurance responsibilities, these will not get done. If the assurance activities are not delegated, Project Board members must seriously consider how the work associated with these responsibilities will get done, when they will find the time and how well those responsibilities will be carried out.

Roles may be combined but never eliminated.

There may be questions of confidentiality or conflicts of interest. The Project Board representatives of the Customer may not wish to discuss everything in front of the Supplier, and vice versa. There is nothing to prevent the Customer or Supplier having private meetings to discuss their position before meeting with the other party.

It is not advisable to combine the roles of Senior User and Senior Supplier because of potential conflict of interest.

According to the project's business environment, any combination of the Executive and Senior User roles should be considered carefully.

Project Boards are the major decision makers. It is important that the business, User and Supplier are represented, because they all need to make commitments to the project.

The Supplier may wish to establish an internal management board to debate and manage internal aspects of the project without the presence of the Customer or User.

The Supplier's equivalent of the 'Project Board' may wish to appoint its own business assurance role to monitor the Supplier's Business Case.

Both the Customer and the Supplier may wish to appoint their own assurance roles. In particular, the Customer may feel the need for assurance about the specialist aspects of the project independent of the Supplier.

A large Project Board can become unwieldy and inhibit the decision-making process. If there are too many candidates for a Project Board role, they should be encouraged to appoint a spokesperson to carry out that role. In particular, if there are too many wanting to share the Senior User role, a User Committee can be formed with a Chairperson. The Chairperson represents them as Senior User, reports back to the committee and takes direction from it before Project Board meetings.

Suppliers should not be in a position to overwhelm the business/User representatives by sheer weight of numbers.

The Project Board is not a democracy controlled by votes. The Executive is the key decision maker with advice and commitments from others.

Other interests can be invited to attend Project Board meetings to provide advice etc., but not to take part in the decision making.

All Project Board members need training in Project Board procedures and responsibilities.

Where the project is one of a string of projects, a decision is needed on who is the User. Is it an end-user or is it the next project in the string?

Don't confuse the need for an organisation to manage the project with the need for a communication vehicle.

Project Board members should sign up to their agreed role and responsibilities before taking the job on.

Where the project is part of a programme, the Programme Director appoints the Project Board Executive and has the option of appointing the other Project Board members. Alternatively the Project Board Executive may be asked to select the other Project Board members. Where the latter is the case, the advice and approval of the Programme Director should be sought.

4.2.5 Project Manager

The Project Manager is given the authority to run the project on a day-to-day basis on behalf of the Project Board within the constraints laid down by the board.

The Project Manager's prime responsibility is to ensure that the project produces the required products, to the required standard of quality and within the specified constraints of time and cost. The Project Manager is also responsible for the project producing a result that is capable of achieving the benefits defined in the Project Initiation Document.

Hints and tips for the Project Manager

It may be beneficial to employ high-quality people part time rather than lesser-quality people full time.

It is important to remember that the manual assumes the Project Manager will be from the Customer. It is possible that the Project Manager may be from the Supplier – that is, the interface boundary moves from Project Manager/Team Manager to Project Board/Project Manager.

Where the Project Manager does not have direct authority over personnel required to work on the project, it is strongly recommended that the agreement of the appropriate managers is obtained (and maintained throughout the project) for the commitment of their personnel.

Remember that the Project Manager's role is to manage the work, not do it.

The Project Manager must avoid becoming involved in low-level detail to the extent that sight is lost of the 'big picture', that is, what is going on in every part of the project.

Different Project Manager attributes are needed for different types of project.

In tailoring the Project Manager and Team Manager roles in a Customer/ Supplier environment, consideration must be given to whether it is acceptable for Customer resources to be managed by a Supplier, or Supplier resources to be managed by the Customer representative. If such a situation is permitted, the division of management responsibilities for human resource management should be made clear – for example, appraisals, promotion and training.

4.2.6 Team Manager

The use of this role is optional. The Project Manager may find that it is beneficial to delegate the authority and responsibility for planning the creation of certain products and managing a team of specialists to produce those products. There are many reasons why the Project Manager may decide to employ this role. Among these are the size of the project, the particular specialist skills or knowledge needed for certain products, geographical location of some team members, and the preferences of the Project Board.

The Team Manager's prime responsibility is to ensure production of those products defined by the Project Manager to an appropriate quality in a timescale and at a cost acceptable to the Project Board. The Team Manager reports to and takes direction from the Project Manager.

The use of this role should be discussed by the Project Manager with the Project Board and, if the role is required, planned at Project Initiation time.

4.2.7 Project Assurance

The Project Board members do not work full time on the project; therefore they place a great deal of reliance on the Project Manager. Although they receive regular reports from the Project Manager, there may always be questions at the back of their minds: 'Are things really going as well as we are being told?', 'Are any problems being hidden from us?', 'Is the solution going to be what we want?', 'Are we suddenly going to find that the project is over budget or late?', 'Is the Business Case intact?', 'Will the intended benefits be realised?' There are other questions. The Supplier and/or Customer may have a quality assurance function charged with the responsibility to check that all projects are adhering to the Quality Management System.

All of these points mean that there is a need in the project organisation for monitoring all aspects of the project's performance and products independently of the Project Manager. This is the Project Assurance function.

Specific responsibilities

The implementation of the assurance roles needs to answer the question 'What is to be assured?' A list of possibilities would include:

- maintenance of thorough liaison throughout the project between the Supplier and the Customer

- User needs expectations being met or managed

- risks being controlled

- expenditure and schedule

- adherence to the Business Case

- constant reassessment of the value-for-money solution

- fit with the overall programme or company strategy

- the right people being involved in product creation

- products being checked for quality at the right time and by the right people

- an acceptable solution being developed

- the project remaining viable

- the scope of the project not 'creeping up' unnoticed

- realisation of benefits

- focus on the business need maintained

- internal and external communications working

- the needs of specialist interests, for example, security, being observed

- adherence to quality assurance standards.

It is not enough to believe that standards will be adhered to. It is not enough to ensure that the project is well set up and justified at the outset. All the possibilities listed above need to be checked throughout the project as part of ensuring that it remains consistent with and continues to meet a business need and that no change to the external environment affects the validity of the project.

PRINCE starts by identifying these Project Assurance functions as part of the role of each Project Board member. According to the needs and desires of the Project Board, the work associated with any of these assurance responsibilities can be delegated, as long as the recipients are independent of the Project Manager and the rest of the team(s). Any appointed assurance jobs assure the project on behalf of one or more members of the Project Board.

It is not mandatory that all assurance responsibilities are delegated. Each assurance responsibility that is delegated may be assigned to one individual or shared. The Project Board decides when an assurance responsibility needs to be delegated, and the delegation may be for the entire project or only part of it. The person or persons filling an assurance role may be changed during the project at the request of the Project Board. Any use of other personnel to take on assurance responsibilities needs to be planned at Initiation Stage; otherwise resource usage and costs for assurance could easily get out of control. Anyone appointed to an assurance job reports to the Project Board member responsible for the appointment.

Project Assurance has to be independent of the Project Manager. Therefore the Project Board cannot delegate any of its assurance responsibilities to the Project Manager.

Hints and tips for Project Assurance

The Project Board may carry out its own assurance roles if it so wishes and if there is time. It greatly assists Project Board commitment if the members can be persuaded to undertake their own assurance. The question is whether the members have the time and skill required.

The assurance required may vary according to the type of project. The lists given here and earlier can be used to identify a need for a given project. One possible example is the need to assure the continued business integrity of the project. This role would monitor the continuing validity of the Business Case against external events, changes to the project business risks, the evolution of actuals against the Project Plan and any impact on the Business Case of changes to the specification. Another example is the regular assurance on behalf of the Customer that the project is staying on track to produce an effective and usable solution. A third example is that of assuring that the correct standards are available, are being used and are being used correctly in the development of the products. This might include assurance that there is an audit trail of all the quality-control work being done. Other examples would include security assurance, and assurance that the project is staying within programme strategy and guidelines.

If a role is changed during the project, care must be taken to ensure continuity of the work being done by that role.

It is not advisable to combine any assurance roles where there would be potential conflicts of interest.

Anyone appointed to an assurance role should be independent of the Project Manager and team(s).

In Customer/Supplier projects, there may be a need for two separate assurance roles to monitor the respective interests of the Customer and the Supplier.

4.2.8 Project Support

The Project Manager may need administrative help. This may stem from the sheer volume of work to be done or the mandated use of certain tools where the Project Manager has insufficient expertise, such as in supporting, planning and control, or Configuration Management.

The provision of any Project Support on a formal basis is optional. It is driven by the needs of the individual project and Project Manager. Project support could be in the form of administrative services, advice, and guidance to one or more related projects. Where set up as an official body, Project Support can act as a repository for lessons learned and estimating metrics, and a central source of expertise in specialist support tools. One support function that must be considered is that of Configuration Management. Depending on the project size and environment, there may be a need to formalise this, and it quickly becomes a task with which the Project Manager cannot cope without support. See Chapter 10 *Configuration Management* for details of the work.

It is necessary to keep Project Support and assurance responsibilities separate in order to maintain the independence of Project Assurance.

Hints and tips for Project Support

The physical location of project staff can present problems if they are geographically remote from each other. If at all possible, choose people at a common location. Alternatively, ensure suitable communications technology and training in its use are available.

A Project Support organisation that serves all projects is an ideal way to establish and maintain a number of management standards, such as a common planning and control tool, the management of risk and Configuration Management.

Where the number of projects and size of staff warrant it, the common areas of support may be concentrated into a Project Support Office (PSO). This allows staff to be permanently allocated to this type of work, and therefore become highly skilled at the activities. A PSO can support all projects and set standards, such as the use of planning and control tools, reporting, change control, and Configuration Management.

4.3 Programme Organisation

PRINCE defines a programme as:

> *A portfolio of projects selected, planned and managed in a co-ordinated*
> *way and that together achieve a set of defined business objectives.*
> *Programme management methods and techniques may also be applied to a*
> *set of otherwise unrelated projects bounded by a business cycle.*

Often, a project may be part of a programme. A programme would normally consist of many projects. An example of a programme is the building and commissioning of a new hospital, where various projects would undertake construction of the building and the road infrastructure, the procurement of equipment, staffing, provision of communications, computer systems and many others.

Figure 4–6 illustrates the standard programme management roles and their relationships with the PRINCE project organisation.

The management, direction and objectives of the programme influence each project. In particular, when starting up the project, the programme management will have a say in the selection of the project Executive. It is therefore necessary to understand the organisation of a programme.

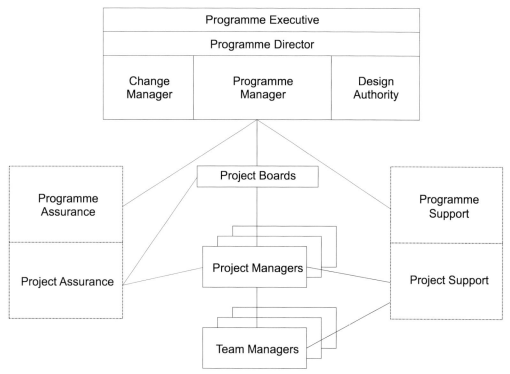

Figure 4–6: Programme organisation

Authority for a programme lies with the Programme Director. Authority for the day-to-day management of a programme is delegated to the Programme Executive.

At the programme level, the assurance role is fulfilled by two roles within the Programme Executive, namely the Change Manager and the Design Authority. At the project level, assurance is the responsibility of the Project Board members, who may delegate some or all of the activities of the role.

The Communication Plan in a project's Project Initiation Document should identify the information needs between the project, the Programme Manager and the Programme Executive.

4.3.1 Programme Director

The Programme Director will have direct, overall control of the programme implementation. This includes delegating the authority for projects to Project Boards.

The role of Programme Director may be part-time, but is responsible for:

- establishing the programme and projects
- Project Board appointments
- securing resources
- monitoring progress
- ensuring the aims of the programme and projects continue to be aligned with evolving business needs
- ensuring the realisation of benefits
- chairing the Programme Executive.

Responsibility for establishing the Project Board lies with the Programme Director. However, having appointed the project Executive, the Programme Director may choose to delegate the appointment of the remainder of the Project Board and Project Management Team to the Executive, rather than making all the appointments personally. Whichever option is followed, serious consideration must be given to the need for programme representation and the need for the project to be seen to be locally owned, so allowing for the adoption of the project's output by the Customer and Users.

The above has an impact on *Starting up a Project (SU)*. If the Programme Director has already appointed the Project Board, then this removes the need to design and appoint the Project Board within the process.

4.3.2 Change Manager

The Change Manager represents the Programme Director's interests in the final outcome of the programme, and is the author and guardian of the final Business Case for funding the programme work. 'Change' in this sense is the change to the customer's way of doing business, which will be brought about by the programme and projects. The role is responsible for the management of change activities, and must ensure that managers and staff in the target business area are informed and involved throughout the life of the programme, and are fully prepared to exploit the new operational business environment once it is put in place. As part of this change responsibility, the role of the Change Manager includes communication with the rest of the organisation and liaison with human resources personnel.

The Change Manager is responsible for assuring that the approach being taken to manage risks is appropriate.

4.3.3 Design Authority

The Design Authority is responsible for compliance with the organisation's strategy and should ensure that, whatever procedures, systems or components are implemented in projects that are part of the portfolio, their designs are consistent and the interfaces between projects are designed consistently. The Design Authority also ensures that all project designs comply with the policies and standards and are consistent with the supporting services and infrastructures that they use or with which they interface. Where the impact of a design change is not perceived at the project management level, the Design Authority should take a proactive role and achieve any necessary design changes to keep the Programme moving forwards.

The Design Authority monitors risks associated with the Programme's products.

4.3.4 Programme Manager

The Programme Manager establishes and manages the Programme Plan. The Programme Manager carries out the day-to-day management of the programme's portfolio of projects on behalf of the Programme Director. To do this the Programme Manager must ensure that an appropriate environment to support the Project Managers is developed and maintained. Once projects are under way, the Programme Manager focuses on monitoring changes within the project portfolio. This will include timely management of exceptions, slippage and issues of priority.

The Programme Manager is responsible for ensuring the management of programme-related risks, particularly those associated with interdependencies between projects and with programme-wide risks.

The Programme Manager is the key link between programme and projects, providing direction to the Project Managers on programme projects.

4.4 Alternative organisation structures

Within a programme, the way in which individual Project Management Teams are defined and how projects interface with a programme may differ from project to project. The following may be considered for some or all of the projects within a programme. The decision must be made during the start-up process of the project, and the roles and responsibilities for that project at both project and programme level defined clearly.

4.4.1 Programme Executive as Project Board members

There is a danger that the two levels of change management (Programme and project) may lead to confusion. One of the ways to avoid this is to have programme representation on the Project Board. This may be done either by appointing a programme representative into a Project Board role or by having a representative of programme management attend the Project Board meetings without taking a formal project role.

For example:

- the Change Manager may take on the role of Senior User

- the Programme Manager may take the Executive role on the Project Board

- the Programme Manager may represent the programme at Project Board meetings without taking a specific Project Board role

- the members of the Programme Executive may share attendance at Project Board meetings between them.

Advantages

Where the individual takes a role on both programme and project, this might result in the joint role becoming full-time. This would allow the individual to concentrate solely on the programme and project, rather than have other day-to-day distractions.

The decisions made are more likely to reflect the central objectives of the programme. As a result, the outputs from projects should be consistent across the programme.

Project decisions that have a programme impact should be made more quickly. The programme representative is more likely to be able to make a decision on the spot, rather than the project having to wait until the Programme Executive is consulted. This should lead to a reduction in delays or re-work caused by having to wait for crucial decisions.

The programme is seen to be proactive in a structured, rather than what might be perceived as a disruptive, meddling way.

Disadvantages

The business area on which the project is focused may feel that the Project Board does not provide it with sufficient representation. This may lead to reluctance to accept the project's products or failure to realise all the predicted benefits. To avoid this situation the flexibility of the Project Board roles can be used to ensure representation of both the programme and end users.

If the Change Manager is occupied full time by having roles at both programme and project level, this person may be taken away from the relevant operational environment, thus becoming unaware of changes taking place within the business.

There will be fewer perspectives than if the Project Board is staffed by individuals who are not part of the programme organisation.

4.4.2 Common programme support and project support staff

Certain functions performed by project support may be filled at programme level for all projects within the programme. Examples of this would be expertise in the planning and control method and software, the management of risk, change control and Configuration Management.

This assumes that programme and project support staff are situated on the same site.

Advantages

Reduction in the duplication of support staff required. A single member of staff may be made responsible for collating all the information for a single area such as risks. The effort needed to maintain Risk Logs across projects will be reduced (or several part-time jobs combined to form one full-time job). Any risks that impact the programme will be identified during appraisals of project risks.

Reduction in the number of experts required. It may be unreasonable or impossible to obtain expertise for each project in Configuration Management or the planning and control tool being used. The problem can be alleviated by concentrating support at programme level.

Central support ensures consistency in the tools being used, the standardised layout of reports and easier summary of reports to programme management.

Where there is continuation of the use of a tool or method into the eventual use of the project's products, such as Configuration Management, centralisation of support helps ensure a smooth passage from projects to operation.

Disadvantages

If the projects are geographically dispersed, central support may be less effective.

Support staff would constantly have to bear in mind the two sides to their roles, programme and project. It would be easier to miss a programme implication of a change or risk because of focusing on doing the job at project level.

5   Plans

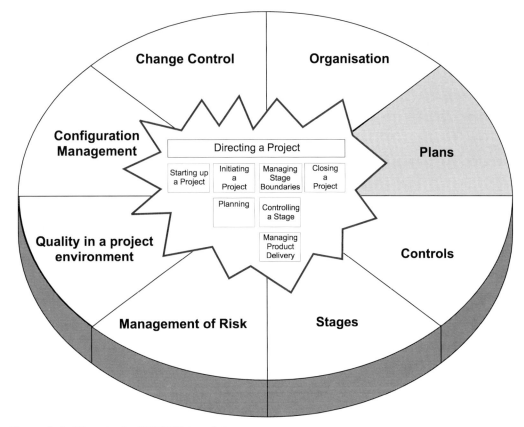

Figure 5–1: Plans in the PRINCE template

5.1   What is a plan?

A plan is a document, framed in accordance with a predefined scheme or method, describing **how**, **when** and **by whom** a specific target or set of targets is to be achieved. A plan is a design of how identified targets for deliverables, timescales, costs and quality can be met.

Plans are the backbone of the management information system required for any project.

A plan requires the approval and commitment of the Project Management Team and must be formally approved by the Project Board.

5.2   What are the components of a plan?

When asked to describe a plan, many people think only of some sort of bar chart showing timescales. A PRINCE plan is more comprehensive. It should contain the following elements (making maximum use of charts, tables and diagrams for clarity):

- the products to be produced

- the activities needed to create those deliverables

- the activities needed to validate the quality of deliverables

- the resources and time needed for all activities (including quality control), and any need for people with specific skills

- the dependencies between activities

- external dependencies for the delivery of information, products or services

- when activities will occur

- the points at which progress will be monitored and controlled.

Plans should be presented as management reports, with key information documented in a way that an audience can understand, interpret and question. A Stage Plan might, therefore, be held in two forms: a summary plan suitable for presentation to the Project Board, and the more detailed one used for day-to-day control of the Stage.

The statement of activities and breakdown of resource requirements must be backed up by text that explains to the reader:

- what the plan covers (for example, delivery of specific products)

- the intended approach to implement the plan

- how adherence to the plan is to be monitored and controlled

- what management reports will be issued

- the quality-control methods and resources to be used

- any assumptions on which the plan is based

- any prerequisites that must be in place on day one of the plan

- what risks there are that may prevent the plan being achieved and what measures should be (or have been) taken to address these risks.

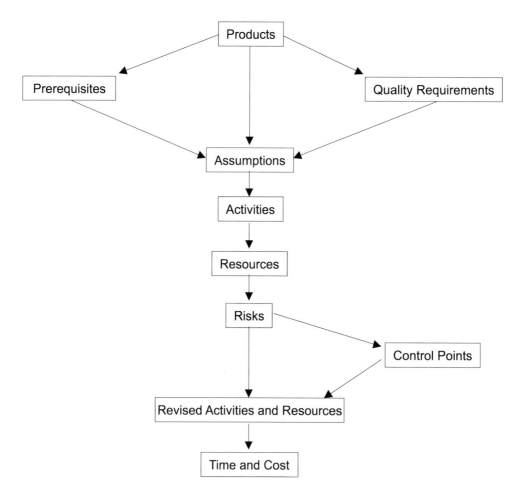

Figure 5–2: The components of a plan

Figure 5–2 shows the components of a plan and illustrates how it might be built up, starting from a list of the products to be produced. Any prerequisites are identified, together with the quality requirements of the products. These three components lead to consideration of what assumptions are being made or are to be made. The next consideration is to define the activities required to generate the products. The dependencies between the activities are identified, then resources to carry out the activities are added. Risks are then considered, followed by the addition of control points. The last two steps might add to the activities and resources required. Finally the overall time and cost are calculated.

5.3   The PRINCE approach

The PRINCE planning structure allows for a plan to be broken down into lower level plans containing more detail. But all plans have the same overall structure and are always matched back to the planned requirements, including quality and benefits, before approval.

5.4   Levels of plan

Activity durations and resource requirements become more difficult to estimate accurately the further into the future they extend. Regardless of this problem, there is still a need to provide a provisional estimate of the duration and cost of the project as a whole in order to gain approval to proceed.

It is seldom desirable, or possible, to plan an entire project in detail at the start. The reasons for this include:

- uncertainty about the detailed nature of later elements of work

- a changing or uncertain environment

- risk factors that could change the situation

- difficulty in predicting resource availability well into the future

- difficulty in predicting business conditions in the future.

However, if the current elements of work are to be controlled, detailed plans containing firm estimates are needed for the realistically foreseeable future. For these reasons, plans need to be produced at different levels of scope and detail.

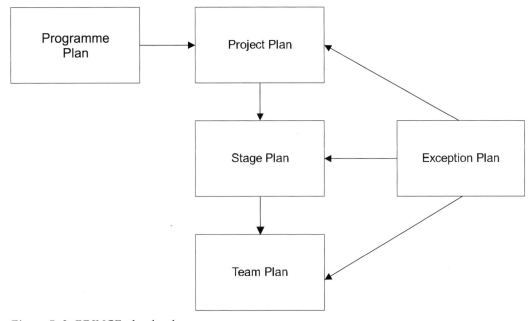

Figure 5–3: PRINCE plan levels

Project Plans may exist within the context of a Programme Plan. If so, the Programme Plan may place constraints on the project.

PRINCE proposes two basic levels of planning, the Project Plan and the Stage Plan, to reflect the needs of the different levels of management involved in the project. Use of the Team Plans illustrated in Figure 5–3 is optional, and will depend on the needs of the individual project. These other levels are explained in more detail later in this chapter, but, briefly:

- a Stage Plan may be broken down into a number of Team Plans (where, for example, a number of teams may be contributing to the work)

- where a Stage or Project Plan is forecast to exceed its tolerances, an Exception Plan is put forward that will replace a Stage Plan or lead to a revised Project Plan.

The principal idea behind the levels is that the lower the level, the shorter the plan's timeframe and the more detail it contains. The project chooses the levels and, therefore, the number of plans it needs according to its size and extent of risk exposure.

5.4.1　Project Plan

An overview of the total project is needed. This is the Project Plan. It forms part of the Project Initiation Document. The Project Plan is mandatory. It provides the Business Case with project costs and is used by the Project Board as a baseline against which to monitor actual costs and project progress stage by stage. The Project Plan identifies key deliverables, resource requirements and the total costs. It also identifies major control points within the project, such as stage boundaries. The Project Quality Plan for the project is documented separately in another part of the Project Initiation Document.

Once the Project Initiation Document has been accepted, the initial Project Plan is 'baselined' and shows the original plan on which the project was approved. As the project moves through its stages subsequent versions of the Project Plan are produced at the end of each stage to reflect:

- progress already made

- any agreed changes in circumstances

- any revised forecast of cost and/or duration of the total project.

The initial and current versions of the Project Plan form part of the information used by the Project Board to monitor how far the project is deviating from its original size and scope.

If the Project Plan is likely to exceed the tolerance laid down by corporate or programme management, the deviation must be referred upwards by the Project Board to get a decision on corrective action. In such cases an Exception Plan (for the entire project) should accompany the submission. The format of an Exception Plan is the same as for any other PRINCE plan and is discussed later in the chapter.

5.4.2　Stage Plan

For each stage identified in the Project Plan, a Stage Plan is required. Each Stage Plan is produced near the end of the previous stage. It will be the basis of the Project Manager's day-to-day control.

It is frequently the case that much of the work in a stage will be done by specialist teams or Suppliers, who will have their own plans for the work they are doing. These plans will not necessarily integrate comfortably with the Stage concepts explained elsewhere. This means that the Project Manager will need to construct the Stage Plan from the various specialist development plans to establish overall resource and timing elements and interdependencies for the work through to the next assessment by the Project Board.

The Stage Plan is similar to the Project Plan in content, but each element will be broken down to the level of detail required to be an adequate basis for day-to-day control by the Project Manager. The validity of assumptions and risk analyses should be reassessed for the Stage, as these may have changed since they were previously considered, or new risks may have arisen or become apparent when looking in more detail.

Stage Plans and Team Plans should contain a Quality Plan, which will identify the method(s) to be used to check the quality of each product and the resources to be used for the checks. The assurance roles have a key part to play here in identifying products of key interest to their role, and in specifying who should be involved in quality checking these products. For example, for any Quality Reviews the names of the review Chairperson and the reviewers would be given. The timing and resource effort will be shown in the graphic plan (typically a Gantt Chart).

Each Stage Plan is finalised near the end of the previous stage. This approach should give more confidence in the plan because:

- the Stage Plan is produced close to the time when the planned events will take place
- the Stage Plan is for a much shorter duration than the Project Plan
- after the first stage, the Stage Plan is developed with knowledge of the performance of earlier Stages.

5.4.3 Exception Plan

When it is predicted that a plan will no longer finish within the agreed tolerances, an Exception Plan is produced to replace that plan. An Exception Plan is prepared at the same level of detail as the plan it replaces. Most Exception Plans will be created to replace a Stage Plan, but the Project Plan may also need to be replaced. An Exception Plan picks up from the current Stage Plan actuals and continues to the end of the Stage.

An Exception Plan has the same format as the plan it will replace, but the text will cover:

- why the Exception Plan is needed
- the impact of the Exception Plan on the Project Plan (if it is a lower level of plan that is being replaced), the Business Case and any risks.

This extra information comes from the Exception Report. The Exception Plan needs the approval of the Project Board.

5.4.4 Team Plan

Team Plans are **optional** and are used to break down activities into a lower level of tasks that are required to produce one or more of the Stage Plan's products. They might be used for separate teams working in a Stage, especially if those teams are from different skill groups, or work for external contractors. The Team Manager would create the Team Plan as part of the sub-process *Accepting a Work Package (MP1)*. The Stage Plan would be a summary of the various Team Plans.

The need for Team Plans will be determined by the size and complexity of the project and the number of people involved. If they are considered necessary, the plans are prepared in parallel with the Stage Plan.

5.5   Benefits of planning

Effective planning identifies:

- whether the targets are achievable

- the resources needed to achieve the targets within a timeframe

- the activities needed to ensure that quality can be built in to the products

- the problems and risks associated with trying to achieve the targets and stay within the constraints.

Other benefits of planning include:

- avoiding muddle and *ad hoc* decisions

- helping the management team to think ahead

- providing a yardstick against which progress can be measured

- communication, through the distribution of a plan to all concerned, of what is to be done, how it is to be done, the allocation of responsibilities, and how progress will be monitored and controlled

- gaining commitment from the contributors and recipients

- the provision of personal targets.

Planning is not a trivial exercise. It is vital to the success of the project. A plan must contain sufficient information and detail to confirm that the targets of the plan are achievable.

It is essential to allocate time for the planning activity. Every project should have an Initiation Stage, in which time is allocated to identify and agree the scope of the project and to plan it in terms of management, resourcing, deliverables, activities, quality and control. Time should also be allocated for the refinement of the Business Case. The Initiation Stage may or may not be formal, depending on the nature and complexity of the project. In addition, during the Initiation Stage and towards the end of every stage in the project except the last one, time should be allowed for planning the next stage in detail.

Without effective planning, the outcome of complex projects cannot be predicted in terms of scope, quality, risk, timescale and cost. Those involved in providing resources cannot optimise their operations. Poorly planned projects cause frustration, waste and re-work.

Hints and tips for planning

When planning, it is easy to forget to add the resources needed to do impact assessment on change requests. Even if a change is subsequently rejected, the assessment will still consume time and effort, probably from the senior team members.

It is important to identify for which products the Customer and Supplier are responsible. An extra heading can be added to the Product Description to record this information.

Plans need to be at an appropriate level to facilitate control. Will the Supplier's and Customer's plans be written at the same level of detail?

6   Controls

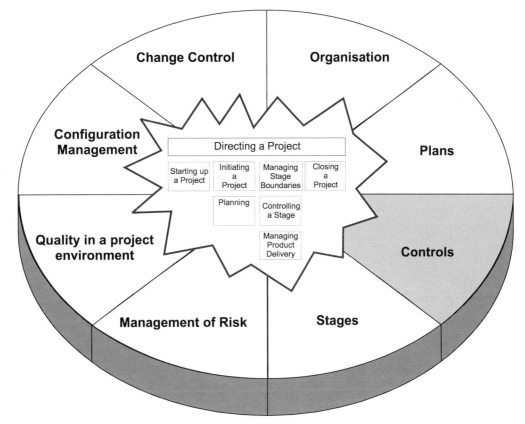

Figure 6–1: Controls in the PRINCE template

6.1   Purpose of control

Control is all about decision making and is the central role of project management.

The purpose of control is to ensure that the project:

- is producing the required products, which meet the defined Acceptance Criteria
- is being carried out to schedule and in accordance with its resource and cost plans
- remains viable against its Business Case.

Figure 6–2 illustrates that monitoring activities facilitate the checking and reporting on progress against the plan. Control activities promote revisions to be made to the plan in response to problems discovered during monitoring.

Controls ensure that, for each level of the Project Management Team, the next level up of management can:

- monitor progress
- compare achievement with plan
- review plans and options against future scenarios
- detect problems
- initiate corrective action
- authorise further work.

Controls must also cover capturing information on changes from outside the project and taking the necessary actions.

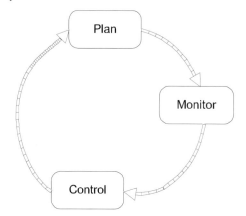

Figure 6–2: The control loop

6.2   Controls overview

There are various levels of control in the project. Most controls in PRINCE are event-driven, including all the decision-making ones. There are some time-driven controls such as regular progress feedback. At the project level there is overall control by the Project Board, which receives information from the Project Manager (and any assurance roles appointed) and has control over whether the project continues, stops or changes direction or scope.

PRINCE applies the concept of 'management by exception' where the Project Board is concerned. That is, having approved a Stage Plan, the Project Board is kept informed by reports during the Stage. There is no need for 'progress meetings' during the Stage. The Project Board knows that the Project Manager will inform them immediately if any exception situation is forecast.

The major controls for the Project Board are:

- **Project Initiation** (Should the project be undertaken?)

- **End Stage Assessment** (Has the stage been successful? Is the project still on course? Is the Business Case still viable? Are the risks still under control? Should the next stage be undertaken?)

- **Highlight Reports** (Regular progress reports during a stage)

- **Exception Reports** (Early warning of any forecast deviation beyond tolerance levels)

- **Mid-Stage Assessment** (The Project Board jointly considers what action to take in response to a forecast deviation)

- **Project Closure** (Has the project delivered everything expected? Are any follow-on actions necessary? What lessons have been learned?).

The Project Board must also monitor the environment outside the project and bring to the notice of those concerned, such as the Project Manager, any changes that affect the project.

The Project Manager has control on a day-to-day basis within a Stage and can make adjustments as long as the Stage and project stay within the tolerances defined by the Project Board and the adjustments do not change the Business Case. The Project Manager is responsible for monitoring progress, and may be assisted by Project Support roles if these have been appointed.

Work Package authorisation is a control that the Project Manager uses to allocate work to individuals or teams. It includes controls on quality, time and cost and identifies reporting and hand-over requirements. The individuals or teams monitor progress through the Work Package and report back to the Project Manager via Checkpoints or other identified means (such as risk 'triggers').

PRINCE is designed for a variety of Customer/Supplier situations. For clarity, the PRINCE manual has been written on the assumption that the project will be run for a Customer with a single (prime) Supplier involved throughout. This has a bearing on not only the organisation of the project, but also the controls.

Planned achievement includes the required quality of products. The aim is to detect problems early while they can be corrected at least cost. Action should be taken in respect of any deviation from plan that is forecast to be outside tolerance.

The what, why, who, how and when questions must be answered satisfactorily before the project proceeds beyond Initiation.

Progress is monitored against plans, with control actions if adjustments are needed. The Project Management Team is kept informed at its various levels by reports and assessments.

There is a controlled close, to ensure that the project does not drift on for ever but does not finish until the Project Manager can satisfy the Project Board that the objectives specified in the Project Initiation Document have been achieved.

6.3   Controlled Start

6.3.1 Project Start-up

Project Start-up is an important prerequisite of project control. Project Start-up contains the work that PRINCE requires is done **before** the project can begin. Its functions are to:

- set up the project management organisation so that the Project Board and Project Manager can make the necessary initial decisions about the project

- plan the Initiation Stage

- develop what *may* be a rudimentary Project Mandate into the Project Brief.

6.3.2 Authorising Initiation (Sub-process DP1)

After the process *Starting up a Project (SU)*, the Project Board approves progress to the Initiation Stage, which is the official 'start' of the project. This approval may be given at a formal meeting

Depending on the project size, risk status, importance and environment, the obtaining of this approval may be done without a formal meeting. It still needs the documented approval of all members of the Project Board identified so far.

Project Initiation is likely to be a short Stage in comparison with the other project Stages, but the approval of the Project Board is needed before it can be done. Project Start-up must, therefore, create a plan for the Initiation Stage that the Project Board can examine in order to understand the required commitment more clearly. The plan should include a statement of any controls to be applied and reports that the Project Board is to receive, so that the Project Board is assured in advance that the Stage will be under its control.

As the creation of the Project Mandate is out of the control of the project, it often falls short of providing all the information that the project needs. Project Start-up gives the Project Manager the opportunity to flesh it out into a full Project Brief and thus present the objectives of the project to the Project Board at the Project Initiation Meeting for the Board's agreement.

Where the project is part of a programme, the programme should provide a complete Project Brief, thus removing the need to produce it during Project Start-up.

6.3.3 Project Initiation

The purpose of Project Initiation is to ensure that before significant resource is spent on the project, everything involved in the project is agreed on:

- the project objectives
- what products will be delivered
- the reasons (Business Case)
- who the Customer is
- who has which responsibilities and authority
- project boundaries and interfaces to the outside world
- how the objectives will be met
- what assumptions have been or can be made
- what major risks exist that might prevent the project from achieving its objectives
- when the major products will be delivered
- how much the project will cost
- how the project will be controlled
- the division of the project into stages
- how the acceptability of its products will be assessed.

These questions are answered in the Project Initiation Document, which is the main product from the stage. A suggested outline of the contents of the Project Initiation Document is included in *Appendix A – PRINCE Product Description outlines*.

The establishment of a suitable Project Management Team is discussed in *Organisation* (Chapter 4).

Another product of the Initiation Stage is the next Stage Plan, so that if the Project Board is satisfied with the Project Initiation Document, it can also approve progress into the next Stage without further delay.

Once approved at the end of the Project Initiation Stage, the Project Initiation Document is 'frozen'. It is now a reference document to show the original basis of the project. At the end of the project it can be measured against final expectations and results to assess the success of the project and to check, for example, that any changes to the Project Plan were made in a controlled manner. It is an essential part of the audit trail on how the project has been managed.

But changes do occur, and it would be wrong not to record the impact of those changes and keep the Project Management Team up to date and so further versions of the most volatile parts of the Project Initiation Document are created as changes occur. Again, this forms part of the audit trail, showing any moves away from the information in the Project Initiation Document, when and why this happened, and what the impact of the change was. The most volatile parts of the Project Initiation Document are:

- the Project Plan
- the Business Case
- the Risk Log.

As later versions of these are created, they are kept in the management section of the project filing. A suitable structure for the filing is illustrated in *Project filing techniques* (Chapter 24).

These volatile parts will be updated throughout the project, at least at the end of each Stage.

To summarise, the main purpose of the Project Initiation Document is to pull the information together to answer the questions: 'What?', 'Why?' 'Who?', 'When?' and 'How?'.

6.3.4 Stage selection

According to the size and riskiness of a project, the Project Board will decide to break it into a number of Stages. This is agreed during the Initiation Stage. The breakdown of the project into Stages is discussed in the *Stages* chapter (Chapter 7).

The end of each Stage is a major control point for the Project Board (see End Stage Assessment), and thus the selection of the number of Stages and their timing in the project life cycle is an important control for the Project Board.

> ### *Hints and tips for Project Initiation*
>
> *Under the 'Project Controls' section of the Project Initiation Document, it is useful to mention the development of the Lessons Learned Report (see later in this chapter). This alerts readers to the fact that it should be a document ongoing throughout the life of the project. Otherwise it may be left until Project Closure, when memories of some lessons may have faded.*

6.4 Controlled progress

During the project there is a need to ensure that the project stays in line with the expectations defined in the Project Initiation Document and the current Stage Plan.

6.4.1 Tolerance

No project ever goes 100 per cent to plan. Even with a good plan, some things will go a little slower than planned, or cost a little more; other things will go more quickly, cost a little less. Such variations will occur all the way through a plan. Although the Project Board agreed a plan with the Project Manager, it doesn't want the Project Manager to be constantly running back to it, saying 'I've spent a pound more than I planned this week' or 'I'm a day late this week'. On the other hand, the Project Board doesn't want progress to deviate wildly from the plan without being told and being able to react. So where is the dividing line between differences that are permissible and those that require Project Board intervention? The dividing line is called **tolerance**.

The two standard elements to tolerance are:

- time

- cost.

Tolerance is the permissible deviation from a Stage or Project Plan without bringing the deviation to the attention of the Project Board (or higher authority if the deviation is at project level). Separate tolerance figures should be given for time and cost. Tolerance figures need not be the same for over and under cost and time. A tolerance, say, of +5% -20% may be more realistic than +/-10%.

Tolerances for the project as a whole should be set by corporate or programme management in the Project Mandate (or ascertained by the Executive during Project Start-up, to be entered into the Project Brief). Based on these overall figures, the Project Board agrees with the Project Manager a tolerance for each stage, once the Stage Plan has been produced.

If the tolerance for a stage is forecast to be exceeded, the Project Board may set new tolerances around the new forecast as long as these are within the constraints of the overall project figures. Where the forecast is for the project tolerance to be exceeded, the Project Board must refer the matter back to corporate or programme management for a decision.

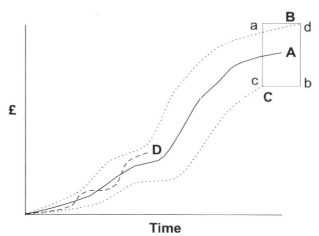

Figure 6–3: Cost/time tolerance graph

Figure 6–3 illustrates cost and time tolerances and the Project Manager's freedom of decision within the tolerances. Line A is the plan. Lines B and C show the limits of the tolerance in cost and time given by the Project Board. Line B illustrates that the plan may cost a little more than forecast or take a little longer. Line C illustrates that the plan may cost a little less, or take a shorter time. Within these two limits the plan is judged to be under control. Line D illustrates how actual progress might be proceeding. Although it is deviating from the plan, it is within the tolerance margins. If at any time the Project Manager can forecast that line D will break through either of the tolerance lines, a special procedure is invoked (see the Exception Report and Exception Plan later in this chapter) that brings in the Project Board to 'manage by exception'. The four corners of the box indicate the tolerance limits on cost and time for the total plan – for example, the bottom left-hand corner of the box (c) indicates the shortest time and least cost of the plan within the tolerance limits. The top right-hand corner (d) represents the tolerance limits for exceeding the planned cost and time.

Hints and tips for tolerance

In most projects, funding is provided by the Customer. But there are situations where the Supplier or a third party either fully or partially funds the project. This may give the Customer fewer rights to intervene or control the project's expenditure. In such situations it is important for the Customer and User to consider and establish controls giving them involvement in quality inspection and approval to proceed at Stage ends. There must also be sufficient progress reporting to assure the Project Board that the project is under control. A tolerance margin for time should still be set.

There are actually four possible elements to tolerance: cost, time, scope, and quality. Where there is a tight or non-existent positive tolerance, for example, the end product must be delivered by date X, the Project Manager would normally look for extra tolerance in one or more of the other elements, such as cost (for example: 'Can more resources or overtime be used to ensure that the time tolerance is not to be exceeded?'). Where there is little or no tolerance on time, cost and scope, the Project Manager must watch out for the temptation for individuals or teams to reduce the quality of work unofficially as a means of saving time.

The Project Board should think, stage by stage (and the figures may change for each stage), 'Under what circumstances do we want to take this stage back from the

Project Manager? Under what circumstances are we happy to let the Project Manager run with it?'

6.4.2 Product Descriptions

A description of each product is written down before that product is developed or obtained – even before it is planned – to ensure that the individual people know:

- why it is needed
- what it will look like
- from what sources it will be derived
- the quality specification to which it must be built.

The Product Description is a control document. It is written as part of the planning process. It defines the deliverable, the standards to be used in its creation, and the quality criteria to be applied to ensure it is fit for its purpose. Not only is this information essential for the creator, but the Product Description also forms the initial checklist for checking the quality of the finished product.

When a product has been identified in a plan's Product Breakdown Structure, its Product Description should be drafted. Outline Product Descriptions of standard PRINCE management and quality products (such as plans, reports, approvals) are provided in *Appendix A – PRINCE Product Description Outlines.*

All Product Descriptions must be approved. In formal terms they are approved by the Project Board. If the assurance roles of the Project Board members are delegated, the assurance of the Product Descriptions may be one of the authorities to be delegated.

The relevant Product Description forms part of a Work Package authorisation given to an individual or team responsible for creation of that product.

Hints and tips for Product Descriptions

Product Descriptions should be written by staff who know the proposed product.

Product Descriptions may not be needed for every level of product. The project Board can make a decision as to which are the major products for which a Product Description is necessary.

6.4.3 Work Package authorisation

Work Package authorisation is the trigger from the Project Manager to an individual or group to undertake a piece of the work of a stage. The implication is that work cannot be undertaken unless the Project Manager has specifically authorised it.

Work is released to a team member or Team Manager in an agreed Work Package. The Work Package will contain the Product Description, constraints such as time, cost and interfaces, reporting and product hand-over requirements, and any other documentation or products necessary for understanding and implementing the Work Package. Work Package authorisation is particularly useful when dealing with contractors or sub-contractors. The two sides to it (giver and receiver) are described in *Authorising Work Package (CS1)* and *Accepting a Work Package (MP1).*

6.4.4 Quality Control

Every project needs procedures and techniques to control the quality of the products being produced. The ideal quality controls will vary according to the type of product and project, and PRINCE makes no effort to define all the possibilities. It does, however, include a generic quality check, which has been found to be effective over a number of years in checking the quality of documents. The check is called a Quality Review.

The Quality Review is one type of quality check. It is a team method of assuring product quality by a review process. The purpose of the review is to inspect the product for errors in a planned, independent, controlled and documented manner. Quality Review documentation, when filed in the Quality section of the project filing, provides a record that the product was inspected, that any errors found were corrected and the corrections themselves were checked. Knowing that a product has been checked and declared error-free provides a more confident basis to move ahead and use that product as the basis of future work.

A Quality Review can be used to control the quality of documents, including those created by the specialists. A Quality Review provides a feedback to the Project Manager on the status of a document (and the performance of the Quality Review technique). It is fully described in its own chapter (Chapter 23).

There are many other types of quality check, depending on the type of product to be tested. PRINCE is compatible with all types of check.

6.4.5 Project Issues

As part of control there must be a procedure that caters for possible deviations from specification. These deviations occur for many reasons:

- the User's requirement changes

- Government legislation changes and the product's specification must be revised to accommodate these changes

- the User or Supplier wants to change or add an acceptance criterion

- during the development, extra features suggest themselves for inclusion

- there are organisational or business changes that alter the scope and objectives of the project

- the Supplier finds that it will be impossible to deliver everything within the agreed cost or schedule

- a question arises on whether the Supplier can meet a particular part of the specification or acceptance criterion

- a sub-contractor or interfacing project fails to meet its planned commitment.

Apart from deviation possibilities, there will also be a need for an avenue into the project for questions or concerns. All of these need a procedure to control them and their effect on the project. In PRINCE all such inputs are handled by the Project Issue procedure.

This procedure ensures that all such questions, problems, concerns or suggestions are answered, but that nothing is undertaken without the knowledge of the appropriate level of management, including the Project Board. Apart from controlling possible changes, it provides a formal entry point through which all questions or requests can be raised.

The Project Issue procedure logs and handles all Project Issues raised during the life of the project. The procedure provides knowledge of the status of all Project Issues, control over their processing, and a feedback to the originator on any actions taken.

6.4.6 Change Control

Every project must have a procedure to handle change. Without Change Control there is no project control.

All requested changes are logged as Project Issues. The procedure includes impact assessment of the request, prioritisation, decision making and action. There is a separate chapter (Chapter 11) describing the control of change and another chapter (Chapter 22) on a suggested approach to Change Controls.

6.4.7 Risk Log

The management of risk is an important control throughout the project.

A Risk Log is kept of all identified risks, their analysis, countermeasures and status. This begins at the start of the project and continues until the project closes. All risks are frequently reviewed. As a minimum, risks are reassessed at the end of each Stage, but they should also be reviewed as part of the assessment of Stage progress.

There is a separate chapter (Chapter 8) on the management of risk.

6.4.8 Checkpoint

A Checkpoint is a time-driven control when the status of work in a Stage or of a team is ascertained. It involves the people carrying out the work and is triggered by either the Project Manager or the Team Manager, whoever is the more appropriate. In larger projects the participants might be the Project Manager, Team Managers and project support people. It may or may not be a formal meeting.

A specific aim of a Checkpoint is to check all aspects of the project against the plans to ensure that there are no nasty surprises hiding. Useful questions are 'What is not going to plan?' and 'What is likely not to go to plan?'

The information gathered at a Checkpoint is recorded for the Project Manager and forms the basis of the Highlight Report. Checkpoints should be taken as frequently as the Project Manager requires in order to maintain control over progress. They may coincide with the Project Manager's need to consider re-planning.

A Checkpoint can also be used for the downward dissemination of information from the Project Board, corporate or programme management to team members.

The suggested content of a Checkpoint Report is given in *Appendix A – PRINCE Product Description outlines*.

6.4.9 Planning and re-planning

Plans are, to a certain extent, guesswork. Activities do not always go as planned. Resources do not always perform as expected. Unplanned activities may emerge. The Project Manager needs to compare the plan regularly against latest information and be ready to re-plan. Failure to re-plan, or re-planning too seldom, can leave it too late to recover from problems. There is, however, a danger of reacting too early or too frequently to the status of non-critical activities. Small deviations may correct themselves and the Project Manager may spend too much time in re-planning rather than in monitoring. When and how often to re-plan will depend on the size and criticality of the project, and is a matter for the Project Manager's judgement.

Re-planning is needed at Stage boundaries and when Exceptions arise.

6.4.10 Highlight Report

A Highlight Report is sent by the Project Manager to the Project Board during a Stage at a frequency dictated by the Project Board. The frequency depends on such factors as the length and perceived risk of the Stage. Typically, the report might be sent fortnightly or monthly.

The Project Board has the right to define the content of the Highlight Report. Minimally, it should contain statements about:

- achievements in the current period
- achievements expected in the next period
- actual or potential problems and suggestions concerning their resolution.

The Project Board may also ask for a copy of the Stage Plan (or parts of it), showing actual progress to date in terms of activities and cost, plus reports on any other item in the Stage that it feels is important. Whatever the content, the style should be concise. Instead of a copy of the Stage Plan the Project Board may prefer to receive an updated copy of the Product Checklist, showing status and any revised dates.

Often the frequency of Highlight Reports is defined for the whole project in the Project Initiation Document, but the frequency can be varied for different stages. For example, the Initiation Stage is normally very short, and the Project Board may request either no Highlight Reports or a lower frequency.

A Highlight Report's purpose is to allow the Project Board to 'manage by exception' between End Stage Assessments. The Project Board is aware of the Stage Plan to which it is committed, and of the tolerance margins that it agreed with the Project Manager. The Highlight Reports confirm that progress is being made within those tolerances. Early warning of any possible problems is reported to the Project Board via the Highlight Report. The Project Board can react to any problems that are reported, as formally or informally as it feels is necessary.

The Project Board can request that copies of the Highlight Report are sent to other interested parties.

Appendix A – PRINCE Product Description outlines contains a suggested outline for a Highlight Report.

Hints and tips for the Highlight Report

The Project Manager can use the Highlight Report to convey concern about items that are under the control of any member of the Project Board. As the report is read by all members of the Project Board, any member whose commitment is the source of the concern will feel pressure from the other members to put the matter right.

The Senior User has part of the responsibility for monitoring project deliverables. This may be difficult to do where a remote Supplier or third party is developing or procuring the product. Monitoring can be assisted by Checkpoint and Highlight Reports and by User involvement in checking the quality of such products.

6.4.11 Exception Report

An Exception Report is a warning from the Project Manager to the Project Board that the Stage (or Project) Plan will deviate outside its tolerance margins. It is a wise precaution for the Project Manager to document the report.

There are situations where it is the tolerance for the whole project that is at risk, and not just that for the Stage. For example, information may be found that shows that a major equipment expenditure, which is to be made much later in the project, will greatly exceed current expectations and take the project outside tolerance.

An Exception Report describes a forecast deviation, provides an analysis of both the exception and the options for the way forward, and identifies the recommended option. There is a suggested content for the Exception Report in *Appendix A – PRINCE Product Description outlines*. An Exception Report usually leads to a meeting (Mid-Stage Assessment), and will be the basis for the production of an Exception Plan for the recommended option.

Where the project is part of a programme, exception situations may occur because of changes or problems at the project or programme level. Examples would be a business change or the late delivery of an externally purchased product, which may impact the whole programme or just a single project. Changes in end dates or to the specification of products to be delivered by the project are likely to have a knock-on effect in the programme. To avoid duplication of effort and to save time, those exception situations likely to impact more than a single project within a programme should be co-ordinated at programme level.

6.4.12 End Stage Assessment

Part of the philosophy of breaking the project into Stages is that the Project Board only commits to one Stage at a time. At the end of that Stage the Project Board takes a good look at the project to decide if it wishes to proceed to the next Stage. This review is called an End Stage Assessment. According to such factors as project size, criticality and risk situation, the End Stage Assessment may be formal or informal.

However it is done, the End Stage Assessment is a mandatory control point at the end of each Stage. The assessment approves the work to date and provides authority to proceed to the next Stage. A Stage should not be considered complete until it has received this formal approval.

The specific objectives of an End Stage Assessment are to:

- check that the need for the project has not changed
- review the results of the Stage against the Stage Plans
- satisfy the Project Board about the quality of the products delivered
- establish that the current Stage has been completed satisfactorily
- check whether any external event has changed the project's premises
- perform a risk analysis and management review of the project and the next Stage Plan and incorporate the results into the next Stage Plan and Project Plan
- review overall project status against the Project Plans (which may now have been revised)
- review the next Stage Plan against the Project Plans
- ensure that a complete and consistent baseline is established for the next stage
- review the tolerances set for the next Stage
- ensure that the specialist aspects of the project are still sound
- review the project against its Business Case and ensure that the project is still viable
- authorise the passage of the project into the next Stage (if the Business Case continues to be viable).

The Project Board has the right to refuse to approve the next Stage Plan if it is unhappy with any of the aspects mentioned in the list above. It can either ask the Project Manager to rethink the next Stage Plan, force closure of the project, or refer the problem to corporate or programme management if the problem is beyond its remit.

6.4.13 End Stage Report

The End Stage Report is the vehicle through which the Project Manager informs the Project Board of the results of a Stage. The Project Board can compare the results in terms of products, cost and time against the Stage Plan that it approved.

The End Stage Report contains all the information described for an End Stage Assessment, except the approval to proceed to the next stage. It forms a record that can be audited at any time in the project, giving a summary of what happened in a stage, the impact on the Project Plan, Business Case and risks, and why decisions about the future of the project were made.

6.4.14 Mid-Stage Assessment

A Mid-Stage Assessment is held between the Project Board and Project Manager after an Exception Report. If any of the Project Board's assurance responsibilities have been delegated, the people to whom assurance has been delegated would also participate. Its purpose is for the Project Manager to present an Exception Plan to the Project Board and obtain its approval for implementation of the plan. As with the End Stage Assessment, it may be formal or informal according to the size, criticality and risk of the project.

The content of an Exception Plan is the same as that of other PRINCE plans. There is some additional text that is described in Chapter 5 *Plans*.

Every exception has an impact on the Stage, project, Business Case and risks. The recommended option will also have an impact on the same items. The Project Board must consider both sets of impact.

6.5   Controlled close

Before the Project Board allows the project to close (unless the project has been prematurely terminated), it has the control to ensure that:

- all the agreed products have been delivered and accepted

- arrangements are in place, where appropriate, to support and maintain the product in its useful life

- any useful statistics or lessons for later projects are passed to the relevant body

- a plan has been made to check the achievement of the benefits claimed in the project's Business Case.

At Project Closure the Project Board must confirm in writing (for the Project Management file) its acceptance that the project has been completed. If necessary, these statements can be qualified – for example, that the products have been delivered with minor deficiencies that can be rectified later.

The following information is generated at the close of the project, which leads to control actions by the Project Board.

6.5.1 End Project Notification

The End Project Notification advises all those who have provided resources or services to the project that the project is coming to an end.

6.5.2 Lessons Learned Report

The Lessons Learned Report is created within the project to disseminate useful lessons learned during the project for the benefit of other projects.

It covers management, specialist and quality processes, techniques and tools, what worked well and what caused problems. It is a useful control as part of the functions of an independent quality assurance or similar group. A suggested content is included in *Appendix A – PRINCE Product Description outlines*.

The Lessons Learned Report is gradually built up (and acted on) during the project and handed over as one of the products at Project Closure.

6.5.3 Follow-on Action Recommendations

At the close of the project there may be a number of actions left undone. For example, there may have been a number of Requests For Change that the Project Board decided not to implement during the project but that were not rejected; not all expected products may have been handed over, or there may be some known problems with what has been delivered.

The Follow-on Action Recommendations document any 'unfinished business' and allow the Project Board to direct them to the person or group whose job it will be to have the recommendations considered for action after the current project has ended.

6.5.4 End Project Report

The End Project Report is similar to the End Stage Report, but covers the entire project. A suggested content is included in *Appendix A – PRINCE Product Description Outlines*.

The End Project Report reviews how well the project has been managed, including actual achievements against the Project Initiation Document. Where the Lessons Learned Report concentrates on the good and bad points in the project management standards, this report concentrates on the performance of the project management team.

Where possible at this point, the achievement by the project of benefits anticipated in the Business Case is reviewed. (Most of this measurement will have to wait until the Post-Project Review.) Any changes made after the Project Initiation Document was agreed are identified, and their impact on Project Plan, Business Case and risks is assessed.

The report provides statistics on Project Issues and their impact on the project, plus statistics on the quality of work carried out.

If the project is part of a programme, the programme will require a copy of the End Project Report. The Programme Executive may provide details of extra statistics and information it needs from the report. This should be covered in the Communication Plan.

6.5.5 Post-Project Review

The Post-Project Review occurs outside the project.

Normally many products need time in use before the achievement of their expected benefits can be measured. This measurement after a period of use is an activity called a Post-Project Review. At Project Closure a plan is agreed on when and how achievement of benefits can be measured.

A Post-Project Review occurs after the project has closed. Any corrective work identified by the Post-Project Review would be done during product use and maintenance. Any problems may not be with the product, but organisational ones, needing such solutions as retraining.

Where a project is part of a programme, the project may simply contribute to the realisation of programme-level benefits.

A suggested content for a Post-Project Review is given in *Appendix A – PRINCE Product Description outlines*.

52

7   Stages

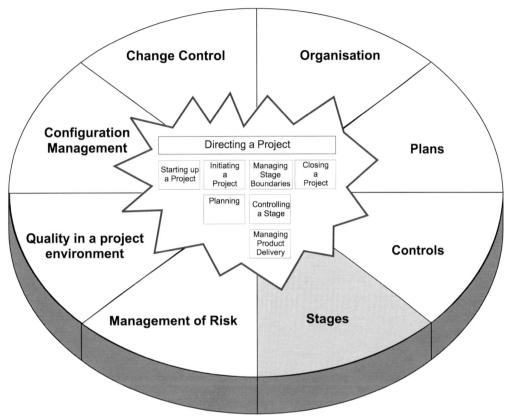

Figure 7–1: Stages in the PRINCE template

7.1   What is a Stage?

Stages are partitions of the project with decision points. A Stage is a collection of activities and products whose delivery is managed as a unit. As such it is a sub-set of the project, and in PRINCE terms it is the element of work that the Project Manager is managing on behalf of the Project Board at any one time. The use of Stages in a PRINCE project is mandatory; the number of Stages is flexible and depends on the needs of the project.

PRINCE Stages are often described as 'management stages' in order to differentiate them from a different use of the word 'stages' in some specific project environments. This is described below.

7.1.1 Phases and Stages

In some methods the word 'phase' is used as an equivalent to the PRINCE Stage. This is not in itself a problem.

It would become a problem if people thought of product life cycle phases, such as:

*   conception
*   feasibility
*   implementation (or realisation)
*   operation
*   termination

as PRINCE Stages. These are phases for the product life cycle, not the project. The last two are outside the project. While a product is 'operational' it may be the subject of any number of projects to enhance or revise it. Most of what in PRINCE terms will be Stages will be divisions of 'implementation' in the product life cycle.

7.2   Why are Management Stages important?

There are various reasons for breaking the project into Stages. They include the following.

7.2.1 Review and decision points

Within any project there will be key decisions, the results of which will have fundamental effects on the direction and detailed content of the project. There is, thus, a need to review direction and ongoing viability on a regular basis.

PRINCE uses stages to deal with these decision points. The decisions form the basis of the End Stage Assessments carried out in *Authorising a Stage or Exception Plan (DP3)*. The benefits that these End Stage Assessments bring to the project are:

- providing a 'fire break' for the project by encouraging the Project Board to assess the project viability at regular intervals, rather than let it run on in an uncontrolled manner

- ensuring that key decisions are made prior to the detailed work needed to implement them. The nature of these decisions can be varied and will include:
  - whether to commit major resources such as capital investment
  - what the impact is of major risk elements
  - the clarification of a previously unknown or ill understood part of the project's direction or products

- clarifying what the impact will be of an identified external influence such as the corporate budget round or the finalisation of legislation.

7.2.2 Planning horizons

Uncertainty can often mean that it is only possible to plan in detail the activities and products of a limited amount of the work of the project. The rest of the project's work can only be planned in broad outline. The adoption of Stages handles this situation by having two different but related levels of plan – that is, a detailed Stage Plan and an outline Project Plan.

7.2.3 Scalability

Every project should consist of at least two Stages. A small project may need only two Stages: an Initiation Stage with the remainder of the project as the second Stage. The Initiation Stage may last only a matter of hours but is essential to ensure that there is a firm basis for the project, understood by all parties.

Most projects need to be broken down into more manageable Stages to enable the correct level of planning and control to be exercised.

7.3   Management versus technical Stages

One method of grouping work together in Stages is by the set of techniques used or the product created. This results in Stages covering elements such as design, build and implementation. Such stages are *technical* Stages and are a separate concept from the *management* Stages introduced above.

Technical Stages are typified by the use of a particular set of specialist skills.

Management Stages equate to commitment of resources and authority to spend.

Often the two types of Stage will coincide; for instance, where the management decision is based on the output from the technical Stage. An example of this might be where the output from the technical Stage is a set of design options.

However, on other occasions the Stages will not coincide. There might be more than one technical Stage per management Stage. For example, the Project Board might decide to combine all the technical Stages that investigate a need and produce a specification into one management Stage. One plan would be approved to cover all the work, with Project Board commitment before the work started and a review at the end. In a risky project – for example, one that is (technically) innovative – a technical Stage might be divided into more than one management Stage.

The PRINCE approach is to concentrate the management of the project on the *management* Stages since these will form the basis of the planning and control processes described throughout the method. To do otherwise runs the risk of the project being driven by the specialist teams instead of the Customer's management.

Where the desired management stages do not coincide with the technical stages, technical work can be broken down so that its activities can be divided over two management Stages. Figure 7–2 gives an example of this break.

Project

Stage 1	Stage 2	Stage 3	Stage 4

```
      Specify
  |—————————————
     A   Overall              Periphery
         Design    Design      Design
        |————————|————————|————————|
          B         C         E
                                      Build
                                   |————————————|
            Training                    F
            Syllabus          Train
            |————————|————————————|
                D                 G
                                            Commission
                                          |——————————————|
                                                H
```

Figure 7–2: Technical activities broken down to fit within management Stages

Figure 7–2 shows that Design has been broken into three activities. Part B now falls within Stage 1. Part C of Design and part D of Training form the second management Stage, and part E of Design is planned to be done in Stage 3.

7.4   How to define Stages

The process of defining Stages is fundamentally a process of balancing:

- how far ahead in the project it is sensible to plan
- where the key decision points need to be on the project
- too many small Stages versus too few big ones.

This will be a balance of the factors identified above, and will be influenced by any Team Plans. However, the Project Manager will have to reconcile these two types of plan. This is discussed in the *Plans* chapter (Chapter 5).

7.5   How to use Stages

The primary use of Stages is as a basis for dictating the timing of the Stage boundary processes covered by *Managing Stage Boundaries (SB)*, and by the associated *Authorising a Stage or Exception Plan (DP3)*. These processes are used to make decisions regarding the continuation or otherwise of the project.

One element of this decision-making process is whether the Stage that has just been completed has been completed successfully. This can be problematic where the *management* Stage ends part-way through one or more elements of specialist work, since it can be difficult to establish whether the specialist work is under control. The PRINCE technique of *Product-based planning (see Chapter 21)* is invaluable here, since by using it the Project Manager can identify the detailed products involved in any element of specialist work, and can hence identify all the products that are due to be produced within the confines of any given management Stage. This can then be used to assess completion or otherwise of the Stage.

Driving this will be *Planning a Project (IP2)*.

8   Management of Risk

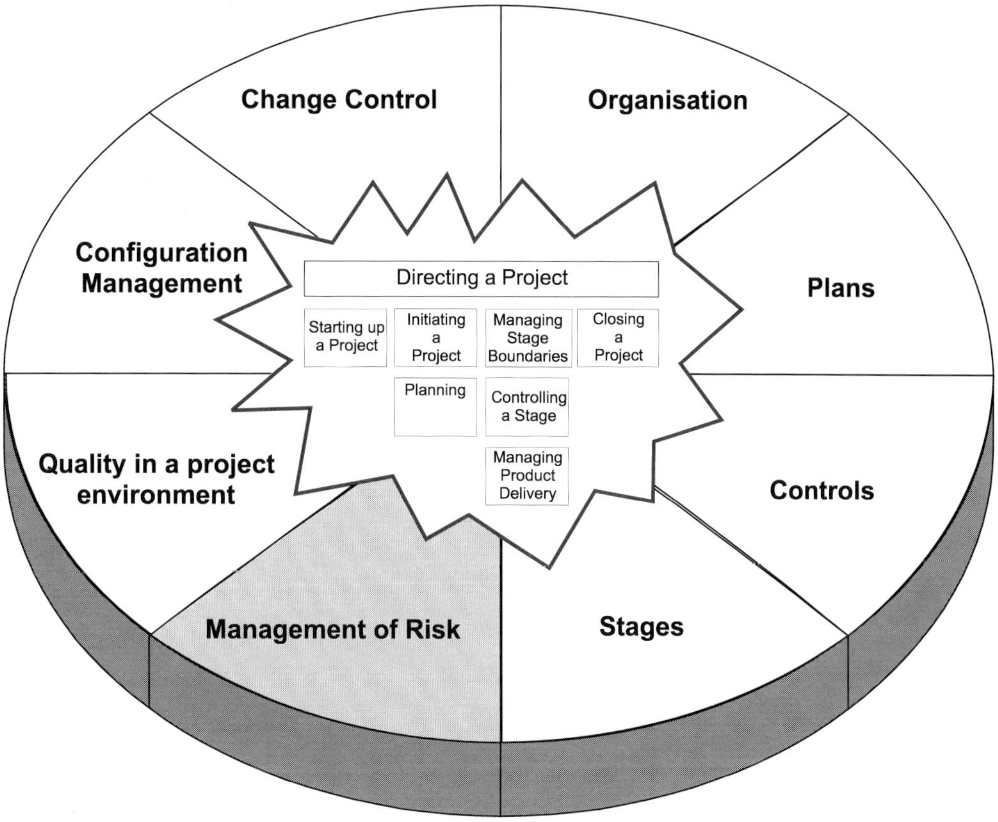

Figure 8–1: The management of risk in the PRINCE template

8.1   Purpose

Risk is a major factor to be considered during the management of a project. Project management must control and contain risks if a project is to stand a chance of being successful.

This section covers the main aspects of the management of risk as they apply to project management

8.2   What is risk?

PRINCE defines risk as:

> ***The chance of exposure to the adverse consequences of future events.***

Projects are set up to bring about change, and hence project work is less predictable than is typically the case with non-project work. The project is unique and usually its objectives have to be achieved within certain constraints. In addition, projects can be large and complex, and can deal with novel or unusual factors.

There are a number of 'standard' risks that may affect the project (that is, they affect all projects). Some examples of these appear under the next heading *Types of risk*. There will be other risks that are project-specific – that is, they exist because of a particular project and its circumstances.

Management of risk is an essential part of project management. There are a number of techniques available that can be used.

8.3 Types of risk

Broadly, there are two types of risk – Business risk and Project risk.

8.3.1 Business risk

This covers the threats associated with a project not delivering products that can achieve the expected benefits. It is the responsibility of the Project Board to manage business risks. This is described in *Directing a Project (DP)* – see Chapter 15. It includes such areas as:

- the validity and viability of the Business Case

- whether the project continues to support the corporate business strategy, including such elements as:
  - strategic direction
  - commercial issues
  - market change

- the consequences to the corporate body of failure or limited success

- the stability of the business areas involved

- programme requirements

- legislative changes

- political factors, including public opinion

- environmental issues

- the impact on the Customer of the results of the project

- the risks of the end result meeting the stated requirements but not fulfilling expectations.

8.3.2 Project risk

This is the collection of threats to the management of the project and hence to the achievement of the project's end results within cost and time. These risks may be managed on a day-to-day basis by the Project Board, Project Manager or Team Manager. Risks will be many and varied, but would include the following broad categories:

- supplier issues, covering those risks caused by being dependent on a third party, including:
  - failure of the third party
  - failure by the third party to deliver satisfactorily
  - contractual issues
  - a mismatch between the nature of the task and the procurement process

- organisational factors such as:
  - additional staff responsibilities alongside project work
  - the project culture, or lack of it, within the Customer organisation
  - personnel and training issues
  - skill shortages
  - potential security implications
  - culture clashes between Customer and Supplier

- specialist issues; there will be a wide variety of issues here because each project has its own particular specialist elements, which bring with them their own risk elements. However, there are some general issues that will apply to many project types, such as:
  - how well requirements can be specified
  - to what extent the requirements can be met using currently available and understood facilities and approaches

- the extent to which a project involves innovative, difficult or complex processes and/or equipment
- the challenges and problems regarding quality testing
- the risks that the specified requirements will not be achievable in full, or that not all requirements will be correctly specified.

It must be stressed that the above lists are given purely to illustrate the areas of risk that need to be considered as part of project management. Each project must be considered in its own right.

Once identified, risks are not kept separate (for example, business, project, Stage Plan). They are all entered in the one Risk Log, which is always reviewed in its entirety.

8.4 Managing risk

The management of risk is one of the most important parts of the jobs done by the Project Board and the Project Manager. The Project Manager is responsible for ensuring that risks are identified, recorded and regularly reviewed. The Project Board has four responsibilities:

- notifying the Project Manager of any external risk exposure to the project

- making decisions on the Project Manager's recommended reactions to risk

- striking a balance between level of risk and the potential benefits that the project may achieve

- notifying programme management of any risks that affect the project's ability to meet programme constraints.

The Project Manager modifies plans to include agreed actions to avoid or reduce the impact of risks. An 'owner' should be identified for each risk, who should be the person best situated to keep an eye on it. The Project Manager will normally suggest the 'owner' and the Project Board should make the decision. Project Board members may be appointed 'owners' of risks, particularly risks from sources external to the project.

In order to contain the risks during the project, they must be managed in a disciplined manner. This discipline consists of:

- risk analysis, which involves the identification and definition of risks, plus the evaluation of impact and consequent action

- risk management, which covers the activities involved in the planning, monitoring and controlling of actions that will address the threats and problems identified, so as to improve the likelihood of the project achieving its stated objectives.

Figure 8–2 shows the major activities in the management of risk.

The risk analysis and risk management phases must be treated separately, to ensure that decisions are made objectively and based on all the relevant information.

Risk analysis and risk management are interrelated and undertaken iteratively. The formal recording of information is an important element in risk analysis and risk management. The documentation provides the foundation that supports the overall management of risk.

Risk analysis requires input from the management of the organisation. The organisation's management, in turn, is kept informed by the analysis in a highly iterative manner. Communication is particularly important between the project and programme levels within the organisation.

Risk Analysis   **Risk Management**

Figure 8–2: The major activities in the management of risk

Where the project is part of a programme, the management of risk procedures used by the project must be consistent and compatible with those of the programme unless there are valid reasons not to do so. Where a risk is uncovered in the programme, any affected projects should be involved in the analysis of that risk. Similarly, project risk evaluation should include staff from the programme.

Project risks that threaten programme milestones or objectives must be escalated to programme management.

8.4.1 Risk analysis

Risk analysis is essential for effective management of risk. It comprises three activities:

- **risk identification**, which determines the potential risks that could be faced by the project

- **risk estimation**, which determines how important each risk is, based on an assessment of its likelihood and consequences to the project and business

- **risk evaluation**, which decides whether the level of each risk is acceptable or not and, if not, what actions can be taken to make it more acceptable.

The actions break into broadly five types:

- **prevention**, where countermeasures are put in place that either stop the threat or problem from occurring, or prevent it having any impact on the project or business

- **reduction**, where the actions either reduce the likelihood of the risk developing or limit the impact on the project to acceptable levels

- **transference**, which is a specialist form of risk reduction where the impact of the risk is passed to a third party via, for instance, an insurance policy or penalty clause

- **contingency**, where actions are planned and organised to come into force as and when the risk occurs

- **acceptance**, where the Project Board decides to go ahead and accept the possibility that the risk might occur (believing that either the risk will not occur or the countermeasures are too expensive).

Any given risk could have appropriate actions in any or all of the above categories. Alternatively, there may be no cost-effective actions available to deal with a risk, in which case the risk must be accepted or the justification for the project re-visited (to review whether the project is too risky).

The results of the risk analysis activities are documented in the Risk Log. If the project is part of a programme, project risks should be examined for any impact on the programme (and vice versa). Where any cross-impact is found, the risk should be added to the other Risk Log.

Risk analysis activities are overlapping, with possibly many iterations involved. Risk analysis is a process that will be conducted continuously throughout the project as information becomes available and as circumstances change. However, there is a need to carry out a major risk analysis at the start of the project as part of the processes:

- *Preparing a Project Brief (SU4)*
- *Planning a Project (IP2)*
- *Refining the Business Case and Risks (IP3)*.

Project risks may, in turn, impact the Business Case. There must also be at least an assessment of all risks during *Managing Stage Boundaries (SB)*. Depending on the individual project, there may be a need to reassess risks on a more frequent basis. The Project Manager and Project Board must constantly be on the lookout for new or changed risks in the business and project environment, which will render the project (as currently planned) wasteful or useless.

8.4.2 Risk management

Once the risks have been identified and evaluated, attention needs to focus on managing them. Risk management logically follows risk analysis, though, as with analysis, the two phases will overlap and often be done in parallel.

Risk management consists of four major activities:

- **planning**, which, for the countermeasure actions itemised during the risk evaluation activities, consists of:
  - identifying the quantity and type of resources required to carry out the actions
  - developing a detailed plan of action to be included in a Stage Plan
  - confirming the desirability of carrying out the actions identified during risk evaluation in the light of any additional information gained
  - obtaining management approval along with all the other aspects of the plans being produced

- **resourcing**, which will identify and assign the resources to be used for the work to carry out the risk avoidance or amelioration actions; these assignments will be shown in Stage Plans; the resources required for the prevention, reduction and transference actions will have to be funded from the project budget, since they are actions that the project is committed to carry out; decisions have to be made on how contingent actions will be funded

- **monitoring**, which consists of:
  - checking that execution of the planned actions is having the desired effect on the risks identified
  - watching for the early warning signs that a risk is developing
  - modelling trends, predicting potential risks
  - checking that the overall management of risk is being applied effectively
  - reporting on risk status, especially on risks with extra-project impact

- **controlling**, which is taking action to ensure that the events of the plan really happen.

Risk management continues in the project, actions being carried out throughout the management cycle.

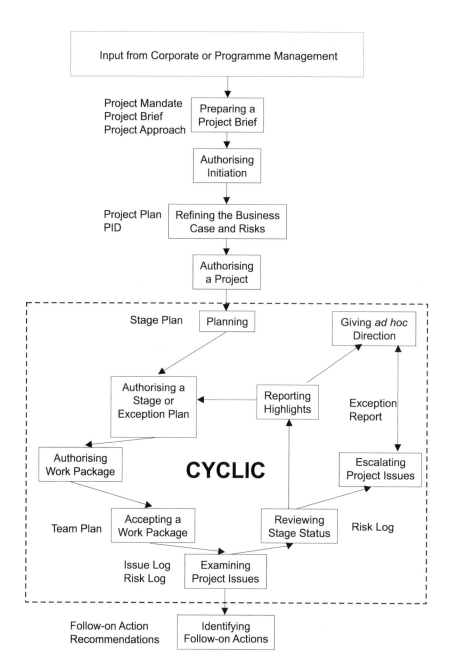

Figure 8–3: Risk flow, showing key points in a project when management is necessary

8.4.3 The Management of Risk throughout the project

At key points in a project, management of risk should be carried out (Figure 8–3).

Preparing a Project Brief (focusing on business risks)

The Project Mandate may have referred to a number of risks facing the potential project. These may be known business risks, such as competitor action, impending or mooted legislation, company policy changes, staff reorganisation or cash-flow problems. Certainly, the preparation of the Project Brief should give rise to an early study of such business risks. Creation of the Project Approach (see Section 13.8) may also have introduced some project risks.

Authorising Initiation

This is the first formal moment when the Project Board can examine the Risk Log as part of deciding whether project initiation can be justified. Pragmatically, the Project Manager should have discussed informally with board members any known risks that seem to threaten the project viability.

Refining the Business Case and Risks (focusing on both business and project risks)

Risks are examined again by the Project Manager as part of preparing the Project Initiation Document. At this time the Project Plan will be created, and this may identify a number of project risks, such as unknown performance of resources, contractor ability and any assumptions being made in the plan. New risks may also come to light as a result of adding detail to the Project Brief. At the same time all existing risks are reviewed for any new information or change in their circumstances.

Authorising a Project

The Project Board now has an updated Risk Log to examine as part of its decision on whether to go ahead with the project. As a result of refining the Business Case, a number of business risks may have been identified. Very often the 'owners' of these risks will be members of the Project Board, and they should confirm their ownership and the actions required of them.

Planning

Each time a plan is produced, elements of the plan may identify new risks, modify existing ones or eliminate others. No plan should be put forward for approval before its risk content has been analysed. This analysis may lead to the plan being modified in order to take the appropriate risk action(s). The Risk Log should be updated with all such details.

Authorising a Stage or Exception Plan

Before authorising a plan, the Project Board has the opportunity to study the risk situation as part of its judgement of the continuing viability of the project.

Authorising Work Package

Negotiation with the Team Manager or team member may identify new risks or change old ones. It may require the Project Manager to go back and amend some part of the original Work Package or change the Stage Plan. Examples here are the assignee seeking more time or needing to change resources.

Accepting a Work Package

This is the point when the Team Manager makes out a Team Plan to ensure that the products of the Work Package can be delivered within the constraints of the agreed Work Package. Like any other plan, it may contain new risks or modify existing ones.

Examining Project Issues

Assessment of a new Project Issue may throw up a risk situation. This may stem from either the technical impact analysis or the business impact analysis. For example, the proposed change may produce a risk of pushing the Stage or project beyond its tolerance margins.

Reviewing Stage Status

This brings together the Stage Plan with its latest actual figures, the Project Plan, the Business Case, open Project Issues, the tolerance status and the Risk Log. The Project Manager (in conjunction with the assurance roles) looks for risk situation changes as well as any other warning signs.

Escalating Project Issues

As well as Project Issues, a risk change may cause the Project Manager to raise an Exception Report to the Project Board.

Reporting Highlights

As part of this task, the Project Manager may take the opportunity to raise any risk matters with the Project Board. Examples here would be notifying the board of any risks that are no longer relevant, warning about new risks, and reminders about business risks that board members should be keeping an eye on.

Giving ad hoc *Direction*

The Project Board is advised by the Project Manager of exception situations via the Exception Report. It has the opportunity to react with advice or a decision – for example, bringing the project to a premature close, requesting an Exception Plan, or removing the problem. *Ad hoc* advice may be instigated by the Project Board on the basis of information given to it from corporate or programme management, or another external source.

Identifying Follow-on Actions

At the end of the project a number of risks may have been identified that will affect the product in its operational life. These should be transferred to the Follow-on Action Recommendations for the information of those who will support the product after the project.

8.4.4 Programme Management and project risks

Where the project is part of a programme, changes in the state of any project risks that are also identified as programme risks must be flagged to the Programme Manager or the designated risk management function in the programme.

Hints and tips for risk

Where the project is part of a programme:

The Programme Manager is responsible for ensuring the management of those risks with interdependencies between projects and programme-wide risks.

The Design Authority monitors risks associated with the programme's outcome.

Where appropriate, the programme should take part in the risk procedure at the project level. This can normally be done by attendance at End Stage Assessments by either the Programme Manager or a designated risk management function.

Risks are frequently common across projects and would benefit from being centralised at programme level. The cost of corrective action can be reduced if it is planned, agreed and actioned only once. Also, problems can result from an inconsistent approach being taken by projects.

9   Quality in a project environment

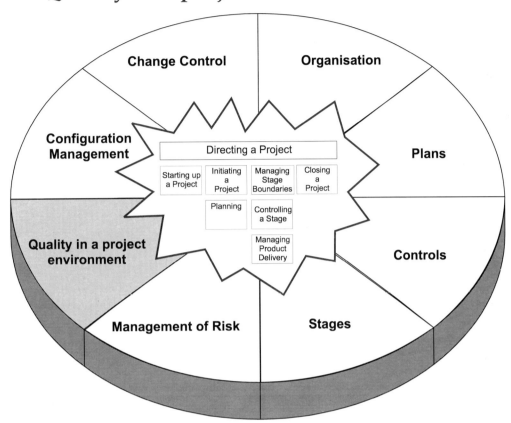

Figure 9–1: Quality in the PRINCE template

9.1   Purpose

The purpose of this chapter is to outline the main elements of quality as they apply to a project, and to put project quality in context with ISO quality standards.

9.2   What is Quality?

Quality is defined in ISO 8402 as the

> *totality of characteristics of an entity which bear on its ability to satisfy stated and implied needs.*

Within projects, quality is a question of identifying what it is about the project's products or services that makes them fit for their purpose of satisfying stated needs. Projects should not rely on implied needs. These lead to uncertainty and, as such, are of little use.

9.3   Quality Management

Quality Management is the process of ensuring that the quality expected by the Customer is achieved. It encompasses all the project management activities that determine and implement the Project's Quality Plan. The various elements of an organisation's quality management interrelate and are as follows:

- a *Quality System* with an organisation structure, procedures and processes to implement quality management. Both the Customer and the Supplier may have quality systems. The project may have to use one of these systems or an agreed mixture of both. PRINCE itself will typically form part of a corporate or programme quality system where it has been adopted as a corporate or programme standard.

- *Quality Assurance*, which sets up the quality system and is the means of assuring that the quality system operates to achieve an end product that meets quality and customer requirements. It creates and maintains the quality system, and audits and evaluates it. A quality assurance function may be set up separate from and independent of the organisation's project and operational activities to monitor use of the quality system across all projects within the corporate body. If such an independent body does not exist, the project assurance function within the project will assume the quality assurance role.

- *Quality Planning* which establishes the objectives and requirements for quality and lays out the activities for the application of the quality system. In the Project Initiation Document the quality approach for the whole project is defined in the Project Quality Plan. It is important that the Customer's quality expectations are understood and documented prior to project commencement. This is done in *Starting up a Project (SU)*. Each Stage Plan specifies in detail the required quality activities and resources, with the detailed quality criteria shown in the Product Descriptions.

- *Quality Control*, which is the means of ensuring that products meet the quality criteria specified for them. Quality control is about examining Products to determine that they meet requirements.

9.3.1 Product Descriptions

The Product Description may need to be updated if a change to the product is agreed.

A Product Description should not be changed, once approved, without passing through change control.

9.3.2 Quality Review

The Quality Review is the primary technique in making project quality work for PRINCE. It is fully described in Chapter 23 the *Techniques* section of the manual.

9.3.3 ISO 9001:1994

ISO 9000 is a range of standards for Quality Management Systems. Many corporate bodies use them as the basis for their Quality Management Systems, and are certificated as to their conformance to it. BS EN ISO 9001:1994 is the specific standard covering Quality Assurance in design and development areas, which includes project management. The use of PRINCE can help an organisation to meet this quality standard, and this help is explained in Appendix B to this manual.

9.4   The quality path

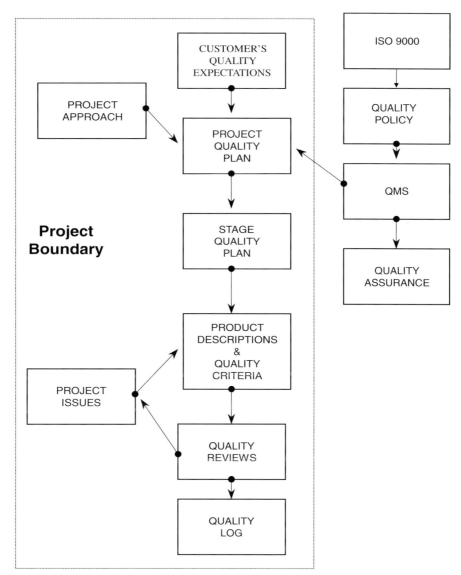

Figure 9–2: The path to Quality

The first approach to quality in PRINCE is shown in Figure 9–2. Each element in this figure is explained below, with cross-references to the areas of PRINCE that relate to it.

Customer's Quality Expectations

In PRINCE, quality considerations begin with discovering what the Customer's quality expectations are. This should be done in the process *Starting Up a Project (SU)*. No plan can be made to provide the customer with a quality product until both Customer and Supplier understand and agree what that quality should be. The Customer and Supplier need a common understanding of quality, cost and time implications and must balance these while ensuring that the end product is fit for its purpose and built within the other constraints.

The colloquial use of the word 'quality' implies use of the best materials, expert craftsmanship, inspection at all points of the product's development, and thorough testing beyond all its expected limits, but this may not be the case. All products do not have the same quality expectations. Quality management usage is focused on meeting the Customer's quality requirements.

Quality expectations could be considered under a number of headings, such as:

- functional requirements
- performance
- practicability
- security
- compatibility
- reliability
- maintainability
- expandability
- flexibility
- clarity
- comparison to another product
- cost
- implementation date.

ISO 9001

ISO 9001 is an international standard for quality systems, issued under the authority of the International Organisation for Standardisation (ISO). It applies to quality assurance in the design/development, production, installation and servicing of a product.

A company can use the quality standard ISO 9001 when:

- setting up a quality assurance function
- examining the quality assurance system of a supplier.

It therefore may have several impacts on the quality considerations for a project.

- It may have been used by the Customer and/or the Supplier as a checklist when creating its Quality Management System.
- The Supplier's development methods may be accredited under ISO 9001.
- The Customer may wish to match a Supplier's quality methods against the requirements of ISO 9001 or insist on a Supplier who holds ISO 9001 accreditation.
- It may have been used as the basis for the corporate quality policy of the Supplier.

Quality Policy

The Customer and/or the Supplier may have a quality policy, laying down the company's attitude towards the quality of anything that it makes or uses. It should direct and influence the Supplier's attitude in construction, testing and reaction to any Customer complaints about quality.

If both Customer and Supplier have quality policies, it is sensible to check that they are in harmony.

Where the project is part of a programme, the programme should provide guidance or direction to the project.

Quality Management System

Two things should support a quality policy; a quality management system (QMS) and a quality organisation structure.

The QMS is a set of standards, which covers all the normal work done by that company. Each standard will cover the techniques, tools, required expertise and steps to be used in the creation of a specific type of product. If the product is a document, the standard will also cover its format or appearance.

If both the Customer and Supplier have quality management systems, there must be agreement on which QMS or what amalgamation of standards from both sets of standards will be used.

The quality organisation structure indicates the responsibilities for quality – that is, who sets the quality policy, who sets the standards to meet the policy, any external body imposing quality constraints, who monitors use of the standards, and any quality training group. Much of this work is often done by a central Quality Assurance function.

Quality Assurance

Site-wide responsibility for setting and monitoring quality standards is often given to a Quality Assurance group. The Project Quality Plan should indicate where this responsibility for setting the quality standards lies. It may be that the independent Quality Assurance group has a representative take a project assurance role in order to monitor the use and effectiveness of agreed standards. If so, this should be stated in the Project Quality Plan.

Project Approach

How the project aims to meet the Customer's quality expectations will be affected by the approach chosen for the provision of the end result. Typical approaches would include:

- the product is built from scratch by the Customer's staff
- an external Supplier builds the product from scratch
- the product is built from scratch with contributions from many external organisations
- an existing product is modified to meet new needs
- an off-the-shelf product is bought.

Quality checking methods and responsibilities will vary according to the approach chosen.

The project approach is confirmed as part of *Starting up a Project (SU)*, therefore it is in place and can be used by the initiation process *Planning Quality (IP1)*.

It is normally impossible to be involved in the testing of an off-the-shelf product. A privileged Customer might be asked to participate in an early test of a product, but this only happens when the organisation is already a Customer. Checks on the quality of such products can be made with existing Customers. Sometimes for more expensive products there is a trial period when testing can be done.

PRINCE offers a good method of checking quality where a product is to be developed by external contractors. This is through use of the Project Assurance function. Each time an external Team Manager plans work for the project, the Project Assurance role should review and approve the draft plan. The purpose is to identify products being developed in the plan that are of interest to the assurance function. Project Assurance then verifies that quality checking arrangements for these products are satisfactory. This covers the method of inspection, the points in the products' development when inspections are to be held, and the people to be involved in the inspection. There should be the option to specify people to be included in the inspections for the purpose of Project Assurance. This is particularly relevant and important for the Customer's assurance of an external contractor's work. This requirement to inspect and modify the contractor's plans should be included in the contract.

Project Quality Plan

This is created in the process *Initiating a Project (IP)*. It forms part of the *Project Initiation Document*. It defines in general terms how the project will meet the Customer's quality expectations.

It will identify the techniques and standards to be used. If there is a QMS in existence, it is normally sufficient simply to point to the QMS manual that contains the standards. If necessary, the Project Quality Plan will identify any standards in the QMS that will not be used, or any extra standards not in the QMS that will be used.

The plan should also identify quality responsibilities for the project. For example, if the Customer or the Supplier has a Quality Assurance function, this would explain how that function would play a part in the project. This links with the *Organisation* component of PRINCE, where the external Quality Assurance function would take a Project Assurance role.

Stage Quality Plan

Encompassed within a Stage Plan will be details of how the Project Quality Plan will be implemented in that Stage. This will go down to the level of each product to be produced in the Stage, defining how its quality will be tested or checked and who will be involved in each check. For example, if the product is a document that is to be Quality Reviewed, the Stage Plan should show the time and effort allocation of the Quality Review chairperson and reviewers to be used. The Stage Plan should show in diagrammatic form when the review will take place and how long it will take.

The Stage Plan is a key time for the involvement of the Project Assurance function. On production of a draft Stage Plan, the Project Manager should discuss the quality requirements with those appointed to an assurance role, particularly user and specialist assurance. They have the opportunity to identify the products that are important to those whose interests they represent. They can then insist on:

- identifying people who should be involved in the check
- the points in the development of the product where it should be reviewed.

This is particularly important where work is being allocated to an external team. Rather than wait until the 'finished' product is handed over for acceptance trials, it is better for the final user to have people checking the product all the way through its design and development. Finding out that a product doesn't meet requirements during its acceptance trials is expensively late – maybe fatally so.

NOTE: Where external teams are to be used, it is important to define in the contract that the Project Assurance function has the right to see draft plans and insist on its people being part of quality checks whenever it wishes.

Product Descriptions and quality criteria

As part of a Stage Plan there should be a Product Description for each major product to be created during that stage. This indicates, among other things, the quality criteria that the product must meet and the method of checking that those criteria exist in the finished product.

It is sensible, often essential, to involve the Customer's staff in defining the Product Descriptions, including the quality criteria. Not only are they the people who should know best, but the product needs to meet their quality expectations.

An inherent quality criterion for every product is that the product should satisfy all the elements of the Product Description. For example, it should contain those elements mentioned under 'Composition' and be capable of satisfying the defined purpose of the product.

Quality Reviews

The detailed steps of a Quality Review are explained in its own chapter. Basically it is a structured review of a document by a group of people in a planned, documented and organised fashion. The people involved should have been identified when creating the Stage Plan. The technique links with the Configuration Management part of the project organisation, which will be responsible for releasing copies of the document to be reviewed, freezing the original copy and updating the status of the product.

There is also a link with the Project Support Office, which might undertake the organisation of the review and the dissemination of the documentation.

Quality Log

The Quality Log is the record of all the quality checking done in the project. The Team Manager or individual team member charged with the development and testing of a product updates it. It forms an audit trail of the quality work done in the project.

The Quality Log is created during *Initiating a Project (IP)*.

Project Issues

Project Issues have many potential impacts on quality. A Project Issue may be reporting a quality problem. It might be thought that such problems would be handled on an Action List as part of a Quality Review or some other test. But a quality problem may be found in a product that has already been approved, or a review might discover a problem in a product that is not the one being inspected. There is also the possibility that an action item from a Quality Review may be found to require a lot of time. It may even be decided, because of time constraints, to approve a product that contains an error. In both these cases the error can be transferred to a Project Issue, so that a record exists and the error will not be overlooked.

If a Project Issue requires changes to one or more products, the relevant Product Descriptions should be checked to see if they also need changing.

9.4.1 What is special about quality in the project environment?

First and foremost, success of the project should be measured by the achievement of the overall objectives of the project – that is, whether it has delivered a quality product.

In a production environment, the elements of quality management discussed above will tend to have been thought through and will be in place on a permanent basis. However, by its nature, the project is a temporary environment created for a particular purpose. As such, any required quality management for the project may have to be created for that project if the organisation does not already have a quality system in place.

9.5 Making project quality work

Project quality planning must cover the following agreements to ensure that the project delivers to an acceptable level of quality:

- *how* each product will be tested against its quality criteria
- *when* each product will be tested against its quality criteria
- *by whom* each product will be tested against its quality criteria.

The first aspect is actioned by *Planning Quality (IP1)* at the outset of the project, during *Initiating a Project*. The last two aspects are actioned in the relevant Stage Quality Plans, created in *Planning a Stage (SB1)*.

Quality is achieved by a combination of actions. The quality criteria for all levels of product are stated in measurable terms in the Product Descriptions (this is described in *Product-based planning*). The process of producing the products and services is controlled via *Authorising Work Package (CS1)* and *Assessing Progress (CS2)*.

The final aspect is the process of using all the quality checking techniques defined in the Quality System. These split largely into two groups:

- **objective methods**, where, after applying them, there is a largely definitive 'yes' or 'no' answer to whether the deliverable is 'to quality'. Examples of these methods are the use of gauges and meters, testing and checklists.

- **subjective methods**, where the criteria involve either judgement or opinion, such as user-friendliness, conformance to business strategy, and market acceptability. To control the process of checking conformance to quality in these areas, the process of Quality Review is available as defined in the *Techniques* section of this manual (Chapter 23).

Hints and tips for quality

It is almost always possible to define objectively measurable criteria. But it is sometimes not worth it – that is, not cost- or time-effective.

10 Configuration Management

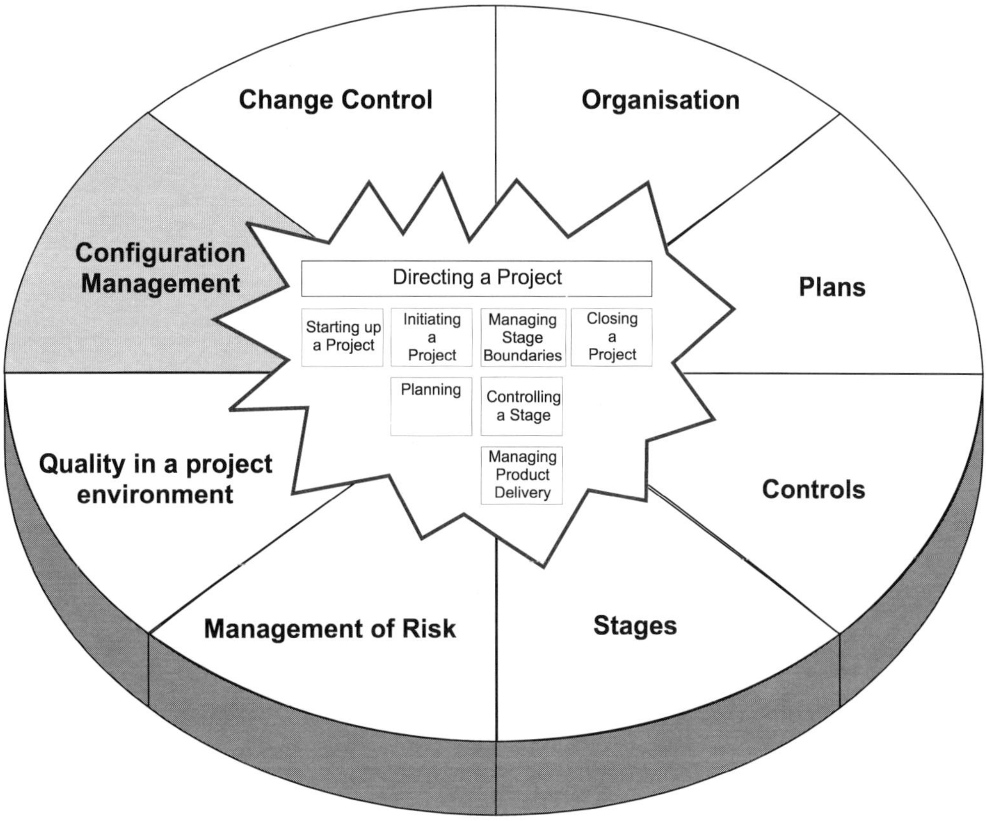

Figure 10–1: Configuration Management in the PRINCE template

10.1 Purpose

No organisation can be fully efficient or effective unless it manages its assets, particularly if the assets are vital to the running of the organisation's business. A project's assets likewise have to be managed. The assets of the project are the products that it develops. The name for the combined set of these assets is a configuration. The configuration of the final deliverable of a project is the sum total of its products.

Within the context of project management, the purpose of Configuration Management is to identify, track and protect the project's products.

Configuration Management is not optional. If more than one version of a product has been created, then Configuration Management is being performed. It is just a question of how formally it needs to be done. Configuration Management for documentation products (both management and specialist) is of equal importance to Configuration Management for deliverables.

Where a project is part of a programme, Configuration Management has even greater importance. Inter-project product transfers may occur during the life of the project, but may also be asynchronous. It is essential that each project's Configuration Management meets the requirements of the programme in addition to the project's internal needs.

10.2 Definition

Configuration Management may be thought of as product control.

The construction of a car is a good example of the need for Configuration Management. What components have to be brought together in order to assemble this version of the car? What about that recent change to the fascia – and the redesigned windscreen wipers? How can the assemblers be sure that they have the correct components? The answer is: from the records held by Configuration Management. If a replacement window winder for a five-year old model is needed, the car's serial number in conjunction with the records kept by Configuration Management will ensure that the right one is supplied.

The job of Configuration Management is, therefore, to provide:

- the mechanisms for managing, tracking and keeping control of all the project's specialist products. It keeps files and libraries of all the products of a project once they have been quality reviewed, controls access to them and maintains records of their status

- the ability to select and package the products that comprise the final working system. This covers releasing the complete system, or updates to it

- a system for logging, tracking and filing all Project Issues.

Configuration Management gives the Project Management Team precise control over the project's assets. The title given to the person (or group) operating the Configuration Management method is Configuration Librarian.

Configuration Management consists of five basic functions:

- **planning** – deciding what level of Configuration Management will be required by the project and planning how this level is to be achieved

- **identification** – specifying and identifying all components of the final product

- **control** – the ability to agree and 'freeze' products and then to make changes only with the agreement of appropriate named authorities. Once a product has been approved, the motto is 'Nothing moves, nothing changes without authorisation'

- **status accounting** – the recording and reporting of all current and historical data concerned with each product

- **verification** – a series of reviews and configuration audits to ensure that there is conformity between all products and the authorised state of products as registered in the Configuration Management records.

Configuration Management is part of the quality control of a project. Without it, managers have little or no control over the products being produced – for example, what their status is, where they are, whether they can be changed, what the latest version is.

The configuration of a project is the sum total of products that will form part of the final deliverable. All the specialist products of a project are part of the configuration. Management and quality documentation *may optionally* be treated as configuration products in order to control the issue of various versions of them. Configuration Management information can be added to Product Descriptions.

A specimen role description for a Configuration Librarian appears below. All the listed functions are necessary for successful projects.

10.3 Configuration Librarian

The Configuration Librarian is the custodian and guardian of all master copies of the project's specialist products. The role may also maintain the Issue Log on behalf of the Project Manager.

Major Tasks

- To control the receipt, identification, storage, and issue of all project products.

- To provide information on the status of all products.

- To number, record, store and distribute Project Issues.

Specific Activities

- Assist the Project Manager to prepare the Configuration Management Plan (during Initiation).

- Create an identification scheme for all products.

- Create libraries or other storage areas to hold products.

- Assist in the identification of products.

- Create Product Description 'skeletons'.

- Maintain current status information on all products.

- Accept and record the receipt of new or revised products into the appropriate library.

- Archive superseded product copies.

- Hold the master copies of all project products.

- When authorised to do so, issue copies of products for review, change, correction or information.

- Maintain a record of all copies issued.

- Notify holders of any changes to their copies.

- Maintain the Issue Log.

- Monitor all Project Issues and ensure they are resubmitted to the Configuration Library after any authorised change.

- Collect and retain information that will assist in the assessment of what products are impacted by a change to a product.

- Produce Configuration Status Accounting reports.

- Assist in conducting Configuration Audits.

- Liaise with other Configuration Librarians where products required by the project are common to other systems.

10.4 Configuration Management method

A Configuration Management method may be manual or automated, whichever is available and most appropriate for the project and the organisation.

Because the system will exist after the project has finished, the Configuration Management method to be used is often mandated on a departmental basis, the same method being used to look after many final products. This is a good reason for having Configuration Librarians in a Project Support Office, providing the method and expertise to all projects.

Configuration Management covers the following functions:

- identifying the individual sub-products of the final product

- identifying those products that will be required in order to produce other products

- establishing a coding system that will uniquely identify each product

- identifying the 'owner' of a product version

- identifing the producer to whom creation or amendment of that version of a product has been delegated

- recording, monitoring and reporting on the current status of each product as it progresses through its own specific life cycle

- filing all documentation produced during the development life of the product

- retention of master copies of all relevant completed products within the Configuration Library

- provision of procedures to ensure the safety and security aspects of the products and to control access to them

- distribution of copies of all products and recording of holders of product copies

- maintenance of the record of relationships between products so that no product is changed without being able to check for possible impact on related products

- administering change to all products, from receipt of Project Issues, through assessment of the impact of proposed changes, release of copies of products, to the eventual receipt of the amended versions

- establishment of Baselines (described later)

- performance of configuration audits.

Apart from the Configuration Management work, the Configuration Librarian also creates and maintains the project and stage files.

Products that are of interest to more than one project may be held centrally.

Items can only be amended or deleted through submission of an authorised Project Issue to the Configuration Librarian.

10.4.1 Configuration Management coverage

The Configuration Management approach should cover all specialist products. The Project Manager decides whether the management and quality products should also come within the scope of the Configuration Management approach.

If the decision is taken to exclude management products from the Configuration Management approach, a means of document control will still need to be devised for the management products, covering identification and version control.

The amount and formality of Configuration Management needed by a project depends on the type and size of the project and the project's environment. It is a question that needs to be faced at the outset of a project.

10.4.2 Choosing the level of product

An important part of Configuration Management is deciding the level at which control is to be exercised – with top-level products broken down into components that are themselves products, and so on. Figure 10–2 shows Product A, which consists of components A1, A2, A3 and A4. Each of these components can be broken down into smaller components. In this example A3 is made up of A3.1, A3.2 and A3.3. Each of the components shown is a product, including the total product.

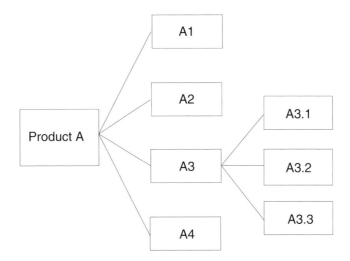

Figure10–2: Configuration breakdown

Normally, products are defined down to the lowest level at which a component can be independently installed, replaced or modified. Each project has to decide on the level at which to stop breaking products down to further levels. Apart from the construction of a car example quoted at the beginning of this chapter, other considerations are cost and effort. The greater the levels of breakdown, the greater the control, but also the greater the cost and effort of Configuration Management.

10.5 Configuration Management Plan

This plan forms part of the Project Quality Plan. It consists of:

- an explanation of the purpose of Configuration Management

- a description of (or reference to) the Configuration Management method to be used. Any variance from corporate or programme standards should be highlighted together with a justification for the variance

- reference to any other Configuration Management systems with which links will be necessary

- identification of the Configuration Librarian

- identification of the products, levels of product, or classes of product that will be controlled under Configuration Management

- a plan of what libraries and files will be used to hold products

- confirmation that the relevant project and next stage files have been set up.

10.6 Configuration identification

As a start, the coding scheme should identify as elements of the unique key required:

- the project

- type of product

- product

- latest version number.

This is apart from the other information needed to fulfil the needs stated above, such as:

- Product Description

- a description of the life cycle steps appropriate to the product

- 'owner'
- date allocated
- library or location where the product is kept
- source – for example, in-house, or purchased from a third-party company
- links to related products
- status
- copy holders
- cross-reference to the Project Issue(s) that caused the change to this product
- cross-references to relevant correspondence.

10.7 Baseline

A Baseline is the moment when the product passes to the Configuration Library after a successful test or Quality Review. This changes its status and 'freezes' the content. It can now be used as a firm basis for the development of any later product.

If the item is to be changed at a later date, the Baseline version stays unchanged. A new version number must be allocated, a copy is issued bearing this new version number, and all the facts are noted in the Configuration Management records. When this amended version is finished and has been quality-reviewed, it is passed into the library and a new Baseline established.

The old Baseline version is never discarded. The Configuration Management method must always permit the recreation of any version of the released system.

A Baseline is also a complete and consistent set of products, which forms a fixed reference point in the development of the end product. The most obvious Baseline is the final product to be handed over at the end of the project. It is normal to establish intermediate system baselines to provide a firm, agreed foundation for later work, preferably at natural breakpoints in the development cycle. This baseline document can be considered as a 'bill of materials' – a list of all products which make up that release or Baseline, showing each item's version number and baseline date.

10.8 Configuration control

Configuration control is concerned with physically controlling receipt and issue of products, protecting finished products and controlling any changes to them.

Product submission

When a product is allocated to an 'owner', that is, the person who will develop it or later amend it, a copy of the identifying information should go with it. When the item or any part of it is submitted to the Configuration Librarian, this information identifies it. Additional information is required on the status of the item and on the names of any reviewers who should receive copies.

Any current holders of the product should receive copies of the new version, with an indication of its status.

Product Issue

A log should be kept, detailing:

- product identity and version number
- recipient's name
- date of issue

- authority for issue

- any sensitivity indication.

All product copies formally issued by the Configuration Librarian should be labelled as such and numbered. This is to ensure that only official copies are in circulation, as only these will be on record to receive any updates. This will reduce the likelihood of people working with out-of-date products. Ideally, copies of old versions should be recalled and destroyed.

10.9 Configuration audits

Configuration audits are comparisons of the recorded Product Descriptions and the current physical representation of them to ensure that they match. The audit also checks that all Product Descriptions are present, complete and to standards. They are normally carried out at the end of each Stage.

Normally, someone with assurance responsibility is responsible for Configuration audits, with help from the Configuration Librarian. If the Project Board is carrying out Project Assurance, the Project Manager must appoint someone else.

10.10 Configuration Management and Change Control

There must be a close liaison between Configuration Management and Change Control staff. A key element is the ability to identify and control different versions of a product.

A Baseline product can only be changed under formal Change Control. This means that a Project Issue has been authorised and presented to the Configuration Librarian. Once a product has been approved, that version of it never changes. If a change is required, a new version of the product is created that will encompass the change. The new version should be associated with documentation of the change that caused the need for the new version.

A product should not be issued for change to more than one person at a time. The changes must be combined in some way and the completion of the product encompassing all changes must be delegated to one of the people involved.

The master copy of any product should never be issued, only a copy.

10.11 Configuration Management and a Project Support Office

Because most final deliverables will exist in operational use long after the project to create them has finished, Configuration Management is usually carried out on an organisation-wide basis, the same approach being used to look after both project and operational products. This is a good reason for providing Configuration Management expertise to all projects from a central Project Support Office.

There may be a requirement for a project to fit in with existing approaches to Configuration Management used by the Customer. Most end products from projects will have a long, useful life, and will be modified many times during that life. Configuration Management is essential to keep track of the changes. If the project has been outsourced, the Configuration Management method used by the Supplier should be compatible with that of the Customer (or whichever group will look after the product in its operational life).

11   Change Control

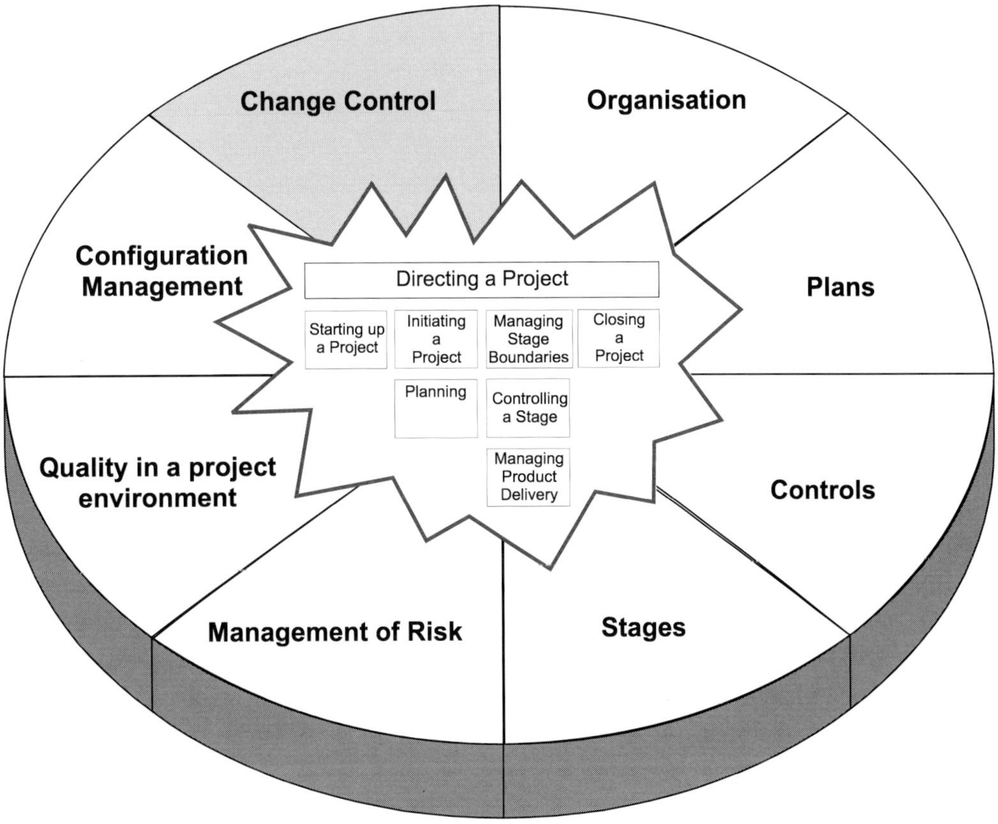

Figure 11-1: Change Control in the PRINCE template

11.1   Purpose

Changes to specification or scope can potentially ruin any project unless they are carefully controlled. Change is, however, highly likely. The control of change means the assessment of the impact of potential changes, their importance, their cost and a judgemental decision by management on whether to include them or not. Any approved changes must be reflected in any necessary corresponding change to schedule and budget.

In PRINCE, all potential changes are dealt with as Project Issues.

An approach to the control of change is given in the *Techniques* section of this manual (see Chapter 22).

In a programme management context, changes within a project that affect the programme must be managed in conjunction with programme management.

11.2   What is being changed?

This chapter looks at the control of changes to specialist products, not management or quality products. Two important points need to be made:

*   if a product is to be changed, its Product Description should be checked for any necessary changes
*   if a product has been approved by the Project Board, that product cannot be changed without the Project Board's agreement.

11.3 Authority levels

One consideration at Project Initiation should be who is permitted to authorise changes to what the project is to produce. In a project where few changes are envisaged, it may be reasonable to leave this authority in the hands of the Project Board. But projects may be in a dynamic environment, where there are likely to be many requests to change the initial agreed scope of the project.

- Is the Project Board prepared to make the time available to review all change requests?

- Does it wish to consider only the top priority changes and delegate decisions on minor changes to another body?

- How will changes be funded?

- Will the Project Board go back to corporate or programme management to vary funding, timetable or scope each time a change is desired?

For projects that exist within a programme, programme management will define the level of authority that the Project Board will have to approve change.

In some projects the Project Board may choose to delegate consideration of changes to a group, here called a 'Change Authority'. A budget to pay for changes is normally given to this Change Authority. This arrangement can avoid a number of Mid-Stage Assessments in projects where the frequency of Project Issues is forecast to be high.

The Project Board needs to decide before the project moves out of Project Initiation where the authority for making changes lies, and these responsibilities must be written into the appropriate job definitions.

11.4 Integrity of change

Project Issues should not be considered in isolation. Some other considerations are as follows.

11.4.1 Benefit/Business Case driven

The Project Issues should be viewed against the benefits they offer, and their impact on the Business Case.

11.4.2 The Risk Log

Project Issues should be considered in two ways under the 'Risk' heading:

- Would the change impact an existing risk?

- Would the change create a new risk?

11.4.3 Time/cost/risk function balance

There must be a balance between the advantage achieved by incorporating the change and the time, cost and risk of implementing it. This is illustrated in Figure 11–2. Can the project afford the delay? Can the extra funds be found? (Or will the change save time and money?) Is this a good way of spending the extra funds? Is it too risky? Should (and can) the change wait until after the current project ends?

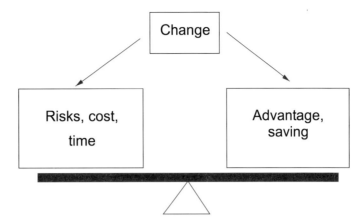

The balancing act between risks, costs and time, and what the customer gets out of it

Figure 11–2: Balancing the decision to change

11.4.4 Where the project is part of a programme

If the project is part of a programme, the impact of the change on the programme as a whole should also be considered. There may also be effects on other projects not necessarily part of the programme.

11.5 Management of change and Configuration Management

If the project is using a Configuration Management method, the procedure used to control Project Issues must be integrated with it. If the project is not in an environment that already has procedures for change control and a Configuration Management method, the Change Control approach in the *Techniques* section of this manual (Chapter 22) can be used.

Project Managers should constantly be looking for ways to take advantage of events to improve on project costs, schedule or performance. These ways should also be recorded as Project Issues (as well as the final outcome being recorded as part of the Lessons Learned Report).

> *Hints and tips on change control*
> *Where a change budget is given to a Change Authority, the Project Board may wish to put a limit on (a) the cost of any single change and (b) the amount spent on change in any one Stage – without reference to the Project Board.*

Processes

12   Introduction to Processes

12.1   Objectives

This chapter of the manual discusses the processes involved in managing a PRINCE project, and how those processes link with each other. The processes indicate the normal content of a PRINCE project.

12.2   The PRINCE process model

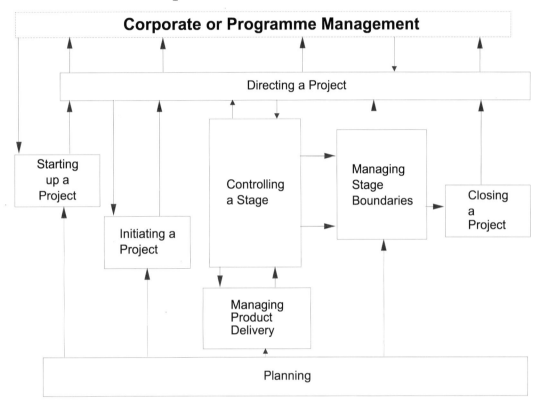

Figure 12–1: Process overview

There are eight processes, each made up of a collection of lower-level processes. The processes are:

Starting up a Project
  Gathering basic information

Initiating a Project
  Getting agreement that everyone knows what the project is about

Controlling a Stage and Managing Product Delivery
  Controlling development

Managing Stage Boundaries
  Taking stock and getting ready for the next part of the project

Planning
  Common planning steps

Directing a Project
  Senior management taking decisions at key points of the project

Closing a Project
  Making sure the project has done the job.

These processes link to a range of project management techniques, some of which are specific PRINCE techniques and are defined within the manual, and some of which are generic and generally used techniques that are not defined within the manual.

Project management is seldom straightforward enough to be a simple, linear process. In a PRINCE context, there are five parallel process levels (see Figure 12–2) to take into account. The first four of these are management process levels. The fifth is of a 'technical' nature.

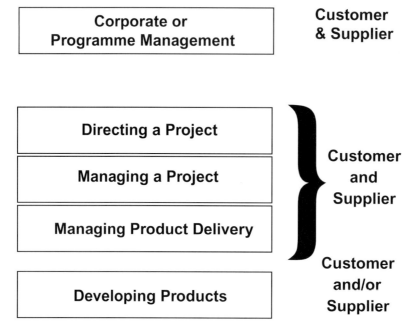

Figure 12–2: The five process levels

- At the highest level is corporate or programme management. While it is not part of project management as such, these higher management levels are important, as they will often set the context for one or more projects.

- Within the project itself the highest level is *Directing a Project* (the Project Board work). This level is for key decision making and direction setting.

- At the level of *Managing a Project* a great deal of management effort is expended in day-to-day planning and control.

- At the lowest management level, *Managing Product Delivery* would be handled by Team Managers.

- Below this, *Developing Products* (which is not part of project management) carries out the tasks that produce the project's interim and final products.

There are two major ways in which these levels interact:

- The higher-level processes exercise control over the lower levels. For example, *Managing a Project* provides the Work Package authorisations that allow work to begin on the 'technical' product in the two levels, *Managing Product Delivery* and *Developing Products*.

- The output of the lower-level processes provides the inputs that allow the higher-level processes to function effectively. For example, *Managing Stage Boundaries* provides essential planning input and control information to allow the effective conduct of the *Directing a Project* activities.

12.2.1 Scalability

Any project run under PRINCE will address each of these processes in some form. **However**, the key to successful use of this process model is its tailoring. Each process must be approached with the question 'How extensively should this process be applied on this project?'

12.2.2 Structure of each Process Description

Below are outline descriptions of each of the processes in the process model. Each Process Description has the following structure and format.

Fundamental principles

Under this heading the following questions are addressed:

- Why have this process?

- What is it aiming to achieve in project management terms?

- Why is this process fundamental to good project management, and hence a minimum requirement of PRINCE?

Context

This section puts each process in context with the other processes, and with activities going on outside the scope of project management as defined by PRINCE. Each context description is supported by a context diagram. The context diagram shows all the information flows into and out of the process. The diagram for each major process only shows the major information flows so as to avoid becoming too complex to read.

Process description

This section describes the process by explaining the objectives and how the process fulfils the fundamental principles, and gives a description of the steps involved in carrying out the process.

No attempt has been made to lay out the steps in a strict sequence, since such a hard-and-fast sequence seldom exists. However, they have been listed in as logical a sequence as possible.

Responsibilities

This section specifies who should be accountable for the successful conduct of the major process and be responsible for its management. These are only stated for the processes, as it is at that level that responsibilities can be decided.

Information needs

This section contains a table of the important information required for the process to function and achieve its objectives. Some entries will be products, such as plans and reports; others are in the nature of decisions.

Key criteria

This section highlights the main issues that will dictate the ultimate success or failure of the process.

Hints and tips

Projects by their nature are very varied. The environments within which they operate also vary tremendously. The PRINCE processes lay out the anticipated requirements for the vast majority of projects in most environments. The *Hints and tips* section provides some guidance on the application of PRINCE in certain circumstances, and indicates how PRINCE might be applied in practice. IT IS NOT EXPECTED TO BE A DEFINITIVE GUIDE. It is strongly advised that this section be fleshed out using best practice and normal approaches for each project environment that adopts PRINCE.

12.3 Summary of the processes

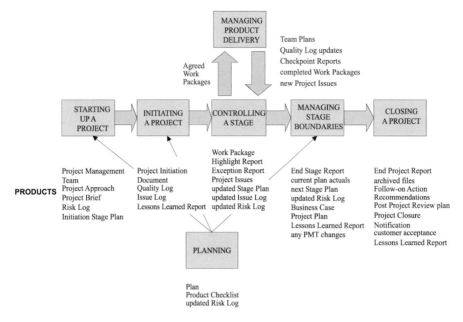

Figure 12–3: Flow of products and processes

12.3.1 Directing a Project (DP)

Directing a Project runs from the start-up of the project until its closure.

This process is aimed at the Project Board. The Project Board manages by exception, monitors via reports, and controls through a number of decision points.

The key processes for the Project Board break into four main areas:

- Initiation (starting the project off on the right foot).

- Stage boundaries (commitment of more resources after checking results so far).

- *Ad hoc* direction (monitoring progress, providing advice and guidance, reacting to Exception situations).

- Project closure (confirming the project outcome and bringing the project to a controlled close).

This process does not cover the day-to-day activities of the Project Manager.

12.3.2 Starting up a Project (SU)

This is the first process in PRINCE. It is a pre-project process, designed to ensure that the prerequisites for initiating the project are in place. The process expects the existence of a Project Mandate that defines in high-level terms the reason for the project and what outcome is sought. The process should be very short.

The work of the process is built around the establishment of five products:

- designing and, as far as possible, appointing the *Project Management Team*

- a *Risk Log*

- the *Project Approach* (in general terms how a solution will be provided)

- the *Project Brief*

- the *Initiation Stage Plan*.

12.3.3 Initiating a Project (IP)

The objectives of *Initiating a Project* are to:

- agree whether or not there is sufficient justification to proceed with the project
- establish a stable management basis on which to proceed
- document and confirm that an acceptable Business Case exists for the project
- ensure a firm and accepted foundation to the project prior to commencement of the work
- agree to the commitment of resources for the first Stage of the project
- enable and encourage the Project Board to take ownership of the project
- provide the Baseline for the decision-making processes required during the project's life
- ensure that the investment of time and effort required by the project is made wisely, taking account of the risks to the project.

The key product of the process is the **Project Initiation Document**, which defines the what, why, who, when and how of the project. It includes the **Project Plan**.

Three other blank products are created in readiness for use during the project. These are:

- the **Quality Log**
- the **Issue Log**
- the **Lessons Learned Report**.

Another required product is the next **Stage Plan**. This, however, comes from the process **Managing Stage Boundaries**, which will occur at the end of the Initiation Stage.

12.3.4 Managing Stage Boundaries (SB)

This process provides the Project Board with key decision points on whether to continue with the project or not.

The objectives of the process are to:

- assure the Project Board that all deliverables planned in the current Stage Plan have been completed as defined
- provide the information needed for the Project Board to assess the continuing viability of the project
- provide the Project Board with information needed to approve the current Stage's completion and authorise the start of the next Stage, together with its delegated tolerance level
- record any measurements or lessons that can help later Stages of this project and/or other projects.

The products of this process are:

- *current plan actuals*, showing performance against the original Stage Plan
- the *next Stage Plan*, for which approval is sought
- a *revised Project Plan*
- the *updated Risk Log*, which together with the next two products are used by the Project Board to review the continuing viability of the project

- a *revised Business Case*

- the *Lessons Learned Report*, updated with any lessons learned from the current Stage

- any changes to the structure or staffing of the *Project Management Team*

- an *End Stage Report*, given by the Project Manager to the Project Board, containing information on the Stage achievements.

12.3.5 Controlling a Stage (CS)

This process describes the monitoring and control activities of the Project Manager involved in ensuring that a Stage stays on course and reacts to unexpected events. The process forms the core of the Project Manager's effort on the project, being the process that handles day-to-day management of the project.

Throughout a Stage there will be a cycle of:

- authorising work to be done

- gathering progress information about that work

- watching for changes

- reviewing the situation

- reporting

- taking any necessary corrective action.

This process covers these activities, together with the ongoing work of risk management and change control. Products produced during the Stage on a cyclic basis are:

- *new Work Packages*

- *Highlight Reports*

- *Project Issues (and updated Issue Log)*

- an *updated Risk Log*

- a regularly *updated Stage Plan.*

There may also be the need for

- an *Exception Report/Exception Plan.*

12.3.6 Managing Product Delivery (MP)

The objective of this process is to ensure that planned products are created and delivered by the project by:

- negotiating details of Work Packages with the Project Manager

- making certain that work on products allocated to the team is effectively authorised and agreed

- ensuring that work conforms to the requirements of interfaces identified in the Work Package

- ensuring that the work is done

- assessing work progress and forecasts regularly

- ensuring that completed products meet quality criteria

- obtaining approval for the completed products.

Products created or updated during this process are:

- *Team Plans*

- *Quality Log* updates, giving the Project Manager a view of quality work being done

- *New Project Issues*

- *Risk Log updates*

- *Checkpoint Reports,* regular progress reports from a team to the Project Manager.

12.3.7 Closing a Project (CP)

The purpose of this process is to execute a controlled close to the project.

The process covers the Project Manager's work to wrap up the project, either at its end or at premature close. Most of the work is to prepare input to the Project Board to obtain its confirmation that the project may close.

The objectives of 'Closing a Project' are, therefore, to:

- check the extent to which the objectives or aims set out in the Project Initiation Document have been met

- confirm the *Customer's acceptance* of the deliverables

- ensure to what extent all expected products have been handed over and accepted by the Customer

- confirm that maintenance and operation arrangements are in place (where appropriate)

- make any recommendations for follow-on actions (*Follow-on Action Recommendations)*

- capture lessons resulting from the project and complete the *Lessons Learned Report*

- prepare an *End Project Report*

- archive the *project files*
  – produce a *Post-Project Review plan*
  – notify the host organisation of the intention to disband the project organisation and resources (*end project notification*).

12.3.8 Planning (PL)

Planning is a repeatable process, and plays an important role in other processes, the main ones being:

- Planning an Initiation Stage (SU6).

- Planning a Project (IP2).

- Planning a Stage (SB1).

- Producing an Exception Plan (SB6).

Apart from a plan, the process produces:

- a *Product Checklist*, which is a table of the products to be produced by the work planned, with space for planned and actual dates for delivery of draft, quality checked and approved products

- the *Risk Log,* updated with any risk situation changes brought about by the plan.

PRINCE provides a product-based start to the planning activity. It also provides a planning framework that can be applied to any type of project. This involves:

- establishing what products are needed

- determining the sequence in which each product should be produced

- defining the form and content of each product

- resolving what activities are necessary for their creation and delivery.

13   Starting up a Project (SU)

13.1 Fundamental principles

- There must be a basic business requirement that triggers the project. Indeed, before any work is commenced or resources are committed, there is a requirement to be able to answer the basic question 'Do we have a viable and worthwhile project?' This question must be answered honestly to ensure that resources are not committed and wasted.

- Certain base information is needed to make rational decisions about the commissioning of the project.

- Nothing can be done in the project until responsibilities are defined and key roles have been filled. Someone has to 'kick-start' the project into being.

- Before approval can be given to enter the Initiation Stage, there should be an Initiation Stage Plan.

13.2 Context

This is the first process within PRINCE. The project begins once this process has been conducted, and the Project Board has approved commencement.

Projects can be identified in a variety of ways and thus have a wide variation in the information available to the Project Management Team at the time of start-up. It is accepted that the Project Mandate may be anything from a verbal request to a complete Project Brief.

The process expects the existence of information explaining the reason for the project and the outcome expected. This set of information has been given the title Project Mandate, to avoid confusion with more rigorously defined sets of information created within PRINCE. *Starting up a Project (SU)* should be of short duration.

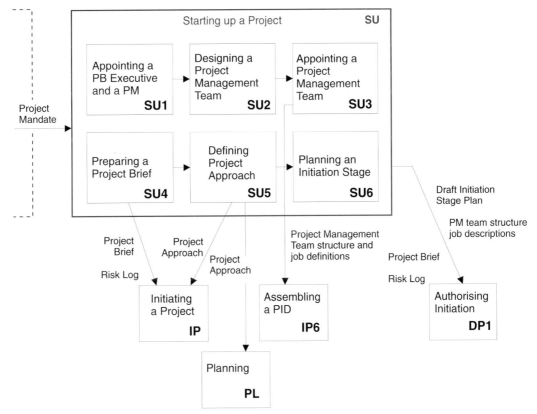

Figure 13–1: Starting up a project

13.3 Process description

The work of the process is built around the production of five elements:

- ensuring that the information required for the *Project Brief* is available

- establishing the *Project Approach*

- designing and appointing the *Project Management Team*

- creating the *Initiation Stage Plan*

- setting up a *Risk Log*.

The objective of the process is to enable a controlled start to the project by ensuring that:

- all the necessary project management authorities exist for undertaking the project

- sufficient information is available to formalise the terms of reference for the project

- individuals are appointed who will undertake the work required in Project Initiation and/or will take significant project management roles in the project

- the work required for Project Initiation is planned

- the organisation that will host the project team is informed of the existence and implications of the new project.

The process begins by receiving from some external source the definition of a problem or opportunity that the project has to satisfy. 'Project Mandate' is a term used for whatever information comes in to trigger the project, be it a Feasibility Study or details on the back of an envelope. The closer the quality of information in the Project Mandate can get to the ideal described in the Product Outline for the Project Mandate, the easier the start-up process will be.

If the project is part of a programme, the programme should provide the Project Brief and appoint some, if not all, members of the Project Board, thus reducing the work required in this process.

The target work location is informed of the impending project, and requests are made for any appropriate logistical support required to carry out Project Initiation. An additional input that will help with the creation of both the Initiation and Project Plans is the project approach, explaining the way in which it is intended that the end products of the project are to be produced.

13.3.1 Scalability

There are a variety of approaches to this process, which fall into three categories.

- This is a stand-alone project and all the steps of this process will apply. If this is the case, there is little problem in deciding which steps to carry out.

- This project is part of a programme. The programme has passed down documentation that is either a complete Project Brief or even a Project Initiation Document. The Project Board may already be defined, the Project Approach and the Risk Log are controlled at programme level. In other words, all the work of *Starting up a Project (SU)* and most of the initiation work have been done. In such a case, the work of this process is simply to check whether any more work needs to be done on the five deliverables.

- The third possibility is that the project is very small. In such cases the process can usually be handled in an informal manner, possibly only taking a matter of minutes. A Project Manager should avoid the temptation to bypass it altogether.

Hints and tips

It will not always be appropriate, or indeed possible, to appoint the entire Project Management Team prior to the start of Initiation. But at least the Executive and the Project Manager should be appointed, so that the input to Initiation can be prepared and decisions can be made.

The Initiation Stage Plan may not have many elements in many cases.

13.4 Appointing a Project Board Executive and a Project Manager (SU1)

13.4.1 Fundamental principles

To get anything done in the project, you need a decision maker and someone to undertake the planning.

13.4.2 Context

Before Initiation of the project can begin, there must be a plan for that Initiation work, and the Project Board has to be appointed to approve the plan.

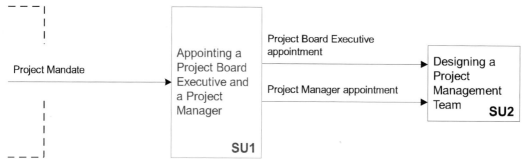

Figure 13–2: Appointing a Project Board Executive and a Project Manager

13.4.3 Process description

The objectives of this process are to:

- identify the Executive from the project's stakeholders
- identify the Project Manager most appropriate for the project
- confirm the selected persons' availability, their acceptance of these roles, and their commitment to carry them out
- appoint them to their respective roles.

A prerequisite of this first process is the existence and availability of a Project Mandate. Because this is the process that precedes the whole of the project, it will be very variable in application, depending particularly on the quality of the Project Mandate information. The following steps will be involved:

- ratify the key elements of the Project Mandate
- establish any missing information
- identify candidates for Executive and Project Manager
- establish the responsibilities for each role
- appoint Executive
- appoint Project Manager
- confirm appointments via agreement to job definitions by corporate or programme management and appointees.

The Project Mandate should indicate the general type of project, its size and complexity, and its political and business sensitivity. This information will help to identify appropriate candidates for the Project Manager role.

There may be a draft Project Plan included in the Project Mandate from earlier work. This would give an idea of the timeframe of the project – useful when confirming the availability of people to fill the roles.

If the project is part of a programme, the Programme Director will appoint the Executive and may influence the appointment of the Project Manager as well.

The outline of the roles of Executive and Project Manager, given in *Appendix C – Project Manangement Team roles*, should be used as the basis for discussion between the Executive and the Project Manager on tailoring and agreement of their roles.

If the project is part of a programme, this work should have been done by the Programme Executive.

13.4.4 Responsibilities

Corporate or programme management.

13.4.5 Information needs

Management information	Usage	Explanation
Project Mandate	Input	The trigger for the Project
Project Board Executive and Project Manager appointments	Output	Agreed job definitions for the Executive and Project Manager

13.4.6 Key criteria

- If the project is part of a programme, will the Programme Manager take the project Executive role on the Project Board?

- Does the proposed Executive have the financial and functional authority necessary to support the project adequately?

- Has the availability of candidates been measured against any forecast duration of the project to ensure that individuals are available for as much of the project as possible?

- Are any candidates likely to change jobs in the near future in a direction that would remove them from the project? If so, has this information been taken into consideration when making the appointments?

- Do the appointees have the skills and knowledge required to undertake their tasks?

Hints and tips

Where the size or importance of the project warrants it, agreed job definitions should be signed by the person or persons undertaking the role plus, where appropriate, their line management; copies should be held by that person or persons and a signed copy also held in the project files.

For small or low-risk projects it may not be appropriate to have formal job definitions, but the people should have read the role descriptions.

A Programme Director has responsibility for establishing the project Executive for each project within a programme. If this is done, the work of this process is reduced. The Programme Director may leave the appointment of the remainder of the Project Board to the Executive.

13.5 Designing a Project Management Team (SU2)

13.5.1 Fundamental principles

- The project needs the right people in place with the authority, responsibility and knowledge to make decisions in a timely manner.

- The Project Management Team needs to reflect the interests of all parties who will be involved, including business, User and Supplier interests.

- Project management requires resources and calls for a range of skills, which must be available within the Project Management Team.

- It is important that consideration is given to all the activities that are involved in managing the project so that no important aspects are overlooked. It is also important that all the skills needed by the project are made available. All the roles identified in the *Organisation* component must be filled in some way in each project.

13.5.2 Context

Having identified an Executive and the Project Manager, the next job is to review the project size, complexity and areas impacted by the final outcome, then design the Project Management Team with appropriate representation of User, Supplier and project support.

In practice it is normal that this process and the next, *Appointing a Project Management Team*, will have considerable overlap.

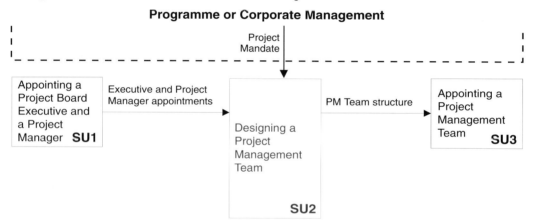

Figure 13–3: Designing a Project Management Team

13.5.3 Process description

The objectives of the process are to:

- design the Project Management Team structure appropriate to the size and nature of the project and the groups involved

- identify candidates for each role in order to produce a recommended Project Management Team

- determine the responsibilities and requisite skills required for each position.

Where the project is part of a programme, the Programme Executive has responsibility for ensuring the establishment of an appropriate Project Board. If this is done, most of this process will not be required. The Programme Director may, however, leave the appointment of the remainder of the Project Board to the Executive.

The PRINCE Project Management Team structure described in *Organisation* and *Appendix C – Project Manangement Team roles* should be used as a basis for the process. There are certain steps that must be undertaken:

- identify candidates for the Project Board roles and create their job definitions

- assess whether any members of the Project Board are likely to delegate any of their assurance responsibilities; this will assist the Project Manager to advise on the design of any assurance roles and the selection of candidates to fill them; this aspect may need to be revisited after the other Project Board roles are actually appointed

- consider whether separate individuals are likely to be needed as Team Manager(s) or whether the Project Manager will be filling this role personally; the final decision on this may not be taken until the planning of each stage

- examine the Project Mandate and Project Manager role definition and propose any project support roles required; a checklist of potential project support responsibilities is shown in *Appendix C – Project Manangement Team Roles*

- assign candidate names to all roles identified; the design should state whether each role will be allocated to one individual, shared, or combined with another role.

13.5.4 Responsibilities

The Executive and Project Manager are jointly responsible for the design. The Executive will take specific responsibility for the Project Board design. If the project is part of a programme, the Programme Director may choose to appoint all members of the Project Board or leave this to the project Executive. In the latter case, the Executive should confirm the acceptability of the design with the Programme Director.

13.5.5 Information needs

Management information	Usage	Explanation
Project Mandate	Input	Indicates the likely User and Customer interests
Project Board Executive and Project Manager appointments	Input	The Executive and Project Manager can identify possible candidates, decide on any necessary support for the Project Manager and assurance support for the Project Board
Project Management Team structure	Output	The basis of discussion with the other appointees and with senior management

13.5.6 Key criteria

- If the project is part of a programme, is there to be programme representation on the Project Board or as some part of the Project Management Team?

- Have the quality assurance functions been catered for?

- Does the organisation design balance with the overall projected cost, criticality and importance of the project?

- Can the proposed Project Board members make the commitments required of them?

- Have all the roles and responsibilities been allocated? If not, are the exclusions justified?

- Does the design allocate roles and responsibilities to individuals with the requisite knowledge, time and authority to carry them out?

- Are all relevant stakeholders represented in the Project Management Team?

- How should the PRINCE model be adapted where the Customer or Supplier uses methods or technology that call for specific organisation-and-control models?

- Does the Project Management Team structure fit in with, and support, any Programme management structure?

- Do any assurance and support roles fit into any overall Programme or strategy assurance and support functions?

Hints and tips

The User and operational interests that will be impacted by the project's deliverable(s) should be considered for Project Board representation.

The Project Board is a decision-making body, not a discussion group. For this reason it is not a good idea to allow the Project Board to grow too large. Ideally it should not grow beyond, say, 3–6 people for even a large project. It may not always be possible to restrict it to this size, but often a separate User Group can be set up, which will appoint one of its members to act as its empowered representative on the Project Board and sort out the voting rights.

While it is important to give consideration to all the items discussed above, it will often not be possible to provide all the information needed to make full and definitive appointments during Start-up, and thus there will often be a need to re-visit this area during Initiation.

Ensuring that quality testing has appropriate User and/or Customer representation is the responsibility of the Senior User. This should be taken into consideration when discussing any delegation of the Senior User's assurance responsibilities.

It is essential to ensure that the project is not adversely affected by delays in Customer or Supplier management chains. This should be considered when thinking of individuals, particularly when filling the various Project Board roles.

Where a third party is funding the project, it may be necessary for the financier to be extensively involved in the management of the project. Project Board roles should reflect this, but also emphasise the User's role in specifying what is needed and monitoring the project to ensure that the solution is going to satisfy these needs.

Where the project is part of a programme, this process can be used to design the lines of communication between project and programme. This may mean programme representation somewhere within the Project Management Team.

13.6 Appointing a Project Management Team (SU3)

13.6.1 Fundamental principles

- An essential for a well-run project is that every individual involved in the management of the project understands and agrees:
  - who is accountable to whom for what
  - who is responsible for what
  - what the reporting and communication lines are.

- There must be agreement and acceptance by everyone of their roles and responsibilities.

- There should be no gaps in responsibilities once the roles have been tailored; someone should be clearly responsible for each given management aspect.

13.6.2 Context

Having created a design for the Project Management Team, this now needs discussion and agreement with the individuals identified.

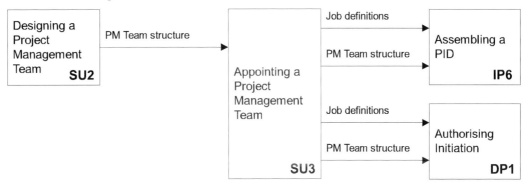

Figure 13–4: Appointing a Project Management Team

13.6.3 Process description

The objectives of the process are to:

- appoint people to:
  - the Project Board
  - Project Assurance (where appropriate)
  - Team Management
  - Project Support (where appropriate)

- ensure that these individuals understand their roles and responsibilities in the management and support of the project

- ensure that the individuals are actively committed to carrying out their roles and responsibilities

- confirm the reporting and communication lines.

These objectives are met by a process of consultation and discussion with all the people involved and, if necessary, their management.

As agreement is reached with Project Board members on their roles, thoughts on the delegation of any of their assurance responsibilities may change from the Project Management Team design. This may lead to a redesign and a further round of appointments or role modifications.

For any assurance or support personnel appointed, the Project Manager needs to confirm what their availability to the project will be.

13.6.4 Responsibilities

The Executive is responsible for the appointments, assisted and advised by the Project Manager. The Executive will have to liaise with corporate or programme management to identify the appropriate personnel and negotiate for their availability.

13.6.5 Information needs

Management information	Usage	Explanation
Project Management Team structure	Input	Identification of the planned allocation of roles
Agreed job definitions	Output	Roles tailored to the project and the individual
Updated Project Management Team structure	Output	Appointed and confirmed Project Management Team

13.6.6 Key criteria

- Did final agreement on job definitions cause any transfer or change of responsibilities that has an impact on another job?

Hints and tips

Each PRINCE role definition will need to be tailored to the particular environment and individual. The resulting agreed job definitions should be signed by the individual concerned and copies held by that individual and the Project Manager.

The Customer or Supplier may have a Project Support Office in existence, from which some or all of the project support identified may be obtained.

If the project is part of a programme that itself has a Programme Support Office, thought will have to be given as to how the project will interface with the programme.

If the project is part of a programme, consideration will need to be given as to how Project Issues are to be handled. For instance, the programme may offer (or insist upon) a central control of all Project Issues. Suppliers may be accustomed to their own arrangements. Is theirs a better practice than the suggested PRINCE procedure? Can all parties be persuaded to use the one procedure?

13.7 Preparing a Project Brief (SU4)

13.7.1 Fundamental principles

- Before proceeding any further, the Project Board needs to satisfy itself that the project is worth doing.

- The project needs to start with a reliable statement of requirements and expectation regardless of the vagaries of any pre-project processes.

13.7.2 Context

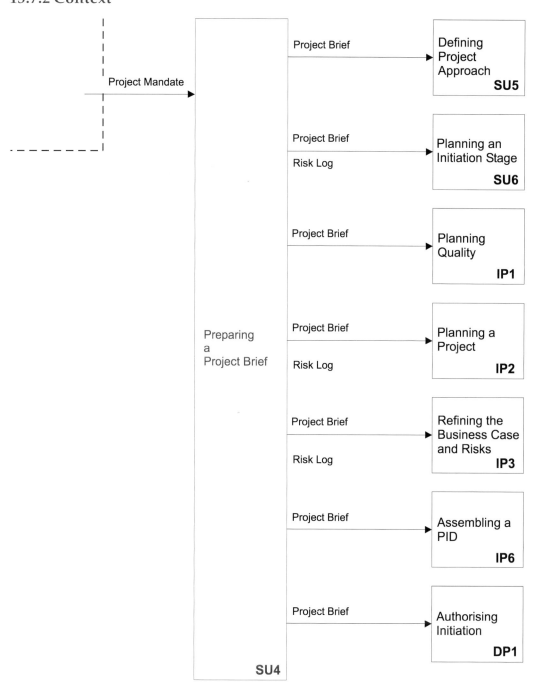

Figure 13–5: Preparing a Project Brief

The external trigger for the project is the Project Mandate. This process checks the content of the mandate and enhances it, where necessary, into the Project Brief.

Where the project is part of a programme, the Project Brief may be created by the programme, thus reducing the work of this process. The project team should validate any provided Project Brief and may need to expand on some of the statements in it. Any changes to the Project Brief provided by a programme must be agreed by the Programme Executive (for example, impacts on constraints, such as delivery dates). Such changes would need impact analysis at programme level and may cause entries in the programme and project Risk Logs.

13.7.3 Process description

The objectives of the process are to:

- prepare the formal Terms of Reference for the project

- ensure there is an outline Business Case based on the information provided in the Project Mandate.

The Project Mandate information may not be complete or accurate. This process achieves a stable statement of project requirement in the form of the Project Brief.

The Project Brief needs to include high-level information on **what** needs to be done and **why, who** will need to be involved in the process, and **how** and **when** it will be done. The aim of the Project Brief is to allow the Project Board to decide whether there is sufficient justification to warrant the expenditure proposed by the Initiation Stage Plan. The Product Outline for the Project Brief, given in *Appendix A – PRINCE Product Description outlines*, lists the information needed for this purpose.

The User requirements should be prioritised. Later, if problems cause reconsideration of the project's scope, funds can then be targeted at those items promising the highest return. Part of the Terms of Reference should be the Acceptance Criteria, given in *Appendix A – PRINCE Product Description outlines*.

The level of detail needed for each element of the Project Brief will vary with different project circumstances. However, each element needs to be considered, even if the result of that consideration is that the element is not needed.

The Business Case will be refined as part of the Project Initiation Document and throughout the project. However, the basic justification for the project needs to be understood, either defined in the Project Mandate or developed in this process and added to the Project Brief.

The Project Brief will also be used in the Initiation Stage to create the Project Quality Plan.

Risks may come to light during this process; therefore a Risk Log should be created.

13.7.4 Responsibilities

The Executive is ultimately responsible for the production of the Project Brief. In practice, much of the actual work may be done by the Project Manager and any appointed project support staff.

13.7.5 Information needs

Management information	Usage	Explanation
Project Mandate	Input	Basis of the Project Brief
Risk Log	Output	Ready to record risks, including any noted in the Project Brief
Project Brief	Output	Submission to the Project Board as part of the justification for Initiation

13.7.6 Key criteria

- Does the Project Brief contain all the required information?
- Is the 'ownership' of the project properly defined?
- Is there any potential disagreement on the Project Brief?
- Is the Project Brief suitable for a decision to be made on whether to authorise Initiation or not?
- If this project is one of a chain of related projects, does the content of the Project Brief conform to any prior projects?

Hints and tips

Check the Project Brief for the project informally with each member of the Project Board before presenting it for formal approval.

Try to determine whether there are any conflicts of interest within the parties to the project.

In small projects the Project Brief may not be produced as a separate document. It may be more appropriate to go straight to producing an outline Project Initiation Document, which would then be refined. In such a case, Starting up a Project (SU) and Initiating a Project (IP) could combine into one process.

13.8 Defining Project Approach (SU5)

13.8.1 Fundamental principles

Before any planning of the project can be done, decisions must be made regarding how the provision of a solution is going to be approached. For example, will the solution be:

- bought 'off the shelf'
- 'made to measure'
- developed in house
- contracted to third parties
- based on an existing product
- built from scratch
- based on specific technologies?

It is also necessary to make sure that the way in which the work is to be conducted is in line with practices and guidelines currently understood between Customer and Supplier, and does not jeopardise the project in any way.

13.8.2 Context

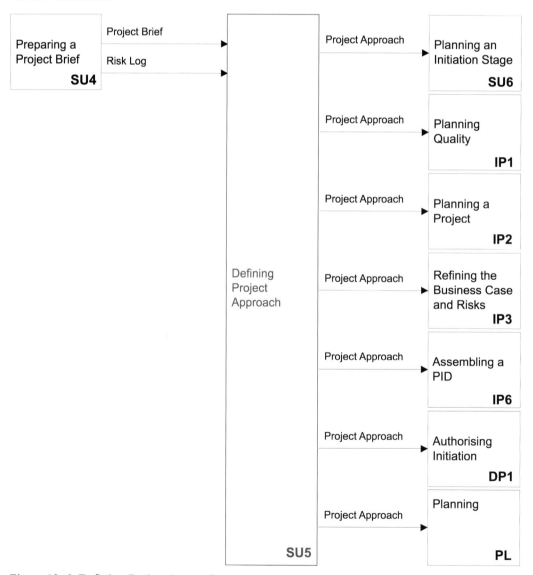

Figure 13–6: Defining Project Approach

The process takes information from the Project Brief, together with information from a range of corporate and industry sources, to produce the defined project approach.

The project approach should also be used when developing the Project Quality Plan.

13.8.3 Process description

The objectives of this process are to:

- decide how the work of the project should be approached
- identify any constraints on the way the work of the project must be carried out or the timing of certain product deliveries
- identify the skills required to conduct the work of the project.

In order to achieve these objectives, various steps have to be undertaken:

- examine, and if necessary refine, how the work is to be approached based on the overall direction given in the Project Brief, particularly within the Project Definition and the Business Case
- identify any constraints on time, money, quality and resource use or availability
- identify any corporate or industry standards that should apply to this project's products or activities
- identify any corporate or industry statements of best practice that could apply to this project's products or activities
- identify any security constraints that apply to the creation and long-term operation of the project deliverables
- identify the range of options open for conducting the work of delivering the project's products and outcomes
- identify any maintenance and operational implications that might have an effect on the choice of approach
- identify any corporate strategies or statements of direction that could have a bearing on this project's products and activities
- put the project in context with any other related work or corporate initiatives by establishing any external dependencies and prerequisites
- identify the current thinking about the provision of solutions within the industry sectors and specialist skill areas involved
- identify the overall business criticality of the project's outcome, and the current assessment of business risk
- consider how the finished product can be brought into use
- identify any training need for User personnel
- evaluate the possible approaches against the identified criteria and parameters
- select the most appropriate approach.

13.8.4 Responsibilities

The Project Manager is responsible for carrying out this process. However, the work will need to be done by people skilled in the specialist areas involved, with input from project support and assurance roles, under the overall direction of the Senior Supplier.

13.8.5 Information needs

Management information	Usage	Explanation
Project Brief	Input	This product contains the information upon which decisions on this process need to be made
Risk Log	Input	Identified risks may affect the approach
Project Approach	Output	This forms part of the Project Plan description within the Project Initation Document and is an input to *Planning Quality (IP1)* and the *Planning Process (PL)*

13.8.6 Key criteria

- Has an approach been selected which maximises the chance of achieving overall success for the project?

- Have the operational and support issues been addressed when selecting the approach to ensure that the benefits have the best chance of being realised?

- Given the approach selected, are risks being taken on a project that is critical to corporate success or that is very high profile?

- Alternatively, are opportunities being missed to experiment, and potentially learn some lessons for the future, on a low-risk and/or non-critical project?

- Have risks to the various approaches been identified and evaluated so that the most appropriate options have been selected?

- Is there a need to bring in external resources? If so, does this have any impact on the mode of working?

Hints and tips

This process will be applied very differently in different environments, and as such it must be actioned thoughtfully. The range of issues will vary tremendously, depending on the nature of the project and the corporate environment. Examples could include:

- *What is the range of construction techniques available?*

- *Should the components or specialist skills required be bought in, or provided in house?*

- *Should existing, tried-and-tested methods be used, or should the project experiment with new leading-edge techniques?*

- *To what extent should decisions be left to a third-party Supplier?*

- *To what extent should there be insistence on adherence to Customer standards?*

If the project creates a product that replaces an existing product, check whether the change-over to using the new product has implications for the project approach.

It may be that not everything can be decided at this stage, and there will be further extension and refinement throughout the project.

The Project Manager's agreement with the Project Board on the technical and quality strategy for the project may need to take account of any planned change of Suppliers during the project.

13.9 Planning an Initiation Stage (SU6)

13.9.1 Fundamental principles

Initiating the project and preparing the Project Plan take time and consume resources. The work should be planned and approved like any other project work. Make sure that Initiation is not aimless and unstructured.

13.9.2 Context

Having already checked that there is a definition of what the project is to do, plus some justification for doing it, the Project Board needs to know what is required to create the Project Initiation Document.

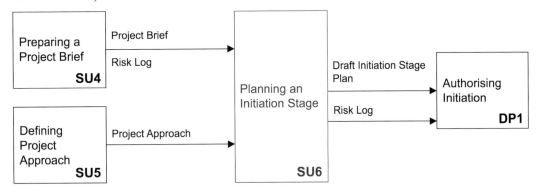

Figure 13–7: Planning an Initiation Stage

13.9.3 Process description

The objectives of the process are to:

- produce a plan (the Initiation Stage Plan) that covers the production of two management products:
  - the Project Initiation Document
  - the Stage Plan for the stage immediately following Initiation

- define the reporting and control arrangements for the Initiation Stage

- create a Risk Log to record and track the project's exposure to risks – if not already created in *Preparing a Project Brief (SU4)*.

The Project Initiation Document is an extension and refinement of the Project Brief with the addition of the Project Management Team details, the Project Plan and the Risk Log. The Initiation Stage Plan needs to show the investigation and development of the extra information required, plus the development of the Project Brief into the format required for the Project Initiation Document. The Initiation Stage should be a short and inexpensive one, compared to the likely total cost of the project.

A Stage structure for the project will be either already defined in the Project Brief or developed during Initiation. At the end of Initiation the Project Board will expect to see not only the Project Initiation Document but a detailed plan for the next Stage, because the extent of their actual commitment will only be for the next Stage.

If the Project is part of a programme, the end date for the Initiation Stage should be checked against that held in the Programme Plan. The Initiation Stage Plan will also give programme management warning of any requirements from the programme and of the need to prepare to review the Project Initiation Document.

The common Planning process (PL) will be used to create the Initiation Stage Plan.

13.9.4 Responsibilities

The Project Manager is responsible for planning the Initiation Stage. The appointed assurance and support roles will assist. In particular, whoever is responsible for business assurance needs to identify in the Initiation Stage Plan how the Business Case and risk assessment will be checked.

13.9.5 Information needs

Management information	Usage	Explanation
Project Approach	Input	This defines the way in which the work of the project will be conducted. This will have a bearing on the scale of work likely to be involved in initiating the project
Project Brief	Input	Details of the job to be done (plus any earlier planning work to be done) are contained in the Project Brief and will help to size the Initiation Stage
Risk Log	Update	Updated with any significant extra activities to counter risk exposure
Draft Initiation Stage Plan	Output	An essential product to gain approval to perform Project Initiation. The Plan for the Initiation Stage should be discussed informally with the Project Board. The assurance and support roles identified will help with creation of the Plan

13.9.6 Key criteria

- Does the Initiation Stage Plan show sufficient resources being available to help the Project Manager develop each of the elements of the Project Initiation Document?

- Has an appropriate level of management reporting been established as required by the size or risk of the Initiation Stage?

- Does the Initiation Stage Plan show how each element of the Project Initiation Document will be produced?

- Is there sufficient information for the corporate or programme management to make the decision on whether to continue with the project or not?

- Have those with assurance responsibilities indicated which parts of the draft Project Initiation Document they wish to be checked, how and by which resources?

Hints and tips

Communication with members of the Project Board should be so frequent in the Initiation Stage that very formal reporting arrangements are not necessary.

The normal reporting frequency may be too long for such a short stage.

While it is always important to plan any work prior to commencement, for some small, low-risk projects it may not be necessary to produce too formal a plan for the Initiation Stage.

The amount of start-up and initiation work, even for large and complex projects, is dependent on what work has gone on before.

14   Initiating a Project (IP)

14.1 Fundamental principles

A successful project should observe the following principles:

- a project is a finite process with a start and end

- all parties must be clear on what the project is intended to achieve, why it is needed, how the outcome is to be achieved and what their responsibilities are in that achievement, so that there can be genuine commitment to the project

- well-managed projects have an increased chance of success.

Following these principles will ensure that the project can be successfully scoped and managed to its completion.

14.2 Context

Initiating a Project (IP) is aimed at laying down the foundations for the fulfilment of the principles described above.

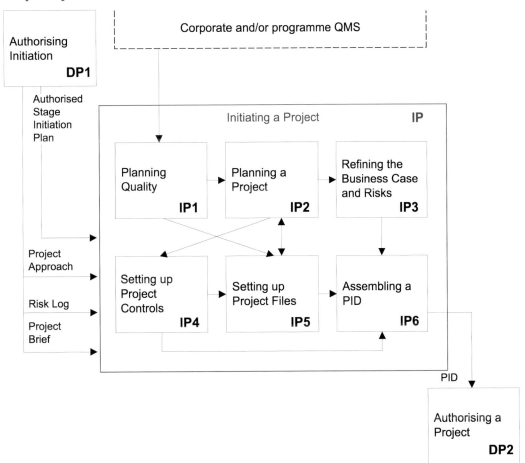

Figure 14–1: Initiating a project

14.3 Process description

The purpose of *Initiating a Project* is to draw up a 'contract' in the form of a Project Initiation Document, so that there is common understanding of:

- the adequacy of reasons for doing the project
- what key products the project will deliver
- how and when these will be delivered and at what cost
- the scope of what is to be done
- any constraints which apply to the product to be delivered
- any constraints which apply to the project
- who is to be involved in the project decision making
- how the quality required will be achieved
- what risks are faced
- how the project is to be controlled
- the next commitment the Project Manager is looking for (the next Stage Plan).

This information can be agreed as informally as the Project Board and Project Manager wish. The Project Manager should always document the understanding, however small the project, and get it signed by the Project Board, even if this is one person. People's recollection of a verbal agreement can differ weeks, or even days, later.

In formal terms, the objectives of *Initiating a Project* are to:

- document and confirm that an acceptable Business Case exists for the project
- ensure a firm and accepted foundation to the project, prior to commencement of the work, via the creation of the Project Initiation Document
- enable and encourage the Project Board to take ownership of the project
- enable and encourage the Project Board to make a decision on whether the project is viable, and to agree to the commitment of resources to the first stage of the project
- provide the Baseline for the decision-making processes required during the project's life
- ensure that by carrying out Initiation in an organised manner, the investment of time and effort required by the project is made wisely, taking account of the risks to the project
- monitor progress of *Initiating a Project (IP)* against the plans for the Initiation Stage.

14.3.1 Scalability

As stated at the beginning of *Starting up a Project (SU)*, the amount of this process needed may be reduced where the project is part of a Programme. At one extreme, the Project Initiation Document may be done already (although this would need to be checked through), and only the next Stage Plan and initial versions of the appropriate logs and files may need to be created. The project still has the responsibility to ensure that any Initiation product provided by the programme is complete and satisfactory.

For small projects, documentation of answers to the questions in Section 13.7.6 might be sufficient for the Initiation Stage (plus, of course, the next Stage Plan). It might have been agreed with the Project Board that the two processes of *Starting up a*

Project (SU) and *Initiating a Project (IP)* can be combined. In such cases *Authorising Initiation (DP1)* may be replaced by a very informal agreement between Project Manager and Project Board.

Hints and tips

Because of the increasing levels of information, and hence understanding, that emerge during the process, Initiation will usually be a set of iterations punctuated by reference to Project Board members for feedback.

Where the project is well-defined and planned from the outset, Initiation can be a very rapid exercise to confirm this and take ownership.

Where the project is part of a programme, the lines of communication and the report structure between project and programme must be made clear in the Project Initiation Document. There are a number of alternative lines of communication between Project Manager and Programme Director. The Project Initiation Document should make these lines as short and as clear as possible.

14.4 Planning Quality (IP1)

14.4.1 Fundamental principles

A key success factor of any project is that the outcome and deliverables of the project conform to the customer's quality expectations. This will only happen if these expectations are both stated and agreed at the beginning of the project, together with the means of assessing achievement of these within the final deliverable.

14.4.2 Context

This process builds on the defined project approach and describes how quality will be achieved in the subsequent planning processes.

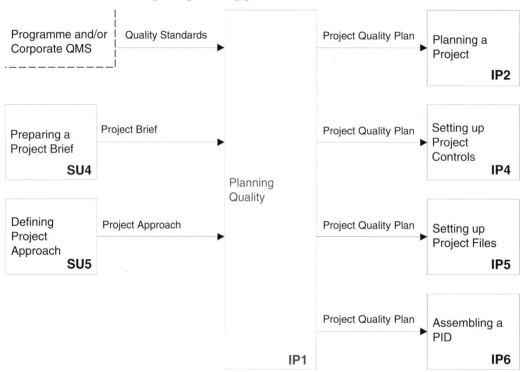

Figure 14–2: Planning Quality

14.4.3 Process description

The objectives of this process are to determine the quality required for the products of the project, and to plan the project's approach to quality (the Project Quality Plan) by:

- establishing the quality regime that will apply to the project
- defining the overall project quality criteria and assurance arrangements to be employed
- establishing the approach to be used within the project for the control of changes.

In order to achieve these objectives, various steps have to be undertaken:

- establish links to any corporate and/or programme quality assurance function and ensure that all project quality activities support, and are supported by, this function. This may include assigning a quality assurance role for the project
- establish any quality assurance needs for the project management products and activities, especially meeting the needs of the Quality Management System where these are applicable

- establish the means by which overall success of the project's ultimate products or outcomes is to be measured, and prioritise them

- identify quality responsibilities both within, and external to, the project

- identify the quality control techniques and procedures to be employed during the conduct of the project

- establish the Configuration Management and change control approaches to be adopted, including:
  - responsibilities
  - procedures
  - documentation.

See the chapters on *Quality in a project environment*, *Change Control* and *Configuration Management* for further information on the above aspects (Chapters 9–11).

Where the project is part of a Programme, the Project Brief passed down from the Programme may have included statements about quality planning. These would form the basis of the Project Quality Plan. If there is any inconsistency between the desired Project Quality Plan and what is contained within the Project Brief, this must be resolved with Programme management. Where the quality plans of the organisation or Programme and project are identical or very similar, the quality plan of the organisation or Programme should be referenced with only variations documented.

14.4.4 Responsibilities

The Project Manager is responsible for the process, assisted by those with project assurance responsibilities, particularly those connected to business assurance. Where a separate quality assurance function exists within a corporate body, the work of this process must be done in close co-ordination with that function.

14.4.5 Information needs

Management information	Usage	Explanation
Project Brief	Input	This document should contain the overall approach to quality and the top-level project quality criteria. These are refined and expanded during this process
Customer and Supplier QMS	Input	Standards with which projects must comply
Project Approach	Input	To establish the most appropriate approach to quality, there is a need to know how the project's work is to be approached as this could have a fundamental effect on the methods and resources used
Project Quality Plan	Output	This will contain the results of *Planning Quality (IP1)* and will be an element of the Project Initiation Document output from *Assembling a PID (IP6)*

14.4.6 Key criteria

- Have all quality standards associated with the project's area of impact been identified and considered?

- Have all those, and only those, standards relevant to the successful outcome of the project been included?

- Are the approaches to assuring quality for the project appropriate in the light of the standards selected?

- Are the quality criteria measurable or assessable by the quality control mechanisms identified?

- Are the change control and quality assurance methods appropriate for the scale, complexity and risk exposure of the project?

- How will quality assurance be provided on projects where the Project Manager is not technically qualified?

- Will 'prepared by the Supplier and checked by the Customer' be a sufficient quality criterion?

Hints and tips

*Much of the information discussed above, such as standards and quality assurance functions, may already be established and documented. It will usually be sufficient for the Project Quality Plan to refer to this documentation, **plus** clear identification and justification of any variation from the standards.*

The Project and Stage Quality Plans may have to take into account any planned change of Suppliers during the project, as they may have different quality standards.

14.5 Planning a Project (IP2)

14.5.1 Fundamental principles

Before committing to major expenditure on the project, the timescale and resource requirements must be established. This information is held in the Project Plan and is needed so that the Business Case can be evaluated and the Project Board can control the project.

14.5.2 Context

The process uses the common *Planning (PL)* process to produce the Project Plan and the detailed plan for the next stage. It includes the implications of the Project Quality Plan from *Planning Quality (IP1)*.

The Project Plan becomes a major element of the Project Initiation Document.

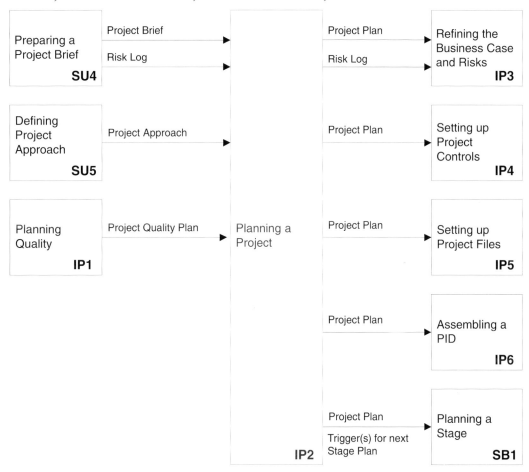

Figure 14–3: Planning a Project

14.5.3 Process description

 The objectives of the process are to:

- understand at a high level the totality of the work that is about to be undertaken, by:
    - identifying and, where possible, defining the major products of the project
    - identifying the major activities to be performed to deliver the products
    - assessing the major risks of the project, and putting in place countermeasures, as highlighted in the *Management of Risk* chapter of this manual (Chapter 8)
    - estimating the effort needed

- identifying the timescales achievable, given the project constraints and any key milestones
- identifying the overall resource requirements and costs

- identify the key decision and review points for the project, and from these decide where the management stage divisions should be (as discussed in *Stages*, Chapter 7)

- use the *Planning* process to produce the Project Plan

- trigger *Planning a Stage (SB1)* to produce a detailed plan for the next stage of the project.

As this process is basically a planning process, the detailed steps needed to carry it out are those explained in *Planning (PL)*.

14.5.4 Responsibilities

The Project Manager is responsible for this process, assisted where appropriate by Project Support roles and guided by those with Project Assurance responsibilities, who also check the results.

14.5.5 Information needs

Management information	Usage	Explanation
Project Approach	Input	This product will explain how the work of the project is to be approached and provides a key input into the planning process
Project Brief	Input	This document contains the base information about the project. It is this information that this process uses as the primary start point for the planning process
Project Quality Plan	Input	This product is needed because the work carried out and the time and resources needed to conduct it will be influenced by the quality required and the quality approach to be adopted
Risk Log	Update	Risks identified in the log may affect the Project Plan
Project Plan	Output	This is the ultimate Deliverable from the process and its production is the prime reason for carrying out the process
Trigger for next Stage Plan preparation	Output	Invokes *Planning a Stage (SB1)* to produce the next Stage Plan

14.5.6 Key criteria

Does the Project Plan show the appropriate balance between being comprehensive and complete, and being sufficiently concise to be understandable? For instance:

- Are all the relevant parts of the Project Brief reflected in the Project Plan?

- Is the level of detail in the Project Plan appropriate for the project, bearing in mind:
  - the duration of the project
  - the levels of certainty or otherwise concerning the project's outcome

- the complexity of the project, for example, the number of dependencies compared with the number of products, the number of departments or groups involved
- the corporate and business risks involved?

- Will it support, and be supported by, the other elements of the Project Initiation Document? Also is it in sufficient detail to support development of the Project Initiation Document?

- Is the Project Plan in a state suitable to support the decisions to be made in *Authorising a Project (DP2)*?

- Is the Project Plan concise enough to be of practical use for the members of the Project Board?

- Has the Customer imposed any quality criteria on the final product that will require quality related work beyond normal expectations?

- Is the Project Plan consistent with corporate and/or programme plans?

Hints and tips

Make sure the Project Brief is understood, as this should provide the base from which the planning is done.

Having understood the way in which benefits are to be realised, there may be implications for how the project should be run.

To arrive at a final Project Plan it will often be necessary to produce a draft plan, then build a detailed next Stage Plan, before refining the Project Plan in the light of the information gained.

There will be a need for a pass through the risk-assessment process to assess the risk scenario of the Project Plan itself.

Where the project is part of a programme, it may be necessary to include provision for interaction between programme and project, for example:

- *periodic audit to ensure reconciliation*

- *programme briefings*

- *project involvement in programme-level risk and change management.*

14.6 Refining the Business Case and Risks (IP3)

14.6.1 Fundamental principles

- When setting up, and particularly while running, the project, it is all too easy to concentrate on *what* is being done and *how* it is to be done, while ignoring *why* it needs to be done. The Business Case states *why* the work is being done, and as such is a crucial element of the project.

- It is also important to anticipate any problems or threats to which the project could be subject, so that appropriate actions can be taken to deal with them.

14.6.2 Context

The process takes the Outline Business Case from the Project Brief and the Project Plan that shows the resource requirements. From these the activities of the process produce a refined Business Case that is later incorporated into the Project Initiation Document. It also expands on risks in the Project Brief, plus any extra risks found since, and produces a Risk Log.

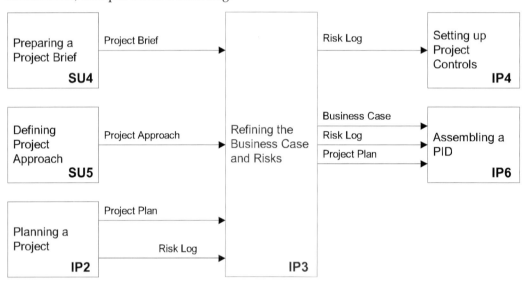

Figure 14–4: Refining the Business Case and Risks

14.6.3 Process description

This process involves creating and refining the Business Case.

The objectives of this process are to:

- refine the Business Case in the light of what is now known about the project

- identify how the achievement of each benefit is to be measured (benefit realisation)

- add to the Risk Log any extra problem or threat to which the project may be subject

- modify the Project Plan in the light of any risk exposure activities.

In order to achieve these objectives, various steps have to be undertaken.

For the Business Case:

- check whether recent external events have affected any of the benefits quoted in the Business Case held within the Project Brief

- check whether the programme, corporate or strategic objectives that this project is expected to address are still likely to be achievable in light of the information gained so far during *Initiating a Project (IP)*

- re-quantify the benefits where appropriate, and identify any disadvantages that might arise from the project's completion

- establish whether any additional business benefits have become apparent

- calculate and/or refine the cost elements based on the Project Plan and the latest information regarding the likely operational and maintenance characteristics of the project's deliverables and outcomes

- refine or calculate the financial case, and re-cast the investment appraisal where appropriate

- establish how the achievement of each claimed benefit will be measured and record this under Benefit Realisation.

For the Risk Log:

- identify any business risks that may impact the project

- assess the likelihood of each business risk occurring within this particular project

- assess the impact on the project if a business risk does occur

- identify possible courses of action to ameliorate the business risk to an acceptable level.

For the Project Plan:

- evaluate the cost of the resolution actions against their value in alleviating the business risk

- add these to the Project Plan and/or the next Stage Plan (NB. This will involve an iteration back through *Planning a Project (IP2)* and possibly a re-visit to the Business Case elements.)

- prepare any appropriate contingency plans for inclusion in the Project Plan.

There will be a step of balancing the agreed benefits with the identified costs and risks in order to make a final decision on project viability. If the steps listed above identify any changes that have a fundamental effect on the Business Case, the Project Board will need to be informed as early as possible, since they may need to escalate the issue to corporate or programme management.

Where the project is part of a programme, identified risks must be fed to the programme support office.

14.6.4 Responsibilities

The Project Manager is responsible for this process, assisted, where appropriate, by the Project Support roles and advised by those with Project Assurance responsibilities. The Project Manager should discuss the Business Case and risks with the Project Board informally before presentation in the Project Initiation Document.

14.6.5 Information needs

Management information	Usage	Explanation
Project Brief	Input	Contains high-level views of the anticipated Business Benefits and risks as identified in *Starting up a Project (SU)*
Project Approach	Input	Will contain information about the way the work is to be conducted and could provide input to both Business Case and risk analysis
Risk Log	Update	Add any identified new risks. Modify with details of any changed risk
Project Plan	Update	Updated with any significant extra activities to counter risk exposure
Business Case	Output	Extract from the Project Brief and update with the latest (more detailed) information

14.6.6 Key criteria

- Are the risk-avoidance costs commensurate with the costs implicit in the threats?

- Is it reasonable that the benefits claimed can be achieved by the anticipated project deliverables and outcomes?

- Is the information in a form that is understandable by the Project Board?

- Are plans in place/to be created by which the Users of the products will realise the benefits?

Hints and tips

The Planning (PL) process will have examined project risks. Concentration in this process should be on business risks.

Each risk effect is itself a potential cause of another effect in a cause–effect chain. The Project Manager has to decide where the chain should be cut to prevent or reduce risks.

The Risk Log can be a large document. It may be appropriate to prepare a high-level extract for presentation to the Project Board.

Where the project is part of a programme, the programme's risk monitoring mechanism must be used unless there are valid reasons not to do so. It may be sensible to combine the maintenance of all the Risk Logs at programme level.

Funding normally comes from the Customer, but there are situations where the Supplier fully or partially funds the project (Private Finance Initiative, for example). This may give the Customer fewer rights to intervene or control the project, and could affect the Customer's ability to insist on the inclusion of risk avoidance or reduction activities.

The Customer and Supplier are likely to have different Business Cases.

The method of payment needs to be considered. Payment may be provided on a regular basis throughout the life of the project, staged according to the delivery of particular products, or in a lump sum at the end.

Benefit realisation often requires measurements of the 'before' situation to be done as part of the project. Once the new product is in place, the old situation has disappeared, making a true comparison impossible. It is sensible to take such measurements close to the time the benefit is claimed.

14.7 Setting up Project Controls (IP4)

14.7.1 Fundamental principles

Each decision on the project has to be made in a timely manner by the person or group most appropriate to make that decision, and must be based on accurate information. This process ensures that an appropriate communication, control and monitoring framework is put in place.

14.7.2 Context

The process builds on the established information to produce a statement of Project Controls.

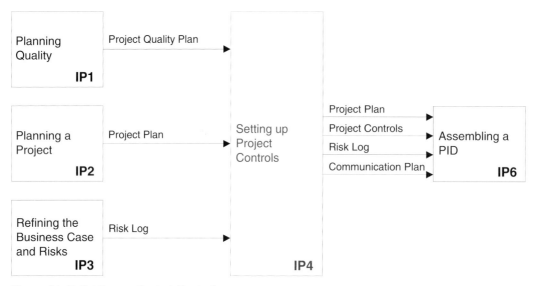

Figure 14–5: Setting up Project Controls

14.7.3 Process description

The objectives of this process are to:

- establish the level of control and reporting required by the Project Board for the project after initiation
- develop controls that are consistent with the risks and complexity of the project
- establish the day-to-day controls required to ensure that the project will be controlled in an effective and efficient manner
- identify all interested parties and agree their communication needs.

In order to achieve these objectives, various steps need to be undertaken:

- allocate the various levels of decision making required within the project to the most appropriate project management level
- establish any decision-making procedures that may be appropriate, possibly by tailoring procedures within existing Quality Management Systems or other standard procedures
- incorporate the control requirements specified in the Project Brief into the overall control environment as created by the above steps
- incorporate decision-making authorities and responsibilities into job definitions where appropriate
- establish the information needs associated with each of the decision-making processes

- identify all stakeholders outside the project management team and agree with them their information needs, plus any information needed from them by the project. Define the communication content, recipient(s) and sender, method and frequency for all these external communications in the Communication Plan

- establish monitoring mechanisms to satisfy these information needs

- establish the resource requirements to provide the monitoring information

- incorporate monitoring mechanisms into resource plans and job definitions where appropriate

- refine and define the reporting requirements as described in the Communication Plan outline Product Description

- establish the procedures required to produce and distribute the reporting information.

Where the project is part of a programme, controls must be put in place to feed information to the programme (part of the Communication Plan).

14.7.4 Responsibilities

The Project Manager is responsible, assisted by project support and advised by those with project assurance responsibilities.

14.7.5 Information needs

Management information	Usage	Explanation
Project Plan	Update	This will need to be updated with resources requirements for control activities
Risk Log	Update	Risk levels will have an impact on the scale and rigour appropriate for control activities. New or changed risks may be noted as a result of defining control and monitoring activities. Also there is a need to put in place monitoring devices for risks as they develop
Project Quality Plan	Input	The achievement of quality is one area that must be monitored and controlled. There is, therefore, a need to co-ordinate Project Controls with the Project Quality Plan
Communication Plan	Output	Identify all communication paths, frequency, methods and reasons
Project Controls	Output	This will form part of the Project Initiation Document

14.7.6 Key criteria

- Are the decisions being allocated to people equipped and authorised to make those decisions?

The next points are there to reinforce the motto 'Not too little, not too much'.

- Are the controls appropriate for the risk, scale and complexity of the project?

- Is the level of formality established appropriate for the risk, scale and complexity of the project? This covers such things as reporting, monitoring, procedures and job definitions.

- Are all the participants committed to providing the information and acting on it?

Hints and tips

When creating the controls for the project, consider the communications requirements of the project as well as the decisions being made.

Make sure that the level of control is appropriate to the project. Don't over-control for the sake of it.

If the project is part of a programme, make sure that any programme reporting requirements will be satisfied by the defined control structure.

Where information has to be fed back to a programme, this may be done by reports from the project being examined by programme staff or by programme representation within the project.

Programme representation is recommended in estimating the impact of change.

When creating the project schedule, appropriate milestones should be identified to allow any required programme monitoring of project progress, such as the ends of stages and the production of reports required for use by either the programme or other projects.

Try to restrict external communication requests to copies of existing project reports.

In a programme context, each project may operate change management within delegated authority levels.

14.8 Setting up Project Files (IP5)

14.8.1 Fundamental principles

Once the project is under way, it is important to keep track of all the information being produced regarding the project and the management and specialist products. There is a need to be able to manage different versions of products and to be able to retrieve information quickly and reliably. These problems can be eased by establishing a sensible and pragmatic project filing system at the start of the project.

14.8.2 Context

This process takes information from the Project Plan and produces the Project Filing structure to add to the Project Initiation Document. It needs to interface with any Configuration Management processes (see *Configuration Management*, Chapter 10).

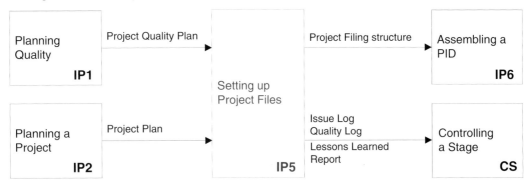

Figure 14–6: Setting up Project Files

14.8.3 Process description

The objectives of the process are to:

- institute a system of storing and retrieving all information relevant to the management of the project, the quality checking work done and the products themselves, which will provide appropriate support to the project team and to the implementation of change management

- assign responsibility for managing this filing system.

It may be that a Configuration Management system is to be used that will provide these facilities for some or all of the project's products.

In order to achieve these objectives, various steps have to be undertaken:

- establish what information will be produced throughout the project and will need filing

- establish what deliverables will be produced throughout the project and the need for associated storage

- establish what retrieval requirements the project team has

- establish filing systems that are appropriate for the identified filing and retrieval needs.

The Issue Log, Quality Log and the Lessons Learned Report are created during this process.

14.8.4 Responsibilities

The Project Manager is responsible for this process, assisted by any project support roles and advised by those with project assurance responsibilities.

Where the project is part of a programme, the project-level Configuration Management method must be consistent with that at programme level.

14.8.5 Information needs

Management information	Usage	Explanation
Project Plan	Input	Contains all the information about the deliverable that the project is expected to produce
Project Quality Plan	Input	Part of the Project Initiation Document
Issue Log	Output	Created in readiness to record all Project Issues
Quality Log	Output	Created in readiness to record all details of quality checks
Project Filing Structure	Output	Part of the Project Initiation Document
Lessons Learned Report	Output	A blank report ready to record aspects of project management that go well or badly

14.8.6 Key criteria

- Is the formality and rigour of the project filing system appropriate for the scale, risk and complexity of the project?

- Will the retrieval system produce all required information in an accurate, timely and usable manner?

- Will the Project Files provide the information necessary for any audit requirements?

- Will the Project Files provide the historical records required to support lessons learned?

Hints and tips

Projects with a wide geographical spread pose particular challenges for information and product control. Computer networks make it very easy for there to be multiple copies of information in varying states of accuracy and timeliness. It is difficult to stop or totally control this.

With sensible design, computerised support can avoid the need for multiple copies and ensure that staff only have access to the latest version of information.

The key to success is complete and rigorous naming conventions and version numbering, so that it is at least clear what information is being looked at, and for the Project Manager to have confidence that there is firm control over all master versions of information and deliverables.

Whether paper-based or automated, create a formal Configuration Management system and the appointment of a Configuration Librarian as discussed in the Configuration Management chapter to this manual (Chapter 10).

Remember that 'files' do not necessarily mean paper. The Project Files will cover a wide range of media, all of which need to be considered.

14.9   Assembling a Project Initiation Document (IP6)

14.9.1 Fundamental principles

There needs to be a focal point at which all information relating to the 'what, why, who, how and when' of the project is gathered for agreement by the key stakeholders, and then for guidance and information for those involved in the project.

14.9.2 Context

The process takes all the information from the other IP processes and produces the Project Initiation Document.

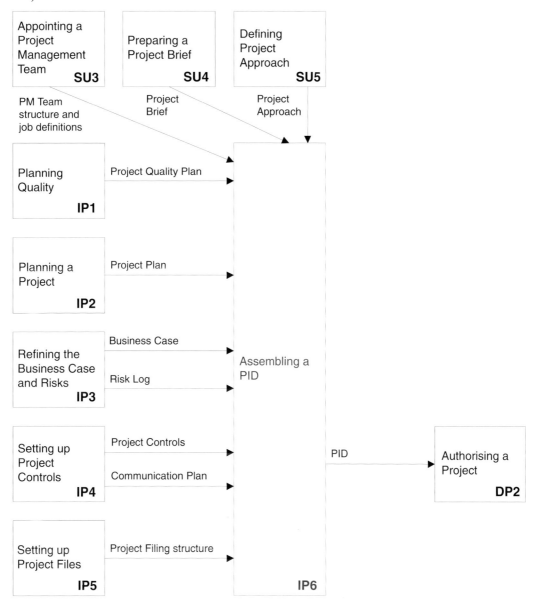

Figure 14–7: Assembling a Project Initiation Document

14.9.3 Process description

The objectives of this process are to:

- provide a basis for the decisions to be made in *Authorising a Project (DP2)*
- provide a basis for all the other management decisions that need to be made during the life of the project

- provide an information base for everyone who needs to know about the project.

In order to achieve these objectives, it is important to understand that the information will need to be held and presented in various ways, and the Project Initiation Document is unlikely to be one physical document.

The steps required to achieve these objectives will include the following:

- decide how the information can best be packaged and held so that the objectives above can be met for this particular project

- assemble the information from the previous processes

- add any narrative, explanatory, or navigational information required

- create the Project Initiation Document

- forward the information required for *Authorising a Project (DP2)*.

The next Stage Plan will be created in parallel with this process, as described in the process *Managing Stage Boundaries (SB)*.

Where the project is part of a programme, the Project Initiation Document must be examined by programme support staff for any changes affecting the programme's portfolio. Where there are changes that have been agreed, these need to be reflected in the portfolio. If the changes are likely to have an impact on other projects (for example, a product required by another project will be produced later than previously scheduled), then the changes should be disseminated.

14.9.4 Responsibilities

The Project Manager is responsible for the production of the document, assisted by project support and advised by those with project assurance responsibilities as required. There should be close consultation with the Project Board on the content as it is developed.

14.9.5 Information needs

Management information	Usage	Explanation
Project Brief	Input	Provides information that will be extracted/developed into the Project Initiation Document (PID)
Project Management Team structure and job definitions	Input	To be developed into part of the PID
Project Approach	Input	To be developed into part of the PID
Project Quality Plan	Input	To be developed into part of the PID
Project Plan	Input	To be developed into part of the PID
Business Case	Input	To be developed into part of the PID
Risk Log	Input	To be developed into part of the PID
Project Controls	Input	To be developed into part of the PID
Communication Plan	Input	To be developed into part of the PID
Project filing structure	Input	To be developed into part of the PID
Project Initiation Document	Output	Final end product of *Assembling a PID (IP6)* and of *Initiation*

14.9.6 Key criteria

- Is the Project Initiation Document going to provide all the information needs of the recipients?
- Is it easy to update those parts of the Project Initiation Document that are dynamic?

Hints and tips

Make sure that the presentational aspects of the Project Initiation Document are thought through. The complete product can be large when all the detailed Product Descriptions and job definitions are included. It can be daunting to receive the whole document, and in some circumstances this could be counterproductive. Use appendices to hold the detail and only publish these when requested.

Where the project is part of a programme, the Project Initiation Document must be created with the needs of the programme in mind. One way to ensure this is for the Programme Executive to play a part in the Project Initiation Document production, rather than waiting to review the assembled document.

If the Project Board prefers to keep the Project Initiation Document as slim as possible, just the Project Management Team structure can be put in the Project Initiation Document, with the job definitions retained in the project management filing.

15 Directing a Project (DP)

15.1 Fundamental principles

Senior project management staff who have the authority and responsibility for:

- defining what is required from the project
- authorising the funds for the project
- committing the resources
- communicating with external interested parties

will typically delegate day-to-day charge of the project to a Project Manager. However, they must exercise overall control and take the key decisions. It is also important that levels of authority and decision-making processes are clearly identified.

15.2 Context

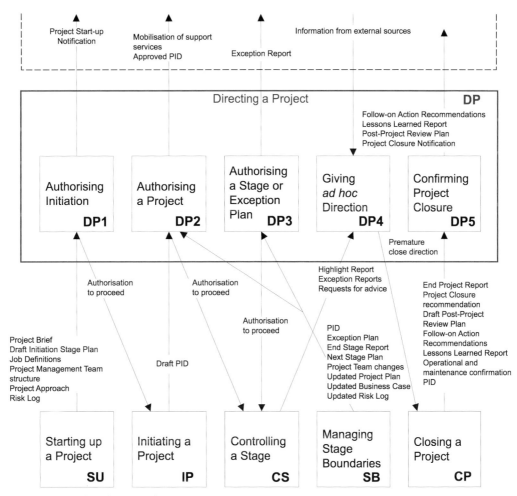

Figure 15–1: Directing a project

Directing a Project runs from after the start-up of the project until its closure and includes the work to:

- authorise the initiation of the project
- provide management direction and control throughout its life
- liaise with corporate and programme management
- confirm project closure.

It does not cover the day-to-day activities of the Project Manager.

This process is aimed at the level of management above the Project Manager, that is, the Project Board. The Project Board manages by exception – that is, it monitors via reports and controls through a small number of decision points. There should be no need for other 'progress meetings' for the Project Board. The Project Manager will inform the Project Board of any Exception situation.

There needs to be a flow of information from the Project Board to corporate or programme management during the project.

15.3 Process Description

The objectives of *Directing a Project* are to:

- ensure the ultimate success of the project, judged by:
  - the ability of the results of the project to deliver the business benefits set out in the Business Case
  - delivery to agreed time, cost and quality parameters

- manage the identified risks to the project

- ensure the effective management of all people and resources concerned with the project

- commit the required resources

- make decisions on any changes when requested by the Project Manager

- provide overall direction and guidance throughout the project

- make decisions on exception situations

- ensure that the project and the products remain consistent with business plans and the external environment

- ensure that the necessary communications mechanisms are in place

- sponsor appropriate external communication and publicity about the project.

This process covers the direction of the project throughout its life cycle. The Project Board proactively manages the project's response to the external environment. Within the project the Project Board should manage by exception. The Project Board members are normally busy executives with a range of responsibilities, and demands on their time should be kept to a minimum, while fulfilling their responsibilities to the project. The key responsibilities are:

- overall directional decision making

- resource commitment.

Where the project is part of a programme, the authority to direct the project is delegated to the Project Board by the Programme Executive. Where decisions are required that are outside the defined authority of the Project Board, these must be referred to the Programme Executive for a decision.

The key processes for the Project Board are predominantly event-driven and target the Project Board members to a small number of key decision points, plus informal discussions where required. These key processes break into four main areas:

- Initiation (starting the project off on the right foot).

- Stage boundaries (commitment to further work after checking results so far).

- *Ad hoc* direction (monitoring progress, providing advice and guidance).

- Project closure (confirming the project outcome and bringing the project to a controlled close).

15.3.1 Scalability

As this process covers the activities of the Project Board and describes its control over the project direction, it is in the hands of the Project Board how formally or informally it wishes to handle its controls. For medium-sized or large projects, and all those dealing with external Suppliers, it is recommended to use this process formally with meetings, written reports and Stage approvals signed by the Project Board.

For small projects, the Project Board may decide to:

- receive some or all reports orally
- have an oral exchange of information and decisions instead of meetings.

As a minimum, all decisions should be documented, so that they are auditable at a later date.

Three points contained within the process are strongly recommended:

- a check (at the end of Initiation) to ensure there is clear understanding of what is needed, preferably in writing
- the establishment of tolerances and the exception procedure
- confirmation at the end that an acceptable product has been delivered and that there are no loose ends.

Hints and tips

The Project Board needs to keep the balance of management by exception between the two extremes of, on the one hand, interfering, and, on the other, deserting the Project Manager once the project is under way.

The success of the process depends to a large extent on performing Setting up Project Controls (IP4) well; therefore that process needs active Project Board participation.

15.3.2 Initiation

Corporate or programme management should confirm the appointment of the Project Board and other Project Management Team members, which is done in *Appointing a Project Board Executive and a Project Manager (SU1)* and *Appointing a Project Management Team (SU3)*. They must ensure that everyone is committed to the work that is to be done.

A plan for the Initiation Stage only, which should be relatively short, is approved by the Project Board at the outset. The purpose of the Initiation Stage is to produce a high-level plan for the entire project, document its Business Case, examine the risks involved, make management decisions about them, and approve the plan for the next Stage. *Planning an Initiation Stage (SU6)* is where the Initiation Stage Plan is prepared.

At the end of the Initiation Stage, the Project Board must agree whether it makes sound business sense to continue with the project. If so, and if they approve the Project Plan, the Project Board gives the go-ahead for the next stage.

15.3.3 Stage boundaries

As part of the Initiation Stage the Project Board and Project Manager will agree on the division of the project into Stages. The division is normally proposed by the Project Manager and accepted by the Project Board during informal discussions after production of a draft Project Plan.

Basically the Project Board only authorises the Project Manager to proceed with one Stage at a time. Between Stages the Project Board reviews the whole project status before approving the next Stage Plan if it is satisfied that the Business Case still stands and the project will deliver what is required.

If problems occur during a Stage, the Project Board may be asked by the Project Manager to approve Exception Plans, which will bring the Stage back under control. This is as part of 'management by exception'.

15.3.4 *Ad hoc* direction

The Project Board's main objectives are to provide overall direction and guidance throughout the project and to ensure that the project and the products remain consistent with business plans. Activities to achieve these objectives are formally defined as part of the Stage Plans, but the Project Board will want to support these activities by receiving appropriate reports on key elements from the Project Manager.

The Project Board must maintain a feedback on project progress to corporate or programme management during the project.

The Project Board must also be mindful of any changes in the corporate strategy or the external environment, and reflect the impact of such changes when directing the Project Manager.

15.3.5 Project Closure

The project ends with confirmation by the Project Board that everything expected has been delivered to the correct level of quality and that, where applicable, it is in a state where it can be used, operated, supported and sustained.

There may be follow-on actions as a result of the project, about which the Project Board must make decisions and refer to the appropriate bodies.

A date and plan for a Post-Project Review can be agreed. This is a point in the future when the benefits of the project and the performance of the finished product can be assessed. Any lessons learned that may be of benefit to other projects are also directed to the relevant body.

Finally, the project's support infrastructure can be disbanded.

The closure process will be modified in situations where the project is terminated prematurely. It is likely that there will be follow-on actions, but all products may not have been produced, and there may be little or nothing to support. It is unlikely that there will be a need for a Post-Project Review, but the review of the End Project Report and Lessons Learned Report may be very important to understand why the project has been prematurely terminated.

15.4 Authorising Initiation (DP1)

15.4.1 Fundamental principles

No one should commit to large expenditure on the project before verifying that it is sensible to do so.

15.4.2 Context

Authorising Initiation is the first major activity for the Project Board, following the process *Starting up a Project (SU)*, to decide whether to allow the project to enter the Initiation Stage. This may be done at a formal Project Board meeting. The Project Board can, however, choose to make the decision without the need for a formal meeting as long as all members are in agreement.

Where the project is part of a programme, a Project Initiation Document may have already been prepared as part of the programme definition activities, thus shortening the normal project initiation process. In such cases, the project may start with *Authorising a Project (DP2)*. It is still the responsibility of the Project Board to ensure that all necessary steps have been taken and documented.

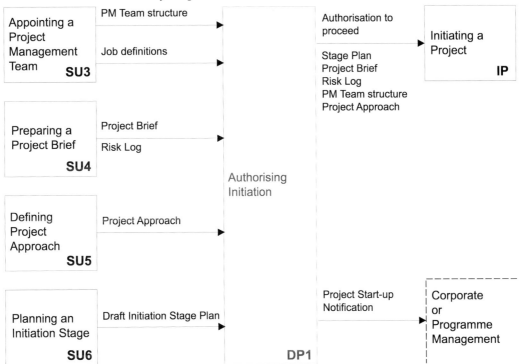

15–2: Authorising Initiation

15.4.3 Process description

The objective is to ensure that the project is properly initiated by:

- ratifying the Project Brief with corporate or programme management

- approving a plan to develop the Project Initiation Document

- obtaining or committing the resources needed by the Initiation Stage Plan

- requesting the necessary logistical support via the Project Start-up Notification to the host organisation (the location where the work is to be done).

The Project Board must ensure that adequate reporting and control mechanisms are in place for the Initiation Stage. A tolerance level should be set for Initiation, just as for the later stages.

The Project Board is responsible for obtaining resources and providing a support infrastructure for the project in line with those requirements identified in the Initiation Stage Plan. The support infrastructure may include accommodation, communication facilities, equipment and any project support.

15.4.4 Responsibilities

Responsibility for the process rests with the Project Board, based on input provided by the Project Manager and those with Project Assurance responsibilities. Corporate or programme management is responsible for ratifying the Project Brief for the Project Board.

15.4.5 Information needs

Management information	Usage	Explanation
Job definitions	Input	Details of job responsibilities
Project Management Team structure	Input	Details of who is to be involved in the management of the project
Project Brief	Update	Contains the 'what' and 'why' of the project and is the document that specifies the Project Board's terms of reference
Draft Initiation Stage Plan	Update	The work to be approved
Project Start-up Notification	Output	Request for logistics support
Authorisation to proceed	Output	The approved plan for the Initiation Stage

15.4.6 Key criteria

- Is there adequate funding for the project?
- Does the Project Brief demonstrate the existence of a worthwhile project, and hence justify the investment involved?
- Are external support and facility requirements available and committed?
- Have the most appropriate standards been applied, particularly if the Customer and Supplier standards differ?
- Are assurance responsibilities allocated and accepted?

Hints and tips

The Project Board should expect to be involved extensively during the Initiation Stage, as this is the stage where the infrastructure of the project is laid down – the foundation for the project's success.

Apart from requesting any staff to support the Project Manager, the process also has to formally agree with the host organisation the logistical support requirements of the forthcoming project. This would include any accommodation, equipment, access, security arrangements, tools and administrative support.

Avoid smothering the Initiation process with excessive formality of reporting during the Stage.

Initiation should be a fast-moving process; hence the need for frequent ad hoc *discussions between Project Board and Project Manager.*

Where a third party is funding the project, it may be necessary for the financier to be extensively involved in the management of the project. Project Board roles should reflect this, but also emphasise the User's role in specifying what is needed and monitoring the project to ensure that the solution is going to satisfy those needs.

Where the Supplier is funding the project, the Executive and Senior Supplier roles will need tailoring to reflect the financial responsibilities.

15.5 Authorising a Project (DP2)

15.5.1 Fundamental principles

No project should commit to significant expenditure without:

- management approval that an acceptable Business Case exists for the project
- checking that it fits with any relevant corporate and programme strategy
- assessment and acceptance of the risks involved
- an estimate of the time and cost involved
- checking that the project will be appropriately controlled.

15.5.2 Context

The process is normally undertaken at the same time as approving the Stage Plan for the stage to follow Initiation. This process can be combined with *Authorising a Stage or Exception Plan (DP3)* to approve both the Project Plan and the next Stage Plan.

The approved Project Initiation Document triggers the next stage of the project.

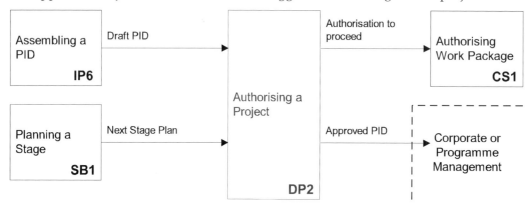

Figure 15–3: Authorising a Project

15.5.3 Process description

The objective of this process is to decide whether to proceed with the project.

This is based on approval or rejection of the Project Initiation Document. The decision-making process is best understood by highlighting the key elements of the Project Initiation Document (see the Product Outline for detailed contents). The Project Initiation Document contains all the important management information about the project. Once the Project Initiation Document is accepted by the Project Board, it is 'frozen' (Baselined) so that a record is preserved of the project's original intentions. Later reviews of how successful the project has been, or whether it diverged from its original aims, can be measured from the Project Initiation Document.

The Project Initiation Document should contain the following:

The Project objectives

The Project Board must satisfy itself that the project objectives are still achievable.

Project Quality Plan

The Project Quality Plan must state how the project intends to meet the Customer's quality expectations, and where quality responsibilities have been allocated. The Project Board must satisfy itself that the quality expectations have been correctly stated in the Project Brief and that the Quality Management System will deliver them.

Business Case

The Project Board has to confirm that an adequate and suitable Business Case exists for the project, and that it shows a viable project. The expected benefits and savings should be supplied and approved by the Customer. The project costs should come from the Project Manager and match the Project Plan.

Risk Log

The Project Management Team should identify any risks (see *Management of Risk*, Chapter 8) facing the project's products. The Project Board should ensure that there is an assessment of the risks, plus appropriate countermeasures and, where appropriate, contingency plans.

Project Plan

The Project Plan gives an overall view of the major products, timescale and cost for the project. Any wide variation between this and any previous forecast for the project (for example, one done as part of a Feasibility Study) should be examined, and the Project Board should assure itself of the continued validity and achievability of the plan and reasons for the variation. The Project Plan needs to be co-ordinated with any relevant strategic and programme management plans.

Project Organisation

Most, if not all, of the appointments of the Project Management Team will have been finalised during the Start-up process. These now have to be formally confirmed, and any late appointments negotiated. Each member of the team should have agreed their role (as described in *Organisation*), and this agreement is one of the items that the Project Board has to confirm.

Controls

The Project Initiation Document will include details of the controls that will enable the Project Board to keep overall control of the project. This will include step-by-step approval for the project to proceed via a series of End Stage Assessments, confirmation of the tolerance level for the project and the Stage after Initiation, and details of what will happen if any stage exceeds its agreed tolerance. There should be information on the frequency and content of reports from the Project Manager to the Project Board, together with details of how the Project Manager intends to control the project on a day-to-day basis. The Project Board must satisfy itself that these controls are adequate for the nature of project.

External Interfaces

The Project Initiation Document will contain details of any required co-operation from outside the project plus links to corporate or programme management. It is the responsibility of the Project Board to obtain this and confirm the availability as part of this process.

Communication Plan

This should reflect the information needs and timing between the Project Manager, the Project Board and any other interested parties. It includes communication in both directions between the parties.

15.5.4 Responsibilities

The Project Board is responsible for this process. Most of the input will come from the Project Manager.

15.5.5 Information needs

Management information	Usage	Explanation
Draft Project Initiation Document	Input	The document to be approved
Next Stage Plan	Input	Validation of the next part of the Project Plan
Approved Project Initiation Document	Output	Baselined after approval by the Project Board for later measurement against actual achievement
Authorisation to proceed	Output	Approval by the Project Board to begin the next stage

15.5.6 Key criteria

- Does the project support corporate strategy and programmes?

- Is the Business Case acceptable?

- Are the risks manageable and acceptable?

- Can the Project Manager show how the Project Plan is achievable?

- Are the differing objectives of all parties clear at the point of initiation?

- Do the defined controls ensure that the differing objectives of all parties will remain clear at each point in the project?

- What happens if one party's decision criteria require cancellation, while others propose continuance? Can contract termination criteria, terms and conditions be agreed to account for this, or should normal contract discharge conditions apply?

- Has PRINCE been adapted correctly to account for Customer or Supplier organisational or control models?

- Do the relevant risks and assumptions clearly identify the Customer and Supplier impacts?

- Can or should the Supplier have sufficient control over the Customer's organisation to be required to bear any of the business risk?

- For each risk and assumption, are the respective Customer's management, monitoring and containment responsibilities defined?

- Where a supply-side risk impacts on the Customer's Business Case, is it clear whether the Supplier or the Customer will manage it?

- Is the project based on staged payments? If so, has an appropriately detailed level of identification of product or outcome delivery been identified? Do the Acceptance Criteria reflect the staged payments approach?

- If funding for the project is variable, has adequate consideration been given to how the Supplier will ensure that the contracted scope is fully funded?

Hints and tips

Time must be allocated by the Project Board to read and understand the Project Initiation Document and to discuss any points at issue (with the Project Manager and others), so that the decisions taken are well informed.

The process is easier if the Project Board and Project Manager have been working closely together during Project Initiation. There will be fewer (ideally no) surprises.

The project organisation structure must allow for communication to decision-making forums which already exist within the Customer and Supplier organisations as well as to temporary ones established to ensure effective management of the project itself. This will normally be a Project Board responsibility. The potential delegation of assurance responsibilities can be used to help achieve the required communication.

In a fixed-funding project, it must still be practical for the Customer to pay for any cost increases caused by scope variations requested by the Customer.

Where the project is funded by the Supplier there may be implications for the organisation and control of the project. This should be carefully described in the job definitions of the Executive and Senior Supplier.

Where there is a wide differential between the Business Cases of the Customer and the Supplier, it is less likely that consistent and compatible decisions and actions will occur. Consider whether knowledge and understanding of the Business Case differentials would assist in assuring compatible behaviour.

Tight time constraints will tend to mitigate against the type of project relationship that requires extensive, formal controls and communications between Customer and Supplier. Review the standard PRINCE controls and their frequency in the light of any time constraints.

When approving the Project Initiation Document, it should not be forgotten that the next Stage Plan also needs approval.

Where funding for the project is variable, Stage approval should include assurance that funds for the Stage are set aside. The choice and timing of Stages may be done to reflect any need to confirm continued funding.

15.6 Authorising a Stage or Exception Plan (DP3)

15.6.1 Fundamental principles

It is important that work commences on a Stage only when the Project Board says it should; this avoids the problems of projects continuing just because no one thinks to stop them.

To enable this to happen, the project should be broken down into manageable sections (Stages), at the end of which the Project Board has to approve whether work is to continue or not.

It is also important to spot problems early and react to them.

15.6.2 Context

This process authorises every Stage (except the Initiation Stage) plus any Exception Plans that are raised.

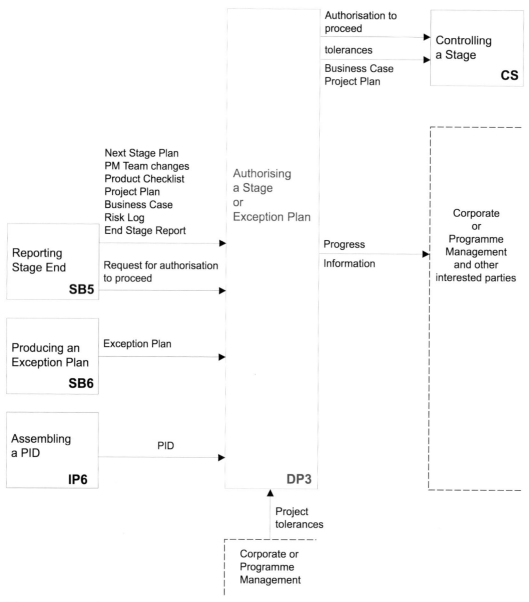

Figure 15–4: Authorising a Stage or Exception Plan

15.6.3 Process description

The objective of this process is to decide whether to authorise the next Stage of work, and hence commit the required resources, based on:

- a view of the current status of the project

- a detailed forecast of the commitment of resources required by, and the products to be created from, the next Stage of the project

- a reassessment of the likely project end date

- a reassessment of the risk situation

- a reassessment of the Business Case and the chances of achieving the expected benefits.

The current status of the project is usually presented by the Project Manager, covering the results of the previous Stage compared with expectations.

The detailed forecast comes from the plan for the next Stage, for which the Project Manager is seeking approval. The detailed forecast should match the updated or revised Project Plan.

The updated Project Plan and Business Case are compared with what they were at the start of the project (and at the start of the previous Stage) to check that the project is still viable.

Any changes to the Business Case defined in the Project Mandate or Project Brief must be communicated to corporate or programme management.

The process may also be invoked when the Stage or project is forecast to exceed its tolerance levels. Early warning of such a situation should have been given to the Project Board via an Exception Report handled in *Giving* ad hoc *Direction (DP4)* – see *Controls*, Chapter 6, for a full explanation. An Exception Report explains the cause of the deviation and the current situation, the options, the Project Manager's recommendation and the impact on the Project Plan, Business Case and Risks.

In the case of a stage being forecast to exceed its tolerances, the Project Manager will ask the Project Board to authorise an Exception Plan. As with a Stage Plan, the Exception Plan should be accompanied by an updated Project Plan, Business Case and Risk Log.

If the forecast is for the project to deviate beyond its tolerances, the Project Board must consider its brief and decide whether the matter has to be referred upwards. As part of the exception process, the Project Board has to secure any necessary decisions from outside the project. For example, if this project is part of a programme, the Programme Support Office will have to examine the likely impact on the programme and take appropriate action following approval by the Programme Executive or Director as necessary.

Once authorised, an Exception Plan becomes the current Stage Plan.

Before authorising a Stage or Exception Plan the Project Board must ensure that changes in the corporate environment, which may impact on the project or its Business Case, are brought to the attention of the Project Manager and dealt with effectively.

15.6.4 Responsibilities

The Project Board has full responsibility for the process, based on information provided by the Project Manager.

15.6.5 Information needs

Management information	Usage	Explanation
Next Stage Plan or Exception Plan	Input	Plan for which the Project Manager is seeking approval
Product Checklist	Input	Summary list of major products to be produced by the plan, with key dates
Updated Project Plan	Input	To allow the Project Board to review the whole project status
Updated Business Case	Input	To allow the Project Board to check that the project is still justified
Project Initiation Document	Input	Used to provide a Baseline against which to assess the advisability of any deviations
Project Management Team changes (included within Stage Plan)	Input	To allow the Project Board to ratify any appointment changes
Updated Risk Log	Input	Check that the risks are still acceptable
End Stage Report	Input	Report of Stage just completed. Helps assessment of current situation. (There would not be one of these for the Initiation Stage)
Request for authorisation to proceed	Input	Usually a stage approval form for the Project Board to sign
Authorisation to proceed and tolerances	Output	Authorisation to proceed with the submitted plan. During Project Initiation, the Project Board decides how formal or informal it wishes the approval to be. The Project Board, of course, has the authority to reject the plan. It may ask for a resubmission or decide to close the project
Progress Information	Output	The Communication Plan may indicate the need to advise an external group of progress

15.6.6 Key criteria

- Was everything expected of the current stage delivered? If not, was this with the approval of the Project Board?

- Are there clear statements about what is to be done about anything not delivered? Is it covered by a Project Issue? Is its delivery included in the next Stage Plan?

- Is the project still viable, and does it remain focused on the same business need?

- Are the risks still acceptable?

- Are the countermeasures still valid, including any contingency plans?

- Does the Project Board want to, and is it able to, commit the resources needed for the next stage of work?

- In projects that have a different Supplier for each stage, is it documented and agreed by all Suppliers that the key project information will be made available to subsequent Suppliers?

Hints and tips

The Project Board members are likely to be busy people. Setting dates for any End Stage Assessments can be difficult because of diary commitments. Get these meetings into diaries as early as possible (at the previous End Stage Assessment) and accept that, in the event, they may not fall exactly at Stage end. Make sure that the Stage boundary issues are discussed somewhere near the end of Stage rather than risk that no discussion is held because people are not available.

Make sure that there are 'no surprises' from the outset; that is, the project situation should be discussed informally between the Project Manager and Project Board and any problems sorted out before any formal request for authorisation of the next Stage.

Where the project is part of a programme, careful co-ordination with programme management may be necessary to ensure the timely achievement of programme-level approvals.

Although a Stage may stay within its tolerances, information may be produced within a Stage that shows that at some time in the future the project will exceed its tolerances. An example would be information that the cost of equipment to be bought a year down the line will exceed the project budget tolerance. It is important that these types of issue are discussed as early as possible, so they should still be raised with the Project Board.

Where the project deviates significantly from its tolerances, it may be better to stop the current project and restart with a Project Initiation Document that reflects the new situation.

In small projects, the Project Board and Project Manager may agree to an informal End Stage Assessment and authorisation to proceed to the next Stage. But a formal sign-off and authorisation by the Project Board is a useful document to have in the management file if problems come along later and the Project Manager is asked why a Stage was undertaken.

If the Supplier is part-funding the project, it may be necessary to modify the normal Executive and Senior Supplier roles to reflect this funding responsibility in their respective authorities at Stage end.

It is essential to ensure that the project is not adversely affected by delays in Customer or Supplier management chains.

15.7 Giving *ad hoc* direction (DP4)

15.7.1 Fundamental principles

Even when a Stage is proceeding according to plan and within tolerance, there may be a need for the Project Board to be consulted. Such occasions might be:

- for advice on direction when options need clarifying

- when the impact of events external to the project needs to be considered

- to resolve resourcing issues that would affect tolerance

- to resolve areas of conflict

- organisational changes within the project.

It is also possible that, during a Stage, the Project Board itself will need to pass information to the Project Manager about external events and its own changing requirements, or pass information to external interested parties.

15.7.2 Context

This is a process that may be needed at any point during the project. It could be prompted by an external event, or by information or circumstances arising from within the project.

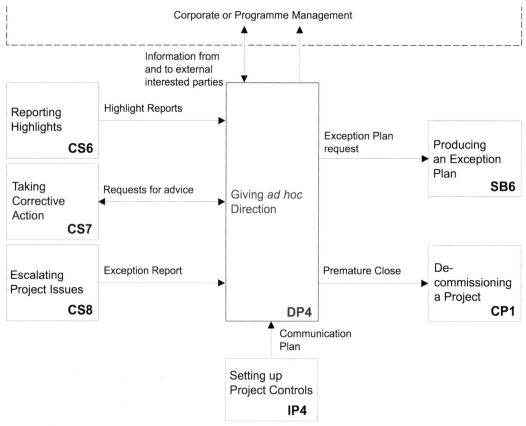

Figure 15–5: Giving ad hoc *Direction*

15.7.3 Process description

The objectives are for the Project Board to:

- ensure that the project remains focused on the business objectives set, and remains justified in business terms

- ensure that the Stage is progressing according to plan

- ensure that changes in the corporate or programme environment that may impact on the project are notified to the Project Manager and appropriate action is taken

- ensure that the project is kept informed of external events that may affect it

- make decisions on Project Issues or Exception Reports that are beyond the Project Manager's authority

- advise the Project Manager of any change to Project Board personnel

- keep corporate or programme management and other interested parties informed about project progress.

The above objectives should be achieved without the need for the Project Board to interfere in the project beyond the controls and reports it has agreed with the Project Manager.

The Project Board should receive regular Highlight Reports from the Project Manager with a frequency agreed for the current Stage.

The Project Board should ensure that any serious risk situations are being monitored sufficiently regularly to keep the risks under control. The Project Manager will refer situations to the Project Board via an Exception Report where a Stage is forecast to exceed its tolerance.

Within its delegated limits of authority, there may be occasions when the Project Board may choose to:

- ask the Project Manager to submit an Exception Plan for the remainder of the stage to reflect the new situation (see *Producing an Exception Plan (SB6)*)

- reduce the scope of project expectations to bring it back within tolerance using change control (see *Producing an Exception Plan (SB6)*)

- abandon the project (see *Decommissioning a Project (CP1)*).

Project Issues may arise on which the Project Manager needs guidance. The Project Board provides this guidance based on the impact of the Project Issue in question on the Business Case and risks. Project Issues include all Requests For Change and Off-Specifications raised. As these represent changes to the agreed Project Initiation Document, it is a Project Board function to approve or reject any changes. Agreed changes may need extra time and/or funds.

Where a Project Issue goes beyond the brief held by the Project Board, the Project Board has the responsibility of seeking a decision from corporate or programme management.

The Project Board has the responsibility to obtain any extra or changed resources that occur as a result of agreements with the Project Manager on issues raised.

The Project Board must ensure that external events that could impact the project are monitored adequately and dealt with effectively.

The Communication Plan may contain details of external interested parties, such as programme management, who need to receive (or are required to provide) information on project matters at given frequencies from/to the Project Board. The Project Board must make itself aware of any such requirements and how, when and by whom such information is to be either given or received.

There will be times when a Project Board has to be changed. This may be because a current member changes job, or extra Customers or Suppliers may be found and they need representation on the Project Board. It is the Project Board's job to notify the Project Manager. The Project Manager must then agree a job definition with the new member(s).

15.7.4 Responsibilities

This is a Project Board responsibility. It may look to share some of the activities with those with project assurance responsibilities.

15.7.5 Information needs

Management information	Usage	Explanation
Highlight Reports	Input	Regular feedback on progress from the Project Manager
Exception Report	Input	Early warning of a deviation. May trigger the creation of an Exception Plan
Request for Advice	Input	Situations where a decision is needed that is beyond the authority of the Project Manager
Information to and from external interested parties	Two-way	Either feedback from a Project Board request or new information that affects the direction of the project
Communication Plan	Input	Details of any interested parties
Corporate or programme management Reports	Output	Feedback on project progress
Exception Plan request	Output	Request in reaction to the inputs noted above
Premature close	Output	Closing the project before its expected end

15.7.6 Key criteria

- Does the Project Manager know how to contact Project Board members in the event of problems arising?

- Are Project Board members aware of the need to react quickly to issues raised?

- Are Project Board members committed to prompt reading of Highlight Reports and to timely response to them?

Hints and tips

There are projects that are so dynamic that there will be many Requests For Change. The Project Board and Project Manager should agree responsibilities, a procedure and possibly a separate budget to handle these.

Expected external changes that can pose a threat to the project should be documented as risks.

The Project Board may delegate among its members responsibility for monitoring particular external sources for any potential impact on the project. Each individual Board member will have prime responsibility for monitoring a particular area to which the project might be sensitive – for example, changing interest rates.

The Project Manager may seek Project Board guidance if any risks materialise.

Where the project is part of a programme, if there is to be a change in the composition of the Project Board, the advice and approval of the Programme Executive should be sought.

15.8 Confirming Project Closure (DP5)

15.8.1 Fundamental principles

There needs to be a formal hand-over of responsibility and ownership of the project's products to the ultimate users.

For most final products there must be a reliable operational and support environment in place.

Every effort should be made to pass on any lessons that have been learned from the project.

15.8.2 Context

The process is triggered by the Project Manager carrying out the activities and producing the management products of *Closing a Project (CP)*. It is the last work done by the Project Board prior to its disbandment.

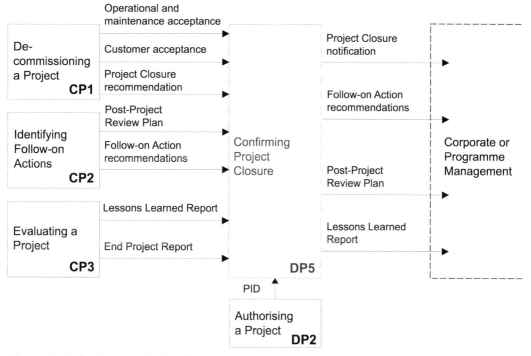

Figure 15–6: Confirming Project Closure

15.8.3 Process description

The project needs to be closed down in an orderly manner.

The objectives of this process are to:

- ensure that the project has a clearly defined end and an organised hand-over of responsibility to the group(s) who will use, support and sustain the products

- release the resources provided to the project

- gain formal acceptance from the Customer that the acceptance criteria set down at the outset have been met adequately

- direct any changes that have not been implemented to an appropriate authority for attention

- establish a future method for verifying that the project has produced the desired benefits

- recommend closure of the project to corporate or programme management.

To achieve these objectives, various steps need to be undertaken.

- Ensure that all the completed products have been approved by the Customer or are covered by approved concessions. (If there have been any concessions, these may also be covered in Follow-on Action Recommendations.)

- Ensure that, where appropriate, the resulting changes in the business are supported and sustainable.

- Ensure Follow-on Action Recommendations have been distributed correctly. These recommendations will have listed all the follow-on actions from the project, those Project Issues that were classified as pending by the Project Board, and any proposals for new work emanating from the project. These have to be directed to the appropriate body. They may be given to the support team to implement, or they may go to a programme board or strategy group for consideration as projects in their own right.

- Where applicable, ensure the hand-over of the products and Configuration Management method to programme management for on-going control.

- Approve the Lessons Learned Report for distribution. A number of lessons may have been learned during the project about weaknesses or strengths of the processes, procedures, techniques and tools used, when they were used, how they were used and by whom. If there is anything that could benefit other projects within the remit of the corporate body, the Project Board has the responsibility of ensuring that this information is passed on to the relevant people, such as quality assurance.

- Prepare a Project Closure Notification. The Project Board advises those who have provided the support infrastructure and resources for the project that these can now be withdrawn.

- Publish and distribute the plans for any Post-Project Review.

15.8.4 Responsibilities

This process is the responsibility of the Project Board, supported by those with project assurance responsibilities.

If a Post-Project Review is set up, it is the responsibility of the Project Board to ensure that the person responsible for its conduct is properly briefed and that accountability is passed to that person.

Where the project is part of a programme, it may be necessary to obtain programme management approval for Project Closure.

Programme management may also wish to direct the hand-over of any follow-on work from the project.

15.8.5 Information needs

Management information	Usage	Explanation
Project Initiation Document	Input	Used as the Baseline against which to assess how far the project deviated from its initial basis. Also contributes some of the information against which to judge the success of the project
Operational and maintenance acceptance	Input	Confirmation that the final product can be used and supported
Project Closure recommendation	Input	Assurance from the Project Manager that everything has been done
End Project Report	Input	More information on which to judge the success of the project
Customer acceptance	Input	Confirmation that the Customer accepts the products
Follow-on Action Recommendations	Approval	Recommendations for all issues classified as pending and other future actions
Post-Project Review Plan	Approval	Suggested plan for assessing the achievement of project benefits. Ratified by the Project Board to be passed on to the people responsible for carrying it out
Lessons Learned Report	Approval	Project lessons that have been learned that might be useful to pass on to other projects
Project Closure Notification	Output	Notification that facilities and support can be withdrawn

15.8.6 Key criteria

- Have the results and products been accepted, and are they no longer dependent on work that is part of this project?
- Is the business ready to support, sustain and further develop the environment and products delivered?
- Are the customers *content* with the results and products?
- Have any necessary programme management requirements been met?

Hints and tips

Give recognition to teams and individuals for significant project achievements and success.

Even if it is not obligatory, it is a sensible precaution to have written confirmation of acceptance from those who will be responsible for the operation and maintenance support of the delivered product.

16   Controlling a Stage (CS)

16.1   Fundamental principles

Once a decision has been taken to proceed with work, and resources have been committed, the Project Management Team must be focused on delivery within the tolerance laid down.

This means controlled production of the agreed products:

- to stated quality standards
- within cost, effort and time agreed
- ultimately to achieve defined benefits.

To achieve this success, the project must:

- focus management attention on delivery of the Stage's products or outcomes
- focus the resources used during the Stage towards this end
- keep the risks under control
- keep the Business Case under review
- carefully monitor any movement away from the direction and products agreed at the start of the Stage to avoid 'scope creep' and loss of focus.

16.2   Context

This process handles day-to-day management of the project. It is started after approving the Stage Plan in *Authorising a Stage or Exception Plan (DP3)*. It describes the work of the Project Manager

Controlling a Stage (CS) drives *Managing Product Delivery (MP)*, the interfaces being the authorisation of a Work Package, any specified reports, and the return confirmation that the Work Package has been completed satisfactorily.

Figure 16–1, plus the following processes, show the 'natural' pattern of events and ensure that all necessary actions are carried out on a regular basis. **However**, much of project management is of an *ad hoc* nature, driven by problems and circumstances as they arise. This means that any or all of *Controlling a Stage (CS)* may be used in an event-driven manner as well as on the regular basis indicated.

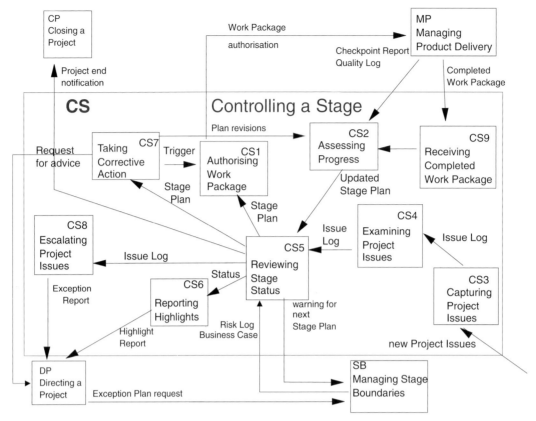

Figure 16–1: Controlling a Stage

16.3 Process Description

The objectives of *Controlling a Stage (CS)* are to:

- deliver the right products

- ensure that quality is achieved as planned

- deliver products on time and to cost within agreed tolerances

- correctly direct and conduct work on products

- properly direct and utilise resources

- update plans with actuals, enabling progress to be checked against the plan

- correctly cost resource usage

- correctly manage any deviations from Stage or Project Plans

- inform all interested parties about project progress in a timely manner

- ensure that projects are stopped or redirected if the reasons for setting them up have been invalidated by internal or external events.

Central to the ultimate success of the project is the day-to-day control of the work that is being conducted. Throughout a Stage, this will consist of a cycle of:

- authorising work to be done *(CS1)*

- monitoring progress information about that work *(CS2 and CS9)*

- watching for changes *(CS3 and CS4)*

- reviewing the situation and triggering new work authorisations *(CS5)*

- reporting *(CS6)*

- taking any necessary corrective action *(CS7).*

If changes are observed that are forecast deviations beyond agreed tolerances, *Escalating Project Issues (CS8)* covers the activities of bringing the situation to the attention of the Project Board.

Other factors that must be borne in mind are as follows.

- The current Stage contains work and involves resource expenditure that have been authorised by the Project Board. It is therefore important to give the Project Board feedback on progress against its expectations.

- All individual items of work in a Stage should be authorised (see the format of the Work Package in *Appendix A – PRINCE Product Description outlines*).

- Project work can be adequately controlled only against a plan.

- If the project is to be successful, the Project Manager and Project Board must react quickly to changes and deviations from the agreed Stage Plan.

16.3.1 Scalability

The core activities of the process can be summarised as:

- allocate work

- check on progress

- ensure that the quality is appropriate for the project's needs

- ensure that changes are controlled

- monitor risks

- report on progress

- watch for plan deviations.

There should be nothing in this list to alarm the manager of a small project. Even in the smallest of projects, the Project Manager must have sufficient time to manage the project activities and resource usage.

The process suggests a number of reports, the inference being that these should be written reports – for example, Work Packages, Highlight Reports and Exception Reports. In small projects a decision may be taken to make some or all of these oral. Even here the Project Manager must think of what events should be recorded in writing in case of later disputes. Part of the reason for documenting events and decisions is continuity if the Project Manager is suddenly unavailable.

Hints and tips

The emphasis within this process is on the processes and techniques of controlling a management Stage. However, much of the ultimate success of the project will be just as dependent on the handling of the people and 'politics' of the project.

16.4 Authorising Work Package (CS1)

16.4.1 Fundamental principles

It would be chaotic to have the people who are working on the project starting activities whenever they think fit. There must be a level of autonomy within the project team(s), but there will be wider issues involved of which they cannot be expected to be aware. It is therefore important that, in broad terms, work only commences and continues with the consent of the Project Manager.

16.4.2 Context

The process will be running constantly throughout a Stage. It interfaces with *Managing Product Delivery (MP)*, which handles the production of the deliverables involved and provides plan updates to *Assessing Progress (CS2)* during the project.

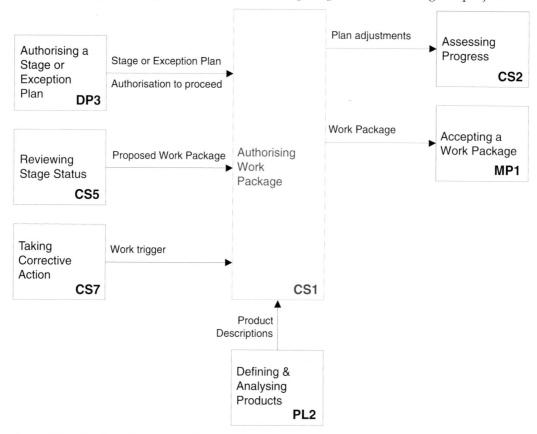

Figure 16–2: Authorising Work Package

16.4.3 Process description

The objective of this process is to keep control over the work of the team(s) by:

- issuing work instructions to the Team Manager(s) to commence work

- revising the instructions as required following management decisions.

The set of documents issued to the Team Manager(s) is known as a Work Package. On some occasions the people working on the project will be directly responsible to the Project Manager. In this case the Project Manager and the Team Manager will be one and the same person.

In order to achieve the above objectives, various steps have to be undertaken:

- review the Product Descriptions for the product(s) to be delivered; ensure that they describe what is required and add any constraints and responsibilities required

- brief the Team Manager(s) and hand out the Work Package with all relevant documentation and information, including the terms of reference covering:
  - the cost and effort that the work is expected to consume
  - the timescale for completion
  - the progress reporting arrangements
  - any individuals, groups or products with whom it is necessary to interface in the performance of the work

- ensure the Team Manager has the correct resources to carry out the work

- identify any problems or risks associated with the work and incorporate any necessary changes or other measures to handle these

- ensure the Team Manager is committed to completion of the work within the terms of reference laid down

- instruct the Team Manager to proceed via an appropriate form of Work Package.

The 'work' discussed in the overview above could be by people and resources within the Customer organisation, by outside Suppliers, or by a combination of the two. It could also cover the supply of products or services that do not involve any actual effort. The objectives and steps outlined apply in all circumstances. The formality of the Work Package will depend on the project situation. The suggested contents of the Work Package are given in *Appendix A – PRINCE Product Description outlines*.

This process must be done in conjunction with Accepting a Work Package (MP1). The overlap covers the negotiation with the Team Manager on dates and other parameters.

16.4.4 Responsibilities

The Project Manager is responsible, assisted by any support roles, and in agreement with the relevant Team Managers.

16.4.5 Information needs

Management information	Usage	Explanation
Stage or Exception Plan	Input	New work from Stage Plan, either expected or as an outcome of *Taking Corrective Action (CS7)*. The Stage Plan may need to be updated by *Assessing Progress (CS2)* in minor areas such as a result of discussions between the Project Manager and the Team Manager during *Authorising Work Package (CS1)*
Product Description(s)	Input	Description of the required product(s), including quality criteria
Proposed Work Package	Input	Details of the work required, including dates and information on any constraints
Work trigger	Input	Corrective actions arising from work triggered by process CS7
Authorisation to proceed	Input	Authorisation by the Project Board to proceed with the Stage
Work Package	Output	Formal hand-over of responsibility for the detailed conduct of the work and delivery of any products from the Project Manager following agreement with the Team Manager
Plan adjustments	Output	Any adjustments after negotiation with the Team Manager

16.4.6 Key criteria

- Is the Team Manager clear as to what is to be produced, and what has to be done to produce it?

- Is the Team Manager clear about the effort, cost and timescale expectations in connection with the work involved?

- Is the Team Manager clear about the expected quality of the work and products, and also clear about how that quality is to be checked, as defined in the relevant Product Descriptions?

- Is the work achievable within the terms of reference laid down?

- Is the Team Manager committed to the achievement of the work?

- Has the Stage Plan been updated as required, based on the agreement on the Work Package?

- Should any Project Assurance involvement be planned, especially in quality checking?

Hints and tips

In a simple, low-risk project, Work Package authorisation may be reasonably informal, although thought should be given to recording an individual's work and performance for appraisal purposes.

If a third party is involved, Work Package authorisation should always be formally documented.

A Work Package may spread over more than one Stage. Where possible, it should be broken down so that its intermediate parts fit into one management Stage or another.

It is good practice for the people responsible for a Work Package to be involved in writing the relevant Product Descriptions. If this is done, the Product Descriptions should be reviewed by other people.

If there is a contract in operation between Customer and Supplier, this may have an impact on the terms of the authorisation. The reverse is also true, so the authorisation of Work Packages should be considered during contract preparation.

16.5 Assessing Progress (CS2)

16.5.1 Fundamental principles

In order to make informed decisions and exercise rational control, it is necessary to know what has *actually* happened, to be compared with what it was *hoped* would happen. Project management can become dominated by 'fire fighting' and day-to-day problem solving. This can result in Project Managers losing sight of the overall goal. It is vital that this is countered by a steady flow of information that fills in the bigger picture, and simple, robust monitoring systems to supply the information.

16.5.2 Context

Assessing Progress (CS2) monitors the status of resources and allocated work, and reviews the Quality Log (as updated by the quality checks carried out by the team(s)). It also keeps the Stage Plan up to date.

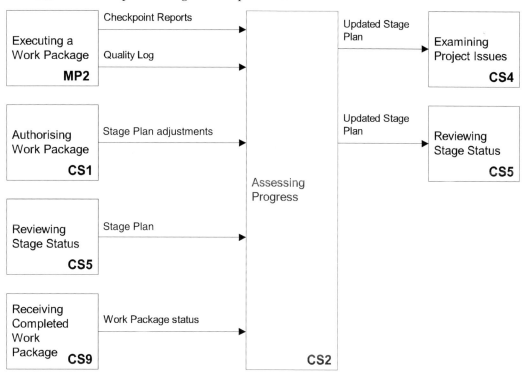

Figure 16–3: Assessing progress

16.5.3 Process description

The objective of assessing progress is to maintain an accurate and current picture of:

- progress on the work being carried out
- the status of resources

by receiving and reviewing progress information from the Team Manager(s).

In order to achieve the objectives, various steps have to be undertaken:

- collect in all progress information for all work currently being undertaken
- collect feedback on recent quality checking activities carried out
- assess the estimated time and effort to complete any unfinished work (including that not yet started)
- assess the availability of resources in the period under review and for the remainder of the stage (or project)

- review with the Team Manager(s) whether work will be completed on time and to budget

- update the Stage Plan with actuals to date

- identify any points that need attention.

The main data-gathering control for the Project Manager is the Checkpoint, described in *Controls* (Chapter 6). The *Assessing Progress (CS2)* process can also be used by Team Managers within their teams. The information is then passed to the Project Manager in a Checkpoint Report.

16.5.4 Responsibilities

The Project Manager is responsible for this process, assisted by any support roles, with input from Team Managers.

16.5.5 Information needs

Management information	Usage	Explanation
Checkpoint Reports	Input	Flows of information, either written or oral depending on the need for formality. The information will cover current status against plan
Quality Log	Input	Confirmation, or otherwise, from the Team Manager(s) that the work and products have been produced to the quality standard specified
Work Package status	Input	To update the Stage Plan
Stage Plan	Update	Updated with actuals to date, forecasts, and adjustments from Process CS1

16.5.6 Key criteria

- Is the level and frequency of progress assessment right for the stage and/or Work Package?

- Is the information timely, useful and accurate?

- Are the estimates of outstanding work objective?

Hints and tips

Progress should be measured and reported in a manner that is suitably accurate and does not allow exaggeration of progress.

Measurement of progress and status is easier if the information collection is product-based, as in Planning (PL).

The use of Earned Value Analysis should be considered in order to obtain an accurate view of expenditure.

Depending on project factors, such as size and geography, the process may be run formally or informally. The Project Manager may hold Checkpoint meetings with Team Managers, and the Team Managers may hold their own Checkpoint meetings with the team.

16.6 Capturing Project Issues (CS3)

16.6.1 Fundamental principles

During the course of managing the project, various problems, queries and changes will occur. They will arrive in a haphazard manner, and will need to be captured in a consistent and reliable way so that they can be assessed and managed properly.

It is also important that Project Issues are not forgotten, especially if there is no immediate solution.

16.6.2 Context

The process of capturing Project Issues is by its nature *ad hoc*, since it takes in details of problems, queries and changes as they occur. These details can come from a wide range of sources–both internal to the project and external.

Capturing Project Issues (CS3) produces information to go forward to *Examining Project Issues (CS4)*. The process should be read in conjunction with the *Change Control approach* defined in the *Techniques* section of the manual (Chapter 22).

This process is the window for all external stimuli, such as changes of scope.

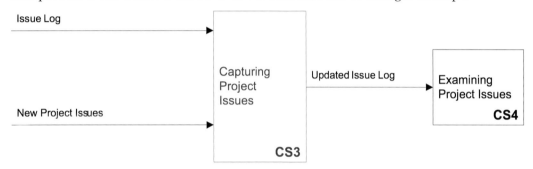

Figure 16–4: Capturing Project Issues

16.6.3 Process description

The objective is to capture, log and categorise all Project Issues. While most will be directly related to the project, the process must allow for Project Issues that have an impact outside the project – for example, on a programme.

A Project Issue is anything that could have an effect on the project (either detrimental or beneficial). Project Issues include:

- a change in requirements, however minor (even apparently very minor changes can have major long-term implications)

- a change in the environment applicable to the project, for example:
  - a legislative change
  - a corporate change of direction
  - a new Customer
  - a new Supplier
  - an unexpected change to a member of the Project Management Team
  - actions by a competitor
  - a programme management directive
  - a corporate reorganisation

- a problem occurring or being identified that was not anticipated during risk analysis

- an anticipated, but unavoidable, risk occurring

- a problem or error occurring in work completed or currently under way.

The *Change Control approach* chapter in the *Techniques* section (Chapter 22) suggests how this logging can be done.

The process of recording Project Issues can be used to note any external developments that affect the project.

Project Issues can arise from a very wide range of sources, can come in many forms, and can show themselves in many ways. The first requirement of this process is, therefore, to provide a consistent and reliable method of capturing all Project Issues.

Once a Project Issue has been identified, it must be logged for future reference and to enable progress on its resolution to be tracked.

Apart from general problems and questions, two specific types of outcome can result:

- A Request For Change, which, for whatever reason, will cause a change to the specification or Acceptance Criteria of the project; any additional cost to carry out the change will normally have to be funded by the Customer.

- An Off-Specification, covering errors or omissions found in work already conducted or planned for the future; additional costs to carry out this work will normally fall on any Suppliers involved.

A final requirement of this process is to provide a consistent output to the following process, *Examining Project Issues (CS4)*.

All Project Issues should be entered into the Issue Log as soon as they are identified.

Suggested structures for a Project Issue, Request For Change, an Off-Specification and an Issue Log are given in *Appendix A – PRINCE Product Description outlines*.

16.6.4 Responsibilities

The Project Manager is responsible for this process, although a project support role may be nominated to act as the central focus for receiving and documenting Project Issues.

16.6.5 Information needs

Management information	Usage	Explanation
New Project Issues	Input	Any Project Issues being raised against the project from whatever source, to be logged in the Issue Log and the type of Project Issue to be decided
Issue Log	Update	Repository of all Project Issues and their status

16.6.6 Key criteria

- Are all significant Project Issues being documented?
- Is this a new Project Issue or a previous one differently worded?
- Is the source of the Project Issue identified?
- Does the Project Issue affect the Project Plan as well as the Stage Plan?
- Is the Project Issue an enquiry that can be answered without changing the Stage Plan?

Hints and tips

Sometimes a Project Issue is so complex that it is better to split it into several smaller Project Issues.

Where the project is part of a programme, Project Issues must be copied to the Programme Support Office for it to look for any impact on the programme as a whole or other projects within the programme.

16.7 Examining Project Issues (CS4)

16.7.1 Fundamental principles

Before making a decision on a course of action, each Project Issue should be assessed for its impact and alternative actions considered.

16.7.2 Context

Capturing Project Issues (CS3) captures and catalogues all Project Issues. The capture of a Project Issue should trigger its analysis. All open Project Issues should be reviewed and courses of action be recommended for consideration during *Reviewing Stage Status (CS5)*.

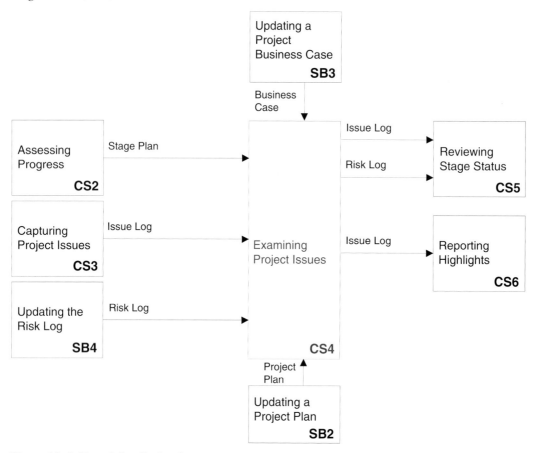

Figure 16–5: Examining Project Issues

16.7.3 Process description

An initial examination of a Project Issue should be performed as soon as it is logged.

On a regular basis, all open Project Issues should be reviewed. Decisions on a course of action should not be taken until the Project Issue can be seen in the wider context of stage status, product delivery and progress against plan. The exception to this delay is where the Project Issue raises an urgent need for action.

In order to prepare Project Issues for review in *Reviewing Stage Status (CS5)*, the following steps need to be taken:

- assemble all available and relevant information about the Project Issue, including anything that pertains to the Project Issue's effect on:
  - costs
  - timescales
  - benefit achievement and/or value
  - risks

– meeting the requirements of the project

– meeting the stated quality standards

- update the Risk Log if the Project Issue relates to a previously identified risk or reveals a new risk

- recommend a course of action.

A recommendation may address a number of Project Issues.

16.7.4 Responsibilities

The Project Manager is responsible for this process. Members of the teams may be required to assess the impact of Project Issues on products, workload, cost, schedule and risk, and devise alternative courses of action. Some of the administrative work may be delegated to an appointed project support role. Those with Project Assurance responsibilities should be involved in the examination of the impact of Project Issues on the products, risks and the Business Case.

16.7.5 Information needs

Management information	Usage	Explanation
Business Case	Input	Reference back to the Business Case to evaluate the impact of the Project Issue
Stage Plan	Input	One of the bases for impact analysis
Project Plan	Input	To check whether an issue affects the project
Issue Log	Update	A list of all outstanding Project Issues and their status, updated with impact analysis information
Risk Log	Update	Current risks that may be affected by a Project Issue. To be updated if any action is recommended that will affect a risk or generate a new one

16.7.6 Key criteria

- Who would be best to evaluate the Project Issue?

- How urgent is the decision? By when does a decision have to be taken?

- Is any special action needed to assure the Customer's best interests during the evaluation?

- Was time and effort for Project Issue evaluation put in the Stage Plan?

- How do any relevant contracts handle changes?

- Is there a separate change budget?

- What products would be affected by the Project Issue?

- Who would be involved in taking any action?

- What alternative courses of action are there?

- What would solution of the Project Issue cost in effort and money?

- What is the impact of the Project Issue on the Business Case?

- Would implementation change the current project objectives, as specified in the Project Initiation Document?

- What would the impact of the Project Issue be on anything in the Risk Log?

Hints and tips

The impact analysis for a new Project Issue should be done as soon as possible after receipt. Time should be built into the Stage Plan for people with the necessary expertise to do the analysis.

Reviews of open Project Issues should occur on a regular and frequent basis.

This process and CS5 (Reviewing Stage Status) need not be formally separated in small-to-medium-sized projects, but information gathering/ talking to the originator might be hard to do during a Stage status review.

The urgency and the importance of a Project Issue are not the same thing. Deal with urgent Project Issues quickly. Deal with important Project Issues comprehensively.

Filter out the trivia as early as possible to allow concentration on the important Issues.

Feed back information on actions to the authors of the Project Issues.

16.8 Reviewing Stage Status (CS5)

16.8.1 Fundamental principles

A Project Manager's job can easily become dominated by day-to-day problem solving. This can mean that overall progress is not checked regularly. If the project is not checked on a timely basis, there is a danger that it will get out of control. There needs to be a balance between planning ahead and reacting to events.

There will often be a need to incorporate unplanned activities.

A regular check must be kept on external events that could affect the project.

16.8.2 Context

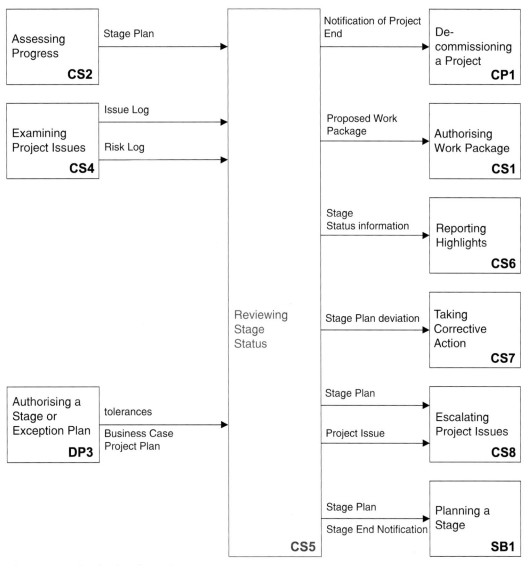

Figure 16–6: Reviewing Stage Status

This process provides the means for a regular assessment of the Stage status. The process decides whether:

- further Work Packages should be proposed

- any plan modifications are required.

If the Stage and project are within tolerance, the next actions are *Reporting Highlights (CS6)* to the Project Board and *Authorising Work Package (CS1)* for the next tranche of work.

If corrective actions are needed, and the Stage and project are predicted to stay within tolerance, the next process will be *Taking Corrective Action (CS7)*.

The Project Manager may seek guidance from the Project Board about any Project Issue (*Escalating Project Issues (CS8)*) and should **always** do so if the Stage or project is predicted to go outside tolerance. Another reason for reference to the Project Board would be that a Project Issue affects policy external to the project.

Under Configuration Management, a status account will be provided for the Project Manager, showing the planned products and their status. If it is the last stage of the project, the Project Manager would ask for a status account for all products to confirm that they are all approved.

16.8.3 Process description

The first objective of this process is to check periodically that the current stage is kept within the tolerances set down by the Project Board by:

- reviewing progress against the Stage Plan

- reviewing resource utilisation and future availability

- reviewing the effect of Project Issues on change budget and Stage and Project Plans

- establishing whether the Stage will go outside the tolerances or not

- passing Project Issues likely to cause tolerance to be exceeded to the Project Board – via *Escalating Project Issues (CS8)* – for consideration.

If corrective action is needed, but the Stage is forecast to stay within tolerance, the action can be taken by the Project Manager, as described in *Taking Corrective Action (CS7)*.

The second objective of the process is to review the project status, specifically:

- checking that the Business Case is still valid

- reviewing the Risk Log for possible changes

- establishing whether or not the project will go outside the tolerances.

In order to achieve these objectives, various steps have to be undertaken:

- identify any variation between plan and actual progress

- check for any variation in the expected future resource availability

- assess any current risk to the Stage Plan for any change to the exposure

- check the updated Stage Plan for any new risks

- review external developments for any impact on the project

- check to see whether anything has happened within the project or externally that will impact the Business Case

- assess whether the Stage will stay within tolerances

- use *Authorising Work Package (CS1)* to authorise any necessary new work required by the Stage Plan.

16.8.4 Responsibilities

The Project Manager is responsible for this process supported by any support roles and those with assurance responsibilities. It may be necessary on occasion to consult Project Board members for guidance, especially with regard to Project Issues or resource shortfalls or external events that may impact the Business Case or Risk Log.

16.8.5 Information needs

Management information	Usage	Explanation
Issue Log	Input	This product will show the current situation regarding all Project Issues. These may be needed for reference when deciding on appropriate action to deal with them
Risk Log	Input	This product shows the current understanding of the problems and threats to the project
Project Plan	Input	Data to check whether any stage problem (or potential change) would have an impact on the Project Plan
Stage Plan	Update	The Stage Plan provides the Baseline against which progress, and the meeting of Stage tolerances, is measured. The product will be updated with any minor amendments arising from progress information on the work currently in hand, or completed since the Stage Plan was last updated
Plan deviation	Output	The information to be passed to *Taking Corrective Action (CS7)*
Stage Status information	Output	This information goes forward to *Reporting Highlights (CS6)*
Stage End Notification	Output	Trigger for *Managing Stage Boundaries (SB)*
Notification of Project End	Output	Trigger for *Closing a Project (CP)*
Project Issue	Output	Trigger, plus information for *Escalating Project Issues (CS8)*
Proposed Work Package	Output	Trigger(s) plus information for *Authorising Work Package (CS1)*

16.8.6 Key criteria

- Have all the aspects of progress, Project Issues and risk been considered?

- Have they been balanced to create a complete picture of the current status of the project?

- Have all reasonable courses of action been considered when deciding on the best way forward?

- Has the project been honest with itself concerning the likelihood of staying within tolerance?

- Do the estimates to complete seem reasonable in the light of all the information available?

Hints and tips

Although this is shown as a discrete process to emphasise the importance of regular progress checking, it will often happen concurrently with other processes. For instance, at the same meeting that carries out this process, Highlights could be produced (Reporting Highlights (CS6)), and the following period's work authorised (Authorising Work Package (CS1)).

Reviewing Stage status is a cyclic/iterative process.

Stage status should be reviewed regularly, the frequency of the reviews being related to the length of activities in the plan and the need (or otherwise) for close control. Small-to-medium projects might be reviewed weekly; large projects might be reviewed each fortnight or monthly.

The status of items on or near the Critical Path (see the Planning process (PL) if this term is not understood) may need to be monitored more frequently than other elements of the plan.

Where the project is part of a programme, any new or changed risks must be fed to the Programme Support Office to check for possible impact on other parts of the programme.

16.9 Reporting Highlights (CS6)

16.9.1 Fundamental principles

The Project Board has overall accountability for the outcome of the project, while delegating day-to-day management to the Project Manager. Good reporting structures keep the Project Board (and all other interested parties) informed and involved.

16.9.2 Context

The process produces Highlight Reports to be passed to the Project Board (see *Giving ad hoc Direction (DP4)*) plus any other information defined in the Communication Plan.

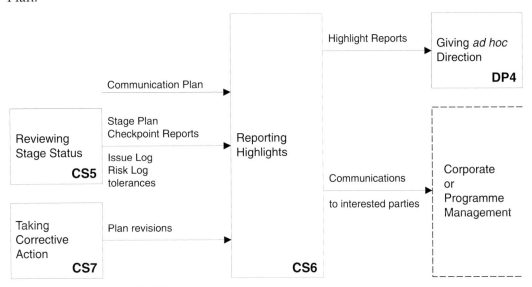

Figure 16–7: Reporting Highlights

16.9.3 Process description

The objectives of this process are:

- to provide the Project Board with summary information about the status of the Stage and project at the frequency defined by the Project Board

- to pass any other information required by the Communication Plan.

In order to achieve these objectives, various steps have to be undertaken:

- assemble the information from the Checkpoint Reports and any significant revisions to the Stage Plan from *Taking Corrective Action (CS7)*

- identify any current or potential problems from *Reviewing Stage Status (CS5)*

- produce the Highlight Report

- distribute the report to the Project Board and any other agreed recipients

- review the Communication Plan for any required external reports and send these out.

16.9.4 Responsibilities

The Project Manager is responsible for this process, assisted by any project support roles.

16.9.5 Information needs

Management information	Usage	Explanation
Stage Plan and tolerances	Input	Information on products delivered and the status of schedule and budget
Plan revisions	Input	Plan revisions resulting from consideration of corrective action
Checkpoint Reports	Input	Information about progress on the project against the plan
Risk Log	Input	Have any risks changed?
Issue Log	Input	Information about any potential problems which need to be brought to the attention of the Project Board
Communication Plan	Input	Identification of interested parties who may need information at this time
Highlight Report	Output	Information formatted as required by the Project Board
Communications to interested parties	Output	Content as defined in the Communication Plan

16.9.6 Key criteria

- Has the information been produced in the form requested by the Project Board?

- Is the report being distributed with the agreed frequency?

Hints and tips

The report should be kept as short as possible, consistent with the information needs of the Project Board. A suggested target length is one to two pages.

16.10 Taking Corrective Action (CS7)

16.10.1 Fundamental principles

Changes and adjustments to the project need to be made in a considered and rational way, even when they appear to be sufficiently manageable to be absorbed within tolerance.

16.10.2 Context

The process is triggered by the identification of a deviation and instigates corrective action. Input may be needed from other members of the Project Management Team.

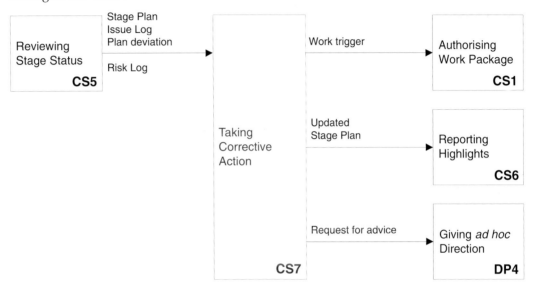

Figure 16–8: Taking Corrective Action

16.10.3 Process description

The objective of this process is to select, and (within the limits of the stage and project tolerances) implement actions that will resolve deviations from the plan. Decisions may be required from the Project Board via *Giving* ad hoc *Direction (DP4)*. The Project Manager has to decide when to seek the advice of the Project Board.

In order to achieve this objective, various steps have to be undertaken. If the input comes from *Examining Project Issues (CS4)*, some of these steps may have been taken in *Reviewing Stage Status (CS5)*. The steps are:

• collect any pertinent information about the deviation

• identify the full cause and effect of the deviation

• identify the potential ways of dealing with the deviation

• select the most appropriate option

• where direction from the Project Board is sought, assemble all information about the problem (it may already be a Project Issue) plus any recommendation

• update the Stage Plan

• trigger corrective action.

16.10.4 Responsibilities

The Project Manager is responsible, supported by project assurance and project support roles, and in consultation with Team Managers if appropriate.

16.10.5 Information needs

Management information	Usage	Explanation
Plan deviation	Input	The plan problem that requires corrective action
Issue Log	Input	This contains details of any Project Issues, Requests for Change or Off-Specifications that could be causing deviations from plan
Risk Log	Update	The change in a risk may be causing the corrective action and its status may need updating with details of the action taken
Stage Plan	Update	Amended with the implications of the corrective action selected
Work trigger	Output	Corrective action
Request for advice	Output	Request for advice on corrective action

16.10.6 Key criteria

- Have all sensible options for corrective action been considered?
- Is there confidence that after the corrective action has been taken, the Stage and project will still stay within tolerance?
- Were the impacts on the Business Case and risks fully considered?
- Has the Stage Plan been updated to reflect the corrective actions?

  Hints and tips

  Beware the cumulative effect on budget and costs of small changes.

  Beware the direction in which some small changes may be taking the project.

16.11 Escalating Project Issues (CS8)

16.11.1 Fundamental principles

A Stage should not go outside the tolerances agreed with the Project Board.

The Project Manager should always present a recommendation when escalating Project Issues.

16.11.2 Context

This process can be advance warning to the Project Board of a deviation before presentation of an Exception Plan. The Project Manager can only take corrective action or maintain the *status quo* alone while the Stage is forecast to stay within the tolerances set by the Project Board. *Escalating Project Issues (CS8)* applies where any corrective action would take the Stage or project beyond the tolerance margins.

The decision by the Project Board in response to the escalation may lead to the production of an Exception Plan, where cost and/or time targets are adjusted, or to the approval of an Off-Specification where a quality concession is required.

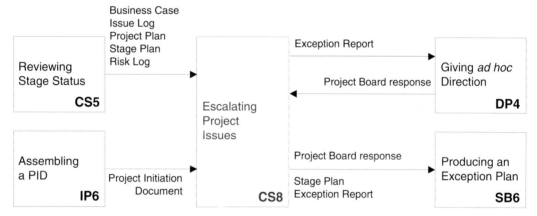

Figure 16–9: Escalating Project Issues

16.11.3 Process description

One of the major controls available to the Project Board is that it sets Tolerances for each Stage. (Tolerance is fully described in *Controls,* Chapter 6.) The Project Manager only has authority to proceed with a Stage while it is forecast to stay within the tolerance margins. If the Stage is forecast to go outside the tolerance margins (possibly as a result of a corrective action), the Project Manager must bring the situation to the attention of the Project Board.

One item likely to cause a deviation is a Project Issue. Project Issues are fully described in Chapter 11 on *Change Control*. There may be one or more Project Issues, the implementation of which would take the Stage (and possibly the entire project) beyond the agreed tolerances. The decision on which (if any) changes to approve for action must be taken by the Project Board.

Other causes may be poor estimation, a change in resource availability, resources under- or over-performing, unplanned tasks, tasks not needed and re-work.

In order to retain the Project Board's overall control, the following steps are taken:

- carry out a full impact analysis of the deviation; the analysis should cover specialist, User and business impacts

- identify and evaluate options for recovery (or to take advantage of good news)

- make a recommendation

- put the situation, options and recommendation to the Project Board in an Exception Report

- the Project Board indicates support or otherwise for the Project Manager's recommendation.

The suggested content of an Exception Report is given in *Appendix A – PRINCE Product Description outlines*.

Where an Exception situation has been identified, an Exception Plan has to be devised which either recovers a situation that is outside tolerance or proposes a new plan with a new target cost and time, plus new tolerances around that target.

The Project Board's advice should be sought before devising the Exception Plan. All current constraints should be investigated with the Project Board to see if they still stand in the light of the new situation. The Project Manager will advise the Project Board of the impact of the deviation on the Project Plan, Business Case and risks. Various options should be identified and a course of action recommended to the Project Board. An Exception Plan should be prepared in line with the recommended actions. The Exception Plan replaces the remainder of the current Stage Plan.

The parts of a plan that can be varied in response to an exception situation are:

- cost

- delivery date

- quality

- scope.

Speed is an important factor in notifying the Project Board of an Exception situation. Some of the above steps can be done in Exception Planning.

It will often be necessary to revise the Project Plan as described in *Updating a Project Plan (SB2)*.

16.11.4 Responsibilities

The Project Manager is responsible for escalating Project Issues. Those with project assurance responsibilities should also be monitoring any situations that could cause a deviation, and should bring the matter to the Project Manager's attention.

16.11.5 Information needs

Management information	Usage	Explanation
Project Initiation Document	Input	This Baseline allows comparison of any change against original expectations
Stage Plan	Update	Updated with the actuals so far, this shows the likely impact on the stage of the deviation in question
Business Case	Input	The latest version allows examination for impact of the Project Issue on the Business Case
Project Plan	Input	This indicates the project status and the overall effect of any deviation
Issue Log	Input	Details of the change(s) that may have caused the exception situation
Risk Log	Input	Details of the risk exposure that may have caused the escalation
Project Board response	In and Out	May pass on to *Producing an Exception Plan (SB6)*
Exception Report	Output	Description of the exception situation, its impact, options, recommendation and impact of the recommendation

16.11.6 Key criteria

- Is the Project Issue within the remit of the project? If not, has guidance been given on how to progress it?

- Is the Stage forecast to go outside its tolerance margins?

- Is there anything within the Project Manager's remit that would bring the Stage back within its tolerances without reducing quality or project scope?

- Have the implications for the Business Case and risks been considered?

- Have all sensible alternatives been considered?

- Is there a recommended course of action for the Project Board to consider?

- Has the impact on the Project Plan been calculated?

Hints and tips

The approval of Project Issues for which work needs to be done in the current Stage may be the factor that drives the Stage outside its tolerances. The Project Board should be made aware of this likelihood when it is considering Project Issue requests.

Such potential deviations should be forecast as far in advance as possible without 'crying wolf'. The Project Manager is expected to try to contain any such situation.

Previous Highlight Reports might have set alarm bells ringing that the Stage might exceed its tolerances.

One option available to the Project Board in response to an Exception situation is to stop the project.

One cause of an Exception might be a Supplier going out of business.

It is necessary to undertake impact analysis on the options to counter a forecast deviation.

User input should be sought on the impact to the user community of the deviation and options.

Specialist input should be sought on the impact on the specialist of the deviation and options.

The business impact should cover the Project Plan, Business Case and risks.

The Project Board may decide to accept an Off-Specification without corrective action, turning the Off-Specification into a concession.

Consider the need for speed in notifying the Project Board. The process can be done in three steps; a brief statement, followed by supporting information, followed by Exception Planning.

16.12 Receiving Completed Work Package (CS9)

16.12.1 Fundamental principles

Where work has been allocated to individuals or teams, there should be a matching confirmation that the work has been completed and accepted.

16.12.2 Context

This process records the successful completion and return of Work Packages. This information is then passed to *Assessing Progress (CS2)*.

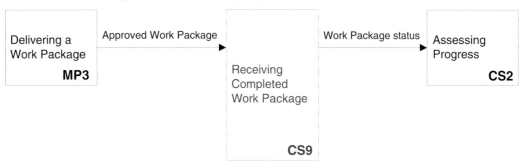

Figure 16–10: Receiving Completed Work Package

16.12.3 Process description

The completed Work Package is checked to see that it conforms to the Product Description and specification, standards, and constraints agreed as part of the authorisation of that Work Package.

Any approvals defined as part of the Acceptance Criteria are checked to be in order.

The completed, accepted product is now Baselined. Any subsequent changes to the product must pass through change control. This would be an automatic part of any Configuration Management method being used.

16.12.4 Responsibilities

The Project Manager is responsible for this process, assisted by any appointed project support staff. Information will be provided by the individual or Team Manager responsible for completion of the Work Package.

16.12.5 Information needs

Management information	Usage	Explanation
Approved Work Package	Input	Signed-off confirmation that the Work Package is complete and acceptable
Work Package Status	Output	To update the Stage Plan

16.12.6 Key criteria

- Are all individuals or teams whose work is to interface with the completed Work Package happy with the product(s)?

- Are the sign-offs sufficiently independent of the creator(s)?

Hints and tips

There is a close link between the management information requirements of this process and the technical requirements of any Configuration Management method being used in receiving and recording completion data. The Configuration Management method will also take charge of the deliverable from the Work Package and be responsible for its storage – see Chapter 10, Configuration Management.

17   Managing Product Delivery (MP)

17.1 Fundamental principles

Managing Product Delivery (MP) allows a controlled break between the Project Manager and product creation/provision by third-party Suppliers. The process needs careful implementation to avoid being over-bureaucratic.

17.2 Context

The third party may not be using PRINCE, and so this is a statement of the required interface between the Team Manager and the PRINCE method being used in the project.

In many projects the Project Manager will allocate work directly to the individual who is to do the work and combine this process with the authorisation of the Work Package.

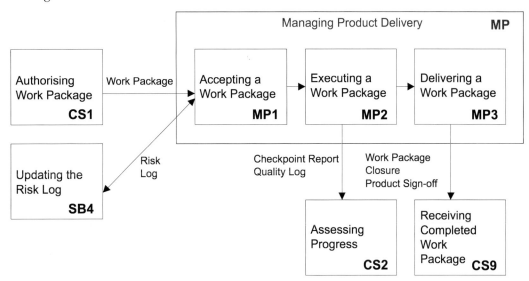

Figure 17–1: Managing Product Delivery

17.3 Process description

The objectives of this process are to allow a Team Manager to:

- agree work with the Project Manager
- get it done
- hand it back to the Project Manager.

Where external Suppliers are involved, the acceptance of Work Packages will be affected by the terms of their contract.

The Team Manager ensures that planned products are created and delivered by the team to the project by:

- making certain that work on products allocated to the team is effectively authorised and agreed
- accepting and checking authorised Work Packages
- ensuring that work conforms to any interfaces identified in the Work Package
- creating a Team Plan for the work

- ensuring that the work is done

- ensuring that work progress and forecasts are regularly assessed

- ensuring that completed products meet quality criteria

- obtaining approval for the completed products.

17.3.1 Scalability

For small projects, or any with just one team reporting directly to the Project Manager, the link between this process and *Controlling a Stage (CS)* will be much less formal.

The process work can be summarised as:

- negotiate work to be done

- plan it

- oversee it being done

- keep track of progress

- report progress

- have it checked

- make a record of quality checks

- control changes

- get the product(s) approved

- return the completed Work Package to the Project Manager.

17.4 Accepting a Work Package (MP1)

17.4.1 Fundamental principles

The fundamental principle of this process is that before a Work Package is allocated to the team, there should be agreement with the Project Manager on:

- what is to be delivered
- what constraints apply
- any interfaces to be recognised
- whether the requirements of the Work Package are reasonable and can be achieved.

17.4.2 Context

This process is the management interface between the Team Manager and the Project Manager for the transfer to the team of work to be done.

The process is the Team Manager's counter to *Authorising Work Package (CS1)*. There will be many instances of the two processes during the project.

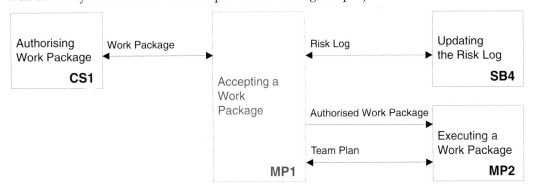

Figure 17–2: Accepting a Work Package

17.4.3 Process description

The suggested content of a Work Package is given in *Appendix A – PRINCE Product Description outlines*. This process identifies the work of the Team Manager to accept a piece of work from the Project Manager.

The Team Manager has to agree the Work Package with the Project Manager. The steps for this are:

- make a clear agreement with the Project Manager on what is to be delivered
- negotiate with the Project Manager on behalf of the team the constraints within which the work is to be done
- agree tolerance margins for the Work Package
- understand the reporting requirements
- understand how, and from whom, approval for the deliverables is to be obtained
- understand how the approved deliverables are to be formally handed over
- confirm how the Project Manager is to be informed of completion of the Work Package
- produce a Team Plan that shows that the Work Package can be completed within the constraints
- perform risk analysis, planning and resourcing.

Product Description(s) should exist that describe the product(s) required, including the quality criteria. The Stage or Team Plan should indicate agreed constraints, such as time and effort.

17.4.4 Responsibilities

The Team Manager is responsible for the agreement with the Project Manager.

17.4.5 Information needs

Management information	Usage	Explanation
Work Package	Update	Package put together by the Project Manager in *Authorising Work Package (CS1)* for the Team Manager's agreement. May be revised in coming to an agreement.
Team Plan	Update	Details of the Work Package are added to the team's workload
Risk Log	Update	The Team Manager adds any risks identified in the Team Plan to the Risk Log
Authorised Work Package	Output	The Work Package is checked and agreed by the Team Manager

17.4.6 Key criteria

- Has there been full consultation on the Work Package between the Project Manager and Team Manager?

- Is there a cost and time allowance for the quality checking work and any re-work that may be required?

- Are the reporting requirements reasonable?

- Are any interfacing requirements achievable within the constraints?

- Are any links to the project's Configuration Management method clear and consistent with the way in which the products will be controlled in the team?

- Has any required interface to project assurance been made clear, and the interface with the team established?

- Are any risks and the means of managing them identified?

- What is the resource availability over the period covered by the Work Package?

- What skills and experience are needed by the Work Package elements?

- Does the individual or group agree with the work allocated?

- Is there adequate description of the quality required?

- Are any standards and techniques to be used defined?

Hints and tips

Where the project has no Team Managers and the Project Manager hands work directly to a team member, this process can be used informally by the individual.

This process 'matches' Authorising Work Package (CS1), and the two will be done together.

17.5 Executing a Work Package (MP2)

17.5.1 Fundamental principles

The fundamental principles of this process are that:

- whatever the type of project, the actual task of creating the required products needs to be managed

- in the same way that work is delegated to a Team Manager, so the tracking of that work is also delegated.

17.5.2 Context

This process may occur at a level that is not using PRINCE – for instance when a third party is involved. There is, therefore, no definition of specific standards or procedures to be used, just a statement of what must be done in order for the Team Manager to liaise within the project.

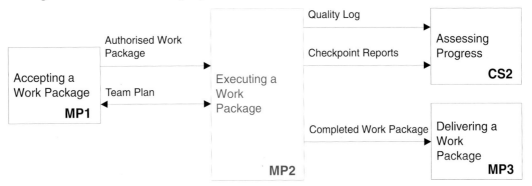

Figure 17–3: Executing a Work Package

17.5.3 Process description

The work on an authorised Work Package has to be monitored at the depth required to provide feedback to the Project Manager as defined in the authorised Work Package. The necessary steps are:

- capture and record the effort expended

- determine the status of each product in the Work Package

- monitor and control the risks associated with the Work Package

- evaluate with the creator(s) the amount of effort still required

- feed the progress and status information back to the Project Manager, in Checkpoint Reports, in the manner and at the frequency defined in the Work Package

- ensure that the required quality checking procedures are carried out and that the product(s) satisfy the quality standards defined in the Work Package

- advise the Project Manager of any problems that might impact the agreed tolerance levels for the Work Package. (Formally, this would be done via a Project Issue.)

17.5.4 Responsibilities

The Team Manager is responsible for the process.

17.5.5 Information needs

Management information	Usage	Explanation
Authorised Work Package	Input	Work agreed with the Project Manager
Team Plan	Update	Record allocation, planned effort, actual effort and progress, plus any modifications required, are all used to update the Team Plan
Quality Log	Update	Details of the checks carried out on the product, to ensure conformance to quality standards, are added to the Quality Log
Checkpoint Reports	Output	Progress reports to the Project Manager at the frequency defined in the Work Package
Completed Work Package	Output	Confirmation that the Work Package is complete and acceptable

17.5.6 Key criteria

- Is the work divided into sufficiently small segments to facilitate the required level of control?
- How will progress be monitored?
- How will the final product(s) be checked?
- Does the Team Plan include the quality checking work?
- Are the team members' progress recording and reporting procedures at the right level for the project reporting requirements?
- Is work being done to the requirements and constraints of the Work Package?
- Are progress recording and reporting in sufficient detail to give early warning of any threat to the tolerance margins?
- Were the quality checks fully carried out?

Hints and tips

The Team Manager may need to add extra information to the Work Package to indicate version control or Configuration Management methods to be used within the team.

Procedures must be put in place to keep the Project Manager up to date on progress.

Even if the team is not using PRINCE, it must provide the Project Manager with the required information in the format stipulated in the Work Package. Therefore, it would be sensible to have recording and reporting procedures that match those of the project (or even use the respective PRINCE reports).

17.6 Delivering a Work Package (MP3)

17.6.1 Fundamental principles

Just as the Work Package was accepted from the Project Manager, notification of its completion must be returned to the Project Manager.

17.6.2 Context

The return of the actual products of the Work Package may be handled by the Configuration Management system used by the project. The essence of this process is that the Team Manager must ensure that the products are handed over correctly and advise the Project Manager that the hand-over has occurred.

The process may trigger *Authorising Work Package (CS1)* (for the next Work Package) or may overlap with it.

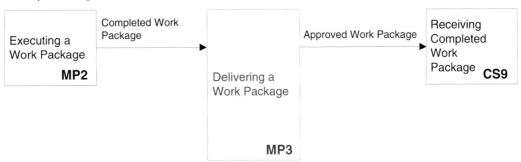

Figure 17–4: Delivering a Work Package

17.6.3 Process description

The process has three elements:

- obtain sign-off by any required quality checkers for the products developed
- hand over the completed products
- advise the Project Manager of completion of the Work Package.

The methods of achieving these elements should have been defined as part of Work Package authorisation.

17.6.4 Responsibilities

The Team Manager is responsible for the process.

17.6.5 Information needs

Management information	Usage	Explanation
Completed Work Package	Input	Details of the work agreed with the Project Manager
Approved Work Package	Output	Products approved as defined in the Work Package

17.6.6 Key criteria

- Has the identified recipient accepted the product(s)?
- Has hand-over been completed, including any Configuration Management aspects?

- Are any agreed statistics available for the Project Manager to record in the Stage Plan?
- Did anything happen during execution of the Work Package that is worthy of addition to the Lessons Learned Report?

Hints and tips

If the Work Package contains a number of products to be developed, they may be handed over to the project's Configuration Management system as they are approved. This may imply a considerable period of time before the Project Manager is notified that the whole Work Package has been completed.

The level of formality required will vary according to the project: formal when third parties are involved, informal when the Project Manager manages the work directly.

18 Managing Stage Boundaries (SB)

18.1 Fundamental principles

Projects, whether large or small, need to be focused on delivering business benefit, either in their own right or as part of a larger programme. The continuing correct focus of the project should be confirmed at the end of each Stage. If necessary, the project can be redirected or stopped to avoid wasting time and money.

18.2 Context

Before the end of each Stage except the final one, the next Stage is planned, together with a review and update of the Business Case, risk situation and overall Project Plan.

There could well be changes of personnel and management, necessitating changes to the Project Management Team.

There is also a requirement to re-visit the Project Quality Plan and Project Approach to check whether they need changing or refining.

The steps of this process will also be used when creating an Exception Plan.

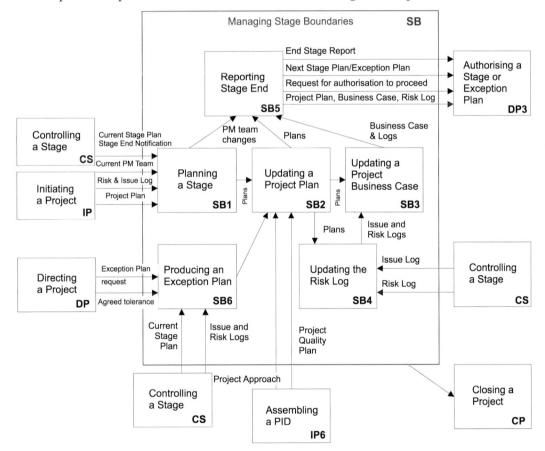

Figure 18–1: Managing Stage Boundaries

18.3 Process description

The objectives of the process are to:

- assure the Project Board that all products in the current Stage Plan have been completed as defined

- provide the information needed for the Project Board to assess the continuing viability of the project

- obtain authorisation for the start of the next Stage, together with its delegated tolerance margins

- record any information or lessons that can help later stages of this project and/or other projects.

The stage immediately post-Initiation is normally approved at the same time as the Project Initiation Document. If so, this process would need customising for that situation.

18.3.1 Scalability

As can be seen from the short list below, the process has a simple purpose, and this can be done as informally as the Project Board and Project Manager wish. The reporting and approval may be informal, if the Project Board is agreeable.

- gather the results of the current stage

- plan the next stage

- check the effect on
  - the project plan
  - the justification for the project
  - the risks

- report and seek approval.

18.4 Planning a Stage (SB1)

18.4.1 Fundamental principles

Planning each Stage of the project ensures that:

- there is sufficient detail for day-to-day control to be exercised against the plan
- each Stage Plan has the commitment of the Project Board and Project Manager
- the Project Board is fully aware of what it is approving at the start of each Stage.

18.4.2 Context

The process is triggered by the approaching end of the current Stage.

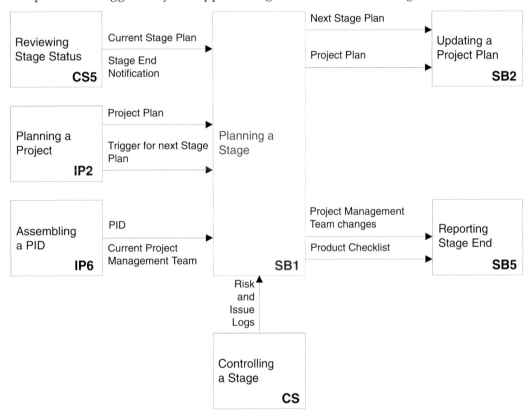

Figure 18–2: Planning a Stage

18.4.3 Process description

The main objective is to prepare a plan for the next Stage of the project. The high-level summary of the next Stage is expanded from the Project Plan into sufficient detail that the Project Manager will be able to control progress against it on a day-to-day basis. The *Planning (PL) Process* is used to develop the plan.

The plan should include all products – not only the specialist ones but management and quality products as well. A typical management product would be the next Stage Plan, which will require preparation towards the end of the Stage. Quality activities and products should also appear in the plan. Whoever is providing project assurance should be consulted about the timing and resourcing of quality activities before the Stage Plan is presented to the Project Board.

The management structure of the next Stage must be specified and any new or changed job definitions prepared.

18.4.4 Responsibilities

The Project Manager is responsible for this process, assisted by project support. The plan should be checked out by those with project assurance responsibilities, particularly with respect to how quality checking will be monitored.

18.4.5 Information needs

Management information	Usage	Explanation
Issue Log	Input	May contain information that affects the next Stage
Current Stage Plan	Input	The results of the current Stage may affect the planning of the new Stage activities
PID	Input	Contains the 'what' and 'why' of the project and is the document that specifies the Project Board's terms of reference
Trigger for next Stage Plan	Input	Invokes *Planning a Stage (SB1)* to produce the next Stage Plan
Project Management Team Structure	Update	This should be updated with any changes for the coming Stage
Project Plan	Update	Provides the major products of the stage and a high-level estimate of its duration and resource needs. Updated as Stages are completed
Risk Log	Update	Update with any new or changed risks revealed by the coming Stage Plan
Draft next Stage Plan and Product Checklist	Output	Produced by this process

18.4.6 Key criteria

- Are the major products shown in the Project Plan for the next stage reflected in the next Stage Plan?

- Are all User, Customer or other resources required to validate the quality of products identified?

- Are the resources used to validate quality in line with the requirements of the Project Quality Plan?

Hints and tips

Ensure that any externally produced products are shown in the Stage Plan, together with sufficient monitoring points to assure the Project Board that these products are both on schedule and to the required quality.

Check any external dependencies to ensure that there has been no change in the scope or constraints of products expected from them.

The Stage Plan will need to be prepared in parallel with any relevant Team Plans.

Ensuring that quality control procedures are used correctly is jointly the responsibility of the Senior Supplier and Senior User. Does the Stage Plan show how this responsibility will be carried out, particularly by the Senior User? The plan needs User involvement in checking products delivered by the Supplier.

Where the project is part of a programme, it is unlikely that programme staff will want to record this level of detail, except for any inter-project dependencies. The Project Plan is a more appropriate level. However, the programme may wish to hold a copy of the Stage Plan for reference.

18.5 Updating a Project Plan (SB2)

18.5.1 Fundamental principles

The Project Board uses the Project Plan throughout the project to measure overall progress. As Stages are completed or planned in detail, the Project Plan must be updated to reflect the latest understanding of the project and to allow the Project Board to revise its expectations.

18.5.2 Context

The Project Plan is updated from information in the Stage Plan for the Stage that is finishing, the next Stage Plan, and any Exception Plan triggered by *Escalating Project Issues (CS8)*. Actuals are taken from the first and the forecast duration and costs from the last two.

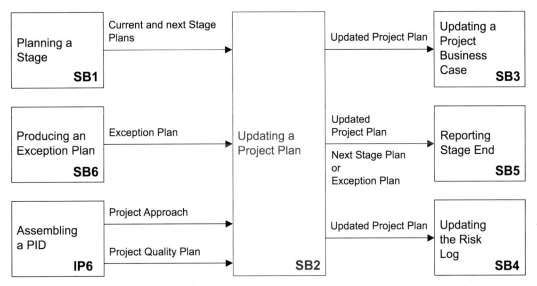

Figure 18–3: Updating a Project Plan

18.5.3 Process description

The Project Quality Plan and Project Approach are reassessed and refined to reflect the current understanding of the project and to form a basis for updating the Project Plan.

The Project Plan is updated based on the actual costs and schedule from a completed Stage Plan or Exception Plan, the new detail of activities and costs from the next Stage Plan (unless there is no next Stage or Exception Plan) and any acquired knowledge about the project. The last might be information about changes that have been agreed by the Project Board and that will cause activities in the next Stage Plan.

The Project Manager should describe in the End Stage Report (or Exception Report) why any change to the Project Plan has occurred.

18.5.4 Responsibilities

The Project Manager is responsible for this process, assisted by project support, and the work checked out by those with Project Assurance responsibility.

18.5.5 Information needs

Management information	Usage	Explanation
Current Stage Plan	Input	The results of the current Stage may affect the project planning
Next Stage Plan or Exception Plan	Input	The extra detail in the Stage Plan or Exception Plan may reveal the need to modify the Project Plan
Project Approach	Update	Events may have occurred that modify the approach
Project Quality Plan	Update	Quality results so far show the need to adjust the Project Plan
Project Plan	Update	Revised in the light of the actuals from the current stage and the forecast of the next Stage Plan. Also updated to reflect any changed or extra products sanctioned by the Project Board

18.5.6 Key criteria

- How reliable are the figures for cost and schedule for the Stage just being completed (especially if fed information from Team Plans)?

- How do the results of the Stage impact the Project Plan?

- How does the next Stage Plan impact the Project Plan, Business Case and risks?

- Did any other information come out of the last Stage that will impact later Stages of the project?

Hints and tips

If the Project Plan is being updated because the scope of the project has changed, make sure that there is an audit trail between cause and effect – for example, ensure that the changes are recorded in the Issue Log.

18.6 Updating a Project Business Case (SB3)

18.6.1 Fundamental principles

Projects do not take place in a static environment. The environment external to the project changes, as do the nature and timing of the project's products. The Business Case needs to reflect these changes and must be reviewed and amended to keep it relevant to the project.

18.6.2 Context

The update of the Business Case and the Project Plan is a cyclical process during Stage-end processes throughout the project.

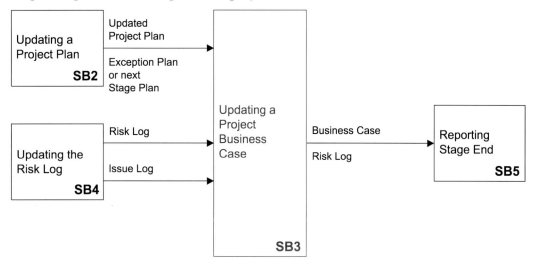

Figure 18–4: Updating a Project Business Case

18.6.3 Process description

The objective is to re-visit and revise, where necessary, the costs, benefits and timings stated in the Business Case. These may have been affected by internal or external events.

Various factors will affect this process:

- the final implementation date of the project may have changed, for better or worse, which might affect some or all of the benefits

- the cost of delivering the outcome might have changed, thus affecting the cost side of the cost/benefit analysis

- approved changes will have affected products, hence benefits

- externally the corporate or programme environment into which the outcome will be delivered may have changed

- the situation with regard to external resources or Suppliers may have changed beyond the control of the project

- it may be an Exception Plan that has caused the Business Case to be re-visited.

A revised Business Case is created. The Risk and Issue Logs are examined to see if anything has changed that might affect the Business Case.

It is worth noting that changes may improve the Business Case, just as well as weaken it.

The Project Board is ordinarily only authorised to continue while the project remains viable (that is, the benefits will be realised within the cost and time parameters set out in the currently agreed Business Case). If costs and/or time are to be exceeded, or it becomes clear that benefits will be substantially lower than those set out in the Business Case, the Project Board needs to have the revised Business Case approved afresh by corporate or programme management.

18.6.4 Responsibilities

The Project Manager is responsible for this process, assisted by project support, and the work should be checked out by those with Project Assurance responsibilities.

The project's benefits are a prime responsibility of the Customer.

18.6.5 Information needs

Management information	Usage	Explanation
Project Plan	Input	Have any changes to the Project Plan been made that affect the Business Case?
Issue Log	Input	Are there any new Issues that threaten (or could improve) the Business Case?
Risk Log	Input	Are there any new risks that threaten the Business Case?
Next Stage Plan	Input	Does anything in the next Stage Plan affect the Business Case?
Exception Plan	Input	If the *SB* process has been triggered by an exception situation, does the Exception Plan affect the Business Case?
Business Case	Update	Revised to account for any changes to the project that may affect it

18.6.6 Key criteria

- Has anything happened external to the project that affects the Business Case?
- Has the Project Plan changed such that it impacts the Business Case – for example, in terms of overall cost or the date of the scheduled outcome?
- Has it become impossible to achieve some or all of the identified benefits?

Hints and tips

Reviewing the Business Case is best done after the Project Plan has been brought up to date.

It is sensible to review the Business Case after any activities caused by reaction to risks have been added to the new Stage Plan. These activities or their cost may have an effect on the Business Case.

18.7 Updating the Risk Log (SB4)

18.7.1 Fundamental principles

Risks change during the life of the project. New risks arise. Old risks change their status. The exposure of the project to risk should be regularly reviewed.

18.7.2 Context

The update of the Risk Log is a cyclical process during Stage-end processes throughout the project. This is the minimum number of times to review risks. Lengthy or risky projects will need to review risks more frequently.

Figure 18–5: Updating the Risk Log

18.7.3 Process description

The objective is to re-visit and revise, where necessary, the risks in the Risk Log. These may have been affected by internal or external events.

Each risk should be examined to see if it has increased, disappeared, decreased, happened or stayed the same.

The next Stage Plan or an Exception Plan may raise new risks or change existing risks. This process should therefore be carried out in conjunction with *Planning a Stage (SB1)* and *Producing an Exception Plan (SB6)*.

Updates to the Project Plan and Business Case may also contain changes that affect items in the Risk Log. The Business Case update may also have raised new Project Issues, which in turn raise new risks or affect risks already recognised.

For further guidance on risk, see Chapter 8, *Management of Risk*.

18.7.4 Responsibilities

The Project Manager is responsible for this process, assisted by Project Support, and the work should be checked out by those with Project Assurance responsibilities.

Each major risk should have an 'owner' – the member of the Project Management Team best placed to observe the risk and the factors affecting it.

18.7.5 Information needs

Management information	Usage	Explanation
Project Plan	Input	Have any changes to the Project Plan been made that affect the risks?
Next Stage Plan or Exception Plan	Input	Does the new plan contain any new or changed risks?
Risk Log	Update	Has anything changed?
Issue Log	Update	Are there any new Issues that are caused by (or could improve) the new risks?

18.7.6 Key criteria

- Has the situation changed with respect to any of the identified risks?

- Have any new risks been identified?

- Have contingency plans been put in place, where possible, for any risks now regarded as serious?

18.8 Reporting Stage End (SB5)

18.8.1 Fundamental principles

The results of a Stage should be reported back to those who provided the resources and approved its execution so that progress is clearly visible to the Project Management Team.

18.8.2 Context

This process is invoked when either the Project Manager identifies that a Stage is nearing its end or an Exception Plan has been created. *Reporting Stage End (SB5)* involves a review of the impact of the Stage on the Project Plan, the Business Case and the identified risks. Except for the final Stage, the process is done as a precursor to the presentation of the next Stage Plan.

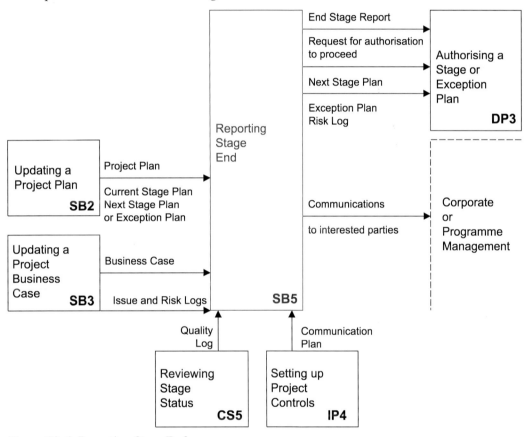

Figure 18–6: Reporting Stage End

18.8.3 Process description

This process should happen as close as possible to the actual end of a Stage. The results of the Stage are presented in an End Stage Report.

The report includes the actual results of the Stage in terms of costs, dates achieved and products produced. These are compared with the original Stage Plan. A statement is made comparing the results with the agreed tolerances for the Stage. A report is given of the quality control activities undertaken and the results of that work.

A summary is given of all Project Issues received during the Stage and what has happened to them.

The report is modified if it has been triggered by an Exception Plan, but it is still needed.

The next Stage Plan and the revised Project Plan (if there is one) accompany the End Stage Report. The report identifies any variations from the previous versions of these plans and assesses any changes to the risk situation. If the project is still viable in the Project Manager's view, a request to proceed to the next stage will accompany the End Stage Report.

Any lessons learned during the stage are added to the Lessons Learned Report. This report is not included in the End Stage Report, but any lessons from the current stage are summarised in the End Stage Report.

The Communication Plan is examined. If any interested party requires information at this time, this information has to be created and sent.

18.8.4 Responsibilities

The Project Manager has the responsibility for this process, with assistance from Project Support. Informal agreement to the report's data and conclusions should be obtained from those responsible for project assurance.

18.8.5 Information needs

Management information	Usage	Explanation
Current Stage Plan	Input	Contains information about the products, cost and dates of the current stage
Business Case	Input	Used to review progress and deliverables of the current Stage
Issue Log	Input	Identifies the issues raised during the stage
Risk Log	Input	Source of information about the status of current risks
Quality Log	Input	Source of information about the activities and results from those who are reviewing products for quality
Communication Plan	Input	May contain a requirement to send information to an external interested party at this time
Next Stage Plan	Input	Data for the End Stage Report
Lessons Learned Report	Update	Updated with any new lessons
Request for authorisation to proceed	Output	This may be formal or informal according to the project's situation
End Stage Report	Output	Performance of the stage against plan
Exception Plan	Output	Alternative to the next Stage Plan

18.8.6 Key criteria

- Have all products identified in the Stage Plan been produced?
- Have they all been checked for quality?
- Have they all been accepted by the Customer?
- What was the actual resource usage and cost in the Stage?
- How many Project Issues were received during the Stage?
- How many changes were approved and implemented, in part or completely, during the Stage and what was their impact on the Stage Plan?

- Have any changes been carried over into the next Stage?

- Does the project still look viable?

- Is the Project Plan still forecast to stay within tolerance margins?

- Does any new or changed risk exposure require a contingency plan?

- Are there any strengths, weaknesses or omissions in the standards and practices used that should be noted for corporate quality management?

- Can any useful measurements be noted from the Stage that would benefit the planning of future Stages or other projects?

Hints and tips

Following the motto 'No surprises', the Project Manager should informally keep the Project Board aware of what the End Stage Report will say. Any problems should, wherever possible, be resolved before presentation of the report.

The level of formality or informality in the presentation of the End Stage Report depends on factors such as the project size and the desires of the Project Board.

Where the project is part of a programme, the Programme Support Office must examine the End Stage Report, the next Stage Plan and the updated Project Plan to ensure that the project stays in tune with the programme.

18.9 Producing an Exception Plan (SB6)

18.9.1 Fundamental principles

A Stage is deemed to be in Exception as soon as current forecasts for the end of the Stage deviate beyond the delegated tolerance bounds. The project is in Exception if the whole project is likely to go beyond tolerance bounds.

If either Stage or project is forecast to deviate beyond its agreed tolerance boundaries, it no longer has the approval of the Project Board. A new plan must be presented to take the place of the current plan.

18.9.2 Context

The deviation should have been recognised during *Controlling a Stage (CS)*. The Project Manager will have brought the situation to the attention of the Project Board through an Exception Report. The Project Board will have requested the Project Manager to produce an Exception Plan. The Exception Plan will then be presented to the Project Board at a Mid-Stage Assessment.

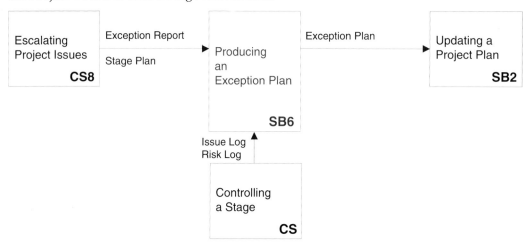

Figure 18–7: Producing an Exception Plan

18.9.3 Process description

If a stage or the project is forecast to go outside the tolerances agreed with the Project Board when the plan was approved, and the situation cannot be rectified, the Project Manager has no further mandate to carry on with the work. The Project Board must be advised of the situation at the earliest possible moment.

The Exception Plan will have the same structure as other PRINCE plans. It should run from the present time to the end of the Stage. If it is the Project Plan that is in Exception, a revised Project Plan should be created, taking into account the actuals to date.

18.9.4 Responsibilities

The Project Manager is responsible for producing Exception Plans with the help of any Project Support, and the Project Manager would work with those responsible for Project Assurance to check it.

18.9.5 Information needs

Management information	Usage	Explanation
Current Stage Plan	Input	This is the plan from which the deviation has occurred and that will define the tolerances and the extent of the deviation. It can also be used to extrapolate what would happen if the deviation were allowed to continue
Issue Log	Input	This may contain details of the reasons for the project or Stage going into Exception
Exception Report	Input	This warning should have been sent to the Project Board at the first indication of a probable deviation. It is the trigger from the process *Escalating Project Issues (CS8)* for the start of this process
Risk Log	Update	What is the impact of the deviation and Exception Plan on the risks?
Exception Plan	Output	The product of the process, a plan that replaces the current Stage Plan

18.9.6 Key criteria

- Has the deviation adversely affected the Business Case for the project?
- What extra risks does the approved option bring?

Hints and tips

If it is the project tolerances that are under threat, a revised Project Plan should be produced.

Where the project is part of a Programme, the Programme Support Office must examine the Exception Plan to ensure that the project remains consistent with the Programme.

The Project Manager should be wary of overestimating the ability to recover from a forecast deviation.

19 Closing a Project (CP)

19.1 Fundamental principles

One of the defining features of the project is that it is finite – it has a start and an end. If the project loses this distinctiveness, then it loses its effectiveness over purely operational management approaches.

So, a clear end to the project:

- is always more successful than the natural tendency to drift into operational management. It is a recognition by all concerned that either the operational regime must now take over, or the products from this project become feeds into some subsequent project or into some larger programme, or the current project has run its course

- helps to achieve business objectives by avoiding waste and by providing a useful opportunity to take stock of achievements and experience

- provides an opportunity to ensure that all unachieved goals and objectives are identified, so that they can be addressed in the future.

19.2 Context

Preparation for closing the project is triggered by the approaching end of the final Stage of the project. All the processes within *Closing a Project (CP)* may be done in parallel – or at least with considerable overlap.

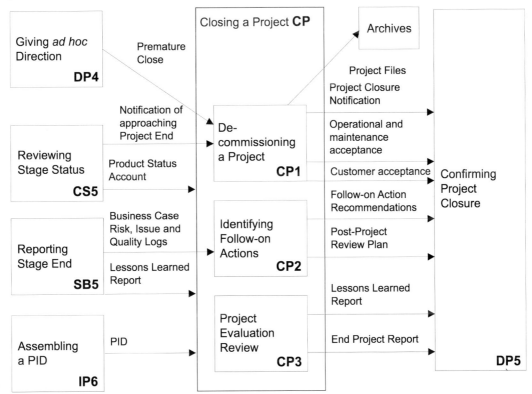

Figure 19–1: Closing a Project

The method of *Closing a Project (CP)* has to be tailored to suit the needs of the particular project. For example, if the project is part of a programme or a series of projects, this may affect how some of the fundamental principles, such as follow-on actions, are handled. The project may be closely connected with a subsequent project and may have been planned ahead that way. All the results of the first project feed into the subsequent one, with no need to be concerned about maintenance, operational or other follow-on actions. If the project has delivered an intangible product – for example to bring about a change in philosophy – then the objective of ensuring operational and support arrangements are in place may not be appropriate.

19.3 Process description

The following is an illustrative list of aims of the process to close the project. According to the type of project, they may not all be required.

- Ensure that the objectives or aims set out in the Project Initiation Document have been met.

- Confirm fulfilment of the Project Initiation Document and the Customer's satisfaction with the products.

- Provide formal acceptance of the products.

- Ensure that all expected products have been handed over and accepted by the Customer or relevant subsequent project.

- Ensure that arrangements for the support and operation of project products are in place (where appropriate).

- If the project has been closed prematurely, document what has been achieved and recommend the way forward.

- Identify any recommendations for follow-on actions.

- Capture lessons resulting from the project.

- Prepare an End Project Report.

- Plan any Post-Project Review required.

- Notify the host location of the intention to disband the project organisation and resources.

The process covers the Project Manager's work to wrap up the project either at its end or at premature close. Most of the work is to prepare input to the Project Board to obtain its confirmation that the project may close.

The Project Initiation Document is examined to check the actual results of the project against the original (or as modified by the Project Board) expectations. All planned products should have been approved and delivered to the Customer or be ready for hand-over.

The Project Manager prepares an End Project Report that comprehensively evaluates the actual project outcome versus that envisaged in the Project Initiation Document.

There may be a number of Project Issues that were held over by the Project Board. These may lead to new projects or enhancements to the products of the current project during its operational life. The Project Manager sorts these out into appropriate follow-on actions.

The Lessons Learned Report, which has been developed during the project, is now completed and made available outside the project.

The host location is notified that the provided resources will no longer be required and release dates are given.

Suggested contents of the management products described in this process can be found in *Appendix A – PRINCE Product Description outlines*.

19.3.1 Scalability

For small projects, the essentials of this process can be summarised as:

- check that everything has been delivered
- check that the product is accepted
- make sure there are no loose ends
- record any follow-on recommendations
- store the project records for audit
- release resources.

The last in the list may not be required.

19.4 Decommissioning a Project (CP1)

19.4.1 Fundamental principles

The main principles are that:

- every project should come to an orderly close

- Customer and Supplier should be in agreement that the project has
  delivered what was expected; this expectation should have been defined at
  the outset of the project

- everyone who has provided support for the project should be warned of its
  close, so that they can plan for the return of the resources provided for that
  support

- project records should be retained to assist with possible audits or the
  production of estimating metrics.

19.4.2 Context

In exceptional cases the process may be used because the Project Board directs the
Project Manager to close the project before its planned end.

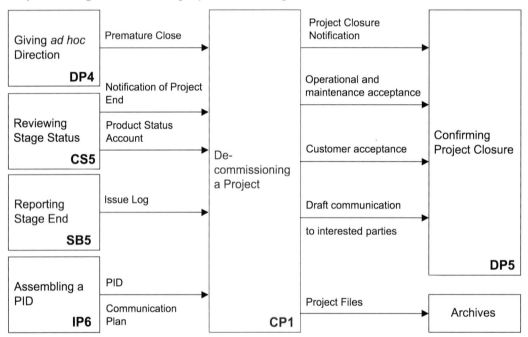

Figure 19–2: Decommissioning a Project

19.4.3 Process description

The objectives of the process are to:

- check that all Project Issues are closed or transferred to Follow-on Action
  Recommendations

- ensure that all project products have been approved and handed over to the
  Customer or User

- confirm that the delivered products meet any needs defined in the
  Customer's specification for operation and support (where applicable)

- confirm that the correct operational and maintenance environment is in place
  (where applicable)

- complete and store all project information

- prepare a notification to all involved organisations and interested parties that
  the project is to be closed and resources disbanded.

The Project Manager prepares the Project Closure Notification to the host location that the project resources and the support services can be disbanded and also prepares notification to any parties identified in the Communication Plan as needing to be told about the project closure. These have to be confirmed by the Project Board.

Before closure of the project can be recommended, the Project Manager must be assured that the expected results have all been achieved and delivered (or have been told by the Project Board that the project is to be closed prematurely).

Where a product has to be supported and sustained during its useful life, there must be confirmation in the report by the people who will use and support the product that they have received the product in a state that allows them to carry out their duties.

To permit any future audit of the project's actions and performance, the Project Files should be secured and archived. The files should include a copy of the Project Closure Notification and Follow-on Action Recommendations.

Where a Configuration Management system is being used, a Status Account should be obtained to confirm that all products have been approved.

19.4.4 Responsibilities

The Project Manager has responsibility for the process, but may need assistance to gather the necessary input and prepare elements of the report. The Project Manager should have informal contact with the Project Board during this time to ensure that there will be no problems with its confirmation of the project closure in *Confirming Project Closure (DP5)*.

Those currently responsible for Project Assurance should also be consulted by the Project Manager for their views on the completeness of work before making the recommendation.

19.4.5 Information needs

Management information	Usage	Explanation
Project Initiation Document	Input	Contains a statement of the project's Acceptance Criteria
Issue Log	Input	Check that all Project Issues have been closed or transferred to Follow-on Action Recommendations
Product Status Account	Input	Confirmation from Configuration Management records that all products are approved
Premature Close direction	Input	Instruction from the Project Board to close the project before its expected end
Notification of Project End	Input	The trigger from Stage monitoring that the normal end of the project is near
Communication Plan	Input	Identification of any other interested party who needs to know
Customer acceptance	Output	Confirmation that the Customer accepts the products
Operational and maintenance acceptance	Output	Confirmation that the product can be operated and supported

Management information	Usage	Explanation
Project Closure Notification	Output	Notice to the host location that the project is about to close, so that plans can be made to disband and re-deploy any provided Project Support services
Draft communication to interested parties	Output	Notification to other parties to be approved by the Project Board
Project files	Archive	Preserve the project records for use by auditors or other enquirer

19.4.6 Key criteria

- Have all products in the Project Initiation Document been approved and delivered? (Remembering that the Project Initiation Document may have been updated during the project to reflect any agreed changes.)

- If there has been deviation from the Project Initiation Document, is the Project Board still prepared to accept the project closure? Are those deviations reflected in the End Project Report and Lessons Learned Report? Where appropriate, are any deviations reflected in the Follow-on Action Recommendations?

- Are there any outstanding Project Issues that have not been put into 'pending' status by the Project Board?

- Have the operational and support teams formally agreed that they are ready to accept hand-over (if appropriate)?

- Are the project resources and support services (if any were provided) no longer required?

- Are there any contractual implications when decommissioning the project?

Hints and tips

The Configuration Management system used on the project to control and record the status of products should check that all products are complete and handed over.

Deviations documented in the End Project Report, the Lessons Learned Report and the Follow-on Action Recommendations should, as far as is sensible, avoid overlap – in other words, the same deviations should not be unnecessarily recorded in several places.

19.5 Identifying Follow-on Actions (CP2)

19.5.1 Fundamental principles

The fundamental principle here is that if there is any unfinished business at the end of the project, it should be formally documented and passed to those who have the authority and responsibility to take action.

19.5.2 Context

Most of the input will be those items on the Issue Log that were held back by the Project Board.

The output is submitted to the Project Board as recommendations.

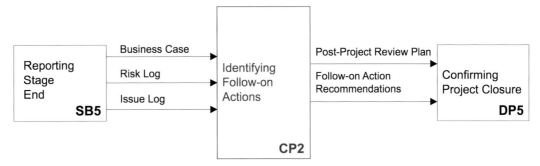

Figure 19–3: Identifying Follow-on Actions

19.5.3 Process description

The aims of the process are to:

- establish actions required following the project

- document any Follow-on Action Recommendations

- recommend a date and plan for any Post-Project Review(s) considered necessary.

A number of actions may be required after the project. The input will come mainly from those Project Issues that were put into 'pending' status by the Project Board during the project. The Risk Log may also contain risks that may affect the product in its useful life.

All unfinished work is documented in Follow-on Action Recommendations.

Many project products should be re-examined after a period of use to check on their quality, effectiveness in use and achievement of benefits. Examination of the updated Business Case will identify whether there are any expected benefits whose achievement cannot be measured until the product has been in use for some time. If this is the case, a recommended date and plan should be made for a Post-Project Review, the benefits to be measured at that time and the measurements to be applied. These benefits should have been defined in the Business Case.

It is not strictly a project activity to produce the Post-Project Review, only to plan it. But in summary the Post-Project Review is to assess achievement of the benefits claimed in the Business Case. The following questions are a sample.

- Has the product achieved the benefits expected?

- Is there an identifiable trend of improving benefits?

- Are the users happy with the product?

- Is the product proving to meet quality expectations?

- Is the product as well supported as was expected?

- Are the support staff happy with what they have been given to support the product?

- Have there been any unexpected problems in the introduction?

- Has the product caused new problems?

The Post-Project Review plan will make use of the information contained under *Benefits Realisation* in the Business Case (see its Product Description outline in Appendix A). This should have stated how the achievement of benefits was to be measured. The plan should be defining:

- what benefit achievements are to be measured

- when benefit achievement can be measured

- how the achievement can be measured

- the pre-delivery situation against which achievement is to be compared

- who is needed to carry out the measurements (individuals or skill types).

Sample questions for a Post-Project Review

1. Is the correct calibre of staff used and supervision exercised?

2. Are any necessary security and standby arrangements satisfactory?

3. Do errors get through undetected?

4. Are errors quickly corrected?

5. Have any unexpected benefits been found?

6. Has any documentation provided been found to be easy to understand and comprehensive?

7. Are there any new techniques available on the market now which could improve the product's efficiency?

8. How many modification requests have there been?

9. How many changes are waiting to be made?

10. What percentage of modifications arise from:
    - auditors
    - error correction
    - new needs
    - efficiency improvements
    - format changes
    - expansion?

11. Is there a formal, working method for registration of complaints/change requests?

12. What is the average time to implement a change request?

13. Is there a bottleneck in incorporating enhancements in the production system?

14. Is there a formal method for testing changes before incorporating them?

15. Was the training adequate?

16. Is there adequate training for new users?

19.5.4 Responsibilities

The Project Manager has responsibility for this process.

216

19.5.5 Information needs

Management information	Usage	Explanation
Issue Log	Input	Unactioned Project Issues will form the basis of any follow-on actions
Business Case	Input	This will reveal benefits whose achievement cannot be measured immediately and will therefore need a Post-Project Review
Risk Log	Input	Check for any risks to the operational use of the end-product(s)
Post-Project Review Plan	Output	Suggested plan for a Post-Project Review for ratification by Project Board
Follow-on Action Recommendations	Output	Recommendations for further work, which the Project Board must direct to the appropriate audience for attention

19.5.6 Key criteria

- Is a Post-Project Review needed to measure achievement of business benefits and re-examine the quality of products after a period of use?

- How much time needs to elapse before these benefits can be measured?

- Are the benefits for this project alone, or combined with the outcomes from other projects?

- Which 'pending' Project Issues should be recommended for follow-on action by the operations and support team?

- Which 'pending' Project Issues should be recommended to be turned into Project Mandates for potential enhancement projects or referred to programme management for further action?

Hints and tips

Arrangements for any Post-Project Review should be discussed informally with the Project Board before making any recommendation, so as to avoid any disagreement in the subsequent process, Confirming Project Closure (DP5).

The date for the Post-Project Review should be set as soon after the project closes as possible. The quality of a product may have appeared fine during testing, but is it still good after a period in the working environment? Also, where some benefits will take much longer to come to fruition, it is worth considering a recommendation to the Project Board that these are the subject of other, later Post-Project Reviews.

Dependent on the type of project product, there may be contractual issues to be resolved for the operational and maintenance support of the products.

Where the project is part of a programme, the Project Board's recommendation to close the project should be reviewed by the Programme Executive in the light of the list of follow-on actions recommended.

Where appropriate, the follow-on actions should be assigned by the Programme Manager, if the project is part of a programme.

19.6 Project Evaluation Review (CP3)

19.6.1 Fundamental principles

Successful organisations learn from their experiences with projects. This is more likely if the lessons learned are somehow preserved beyond the end of the project.

19.6.2 Context

This is the internal project evaluation. There may be a separate external evaluation – for example, from a quality assurance group.

The partially completed Lessons Learned Report is finalised. This is created at the outset of the project and incremented as the project progresses with observations on what aspects can usefully be noted to help future projects. It should include observations on management, technical and quality procedures.

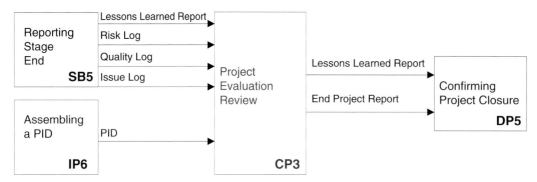

Figure 19–4: Project Evaluation Review

19.6.3 Process description

The objectives of the process are to:

- assess the results of the project against what it was intended to achieve

- examine the records of the completed project to assess the quality of its management, especially quality and risk management

- identify lessons to be learned from the project and applied on future projects.

End Project Report

The updated Project Plan allows the Project Manager to document in the End Project Report the effectiveness of the project management processes, and how well the project has performed against its Project Initiation Document, including the original planned cost, schedule and tolerances.

Not all benefits will be seen to have been achieved by the time of project closure. Any achievements or non-achievements that can be defined should be part of the report. A note of any benefits that need to be measured after operational use of the final product is passed to *Identifying Follow-on Actions (CP2)*.

The report should also take into consideration the effect on the original Project Plan and Business Case of any changes that were approved. The End Project Report should give final statistics on changes received during the project and the total impact of approved changes. Any outstanding ones should match up with follow-on actions defined in *Identifying Follow-on Actions (CP2)*. Statistics may also be appropriate for all quality work carried out.

The End Project Report is concerned with how well the management of the project was done. This includes the performance of all the project management team, the success of any scaling, use of the processes and any tailoring of them, change control and quality results. The Lessons Learned Report, on the other hand, is concerned with the project's use of the project management processes and techniques – that is, PRINCE and any local standards used, and what can be learned from this implementation.

Lessons Learned Report

At the start of the project an embryo Lessons Learned Report should be created. A note should be added to this every time the Project Management Team spot something about the management, specialist or quality processes and procedures that either made a significant contribution to the project's achievements or caused a problem.

In this process, all the notes should be correlated and turned into a report, including any views with hindsight on the project's management. The report should be aimed at answering the question 'What should be done differently next time?'

The report is also the repository of any useful measurements and quality statistics collected during the project that will help in the planning and estimation of subsequent projects.

It is important to identify who should receive the Lessons Learned Report and make sure that the Project Board know where it should go. There is little point in preparing the report, only to find that it will not be used.

19.6.4 Responsibilities

The Project Manager bears overall responsibility for this process, but additional information could come from anyone involved in the project.

19.6.5 Information needs

Management information	Usage	Explanation
PID	Input	Original statement of project objectives, scope and constraints
Issue Log	Input	The reasons for Off-Specifications may provide lessons for future projects
Risk Log	Input	What risks were considered and what happened to them may provide lessons for future projects
Quality Log	Input	This may indicate whether the quality policy and procedures were adequate. Statistics of the number of quality checks made and the errors found are also useful to a quality assurance function
Lessons Learned Report	Update	This should be an ongoing document from the start of the project, completed with relevant notes, but finalised into a report in process *CP3*
End Project Report	Output	Evaluation of the management, quality and technical performance of the project and achievement of objectives as defined in the PID

19.6.6 Key criteria

- Which management processes or procedures have worked well?
- Which management processes have had problems?
- Was it easy to achieve the required quality?

- Which quality procedures have worked well?

- Were there any weaknesses in quality procedures for specific types of product?

- How well did risk strategies work?

- Were there any unforeseen risks?

- How well were the risks managed?

- Was the contingency used?

- Was training in the management, quality and delivery processes and procedures adequate? Were there recognisable benefits from the level of training given, or recognisable problems caused by lack of training?

- How well did any support tools work?

- Could anything have been done to improve skill levels before the relevant work was done?

Hints and tips

Concentrate on items that can be of use to future projects.

Observations on failures and omissions can be as useful as identification of successful elements.

Consider whether there are any lessons about the quality procedures that should be directed to any quality assurance function. These might be weaknesses in current standard practices, new quality testing requirements from the products of the project that are not currently covered by standards, or new ways of testing quality that the project has pioneered.

Where the project is part of a programme, the Programme Support Office should review the Lessons Learned Report for applicability to the programme or individual projects within the programme.

There are a number of possible recipients of the Lessons Learned Report. The aim is to identify the group that will distribute the report to other projects, not just current projects but any that may be starting up in the future. Ideally this should be a group that has the responsibility to maintain project management standards. Some organisations have a Project Management Office; others vest the responsibility as part of the duties of a Quality Assurance group. Elsewhere it may be known as Management Services or the central Project Support Office.

20 Planning (PL)

20.1 Fundamental principles

Effective project management relies on an effective planning and control process. Even small projects require planning.

Planning provides all personnel involved in the project with information on:

- what is required
- why it is required
- how it will be achieved and by whom, using what specialist equipment and resources
- when events will happen.

Product-based planning is a key component of PRINCE and provides a comprehensive approach to effective planning. It is the method that enables the Project Manager to:

- define what the project has to deliver
- provide definitions of success to the people working on the project via measurable statements of the quality required
- objectively monitor and control progress.

20.2 Context

Planning is a repeatable process, and plays an important role in other processes, the main ones being:

- *Planning an Initiation Stage (SU6)*
- *Planning a Project (IP2)*
- *Planning a Stage (SB1)*
- *Producing an Exception Plan (SB6).*

Planning is also an iterative process. There will be a series of loops through the planning steps as extra information becomes available or adjustments are made.

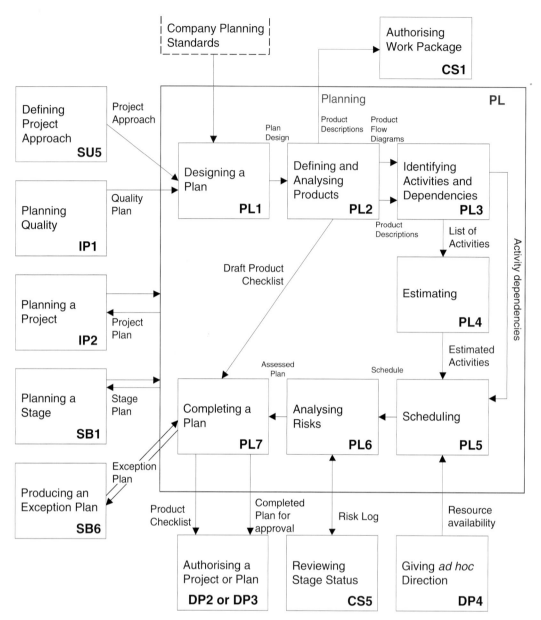

Figure 20–1: Planning

20.3 Process description

In PRINCE, plans are produced on the basis that:

- plans are constructed by identifying the final products required, all requisite intermediate products, and then the activities and appropriate resources necessary to deliver them

- plans should cover management and quality needs as well as the Customer's products

- there should be assurance that all activities are thought through in advance and to a level consistent with the control requirements identified in the Project Initiation Document.

PRINCE provides a product-based start to the planning activity and a planning framework that can be applied to any type of project. This involves:

- establishing what products are needed

- describing those products and their quality criteria

- determining the sequence in which each product should be produced and any dependencies.

After these initial steps, the normal steps of planning are used:

- deciding when the activities should be done and by whom

- estimating how much effort each activity will consume

- estimating how long the activities will take

- agreeing what quality control activities and resources are needed

- calculating how much the overall effort will cost

- producing the budget from the cost of the effort plus any materials and equipment that must be obtained

- assessing the risks contained in the plan

- identifying the management control points needed.

The steps involved are the same for all levels of plan.

Several iterations of the planning process are normally needed.

The Project Approach is a prerequisite for planning. This should have been defined as part of *Starting up a Project (SU)*.

20.3.1 Scalability

Planning is essential, regardless of type or size of project. The amount of detail varies according to the needs of the project.

The Product Checklist is optional in a small project. The Project Board might prefer its tabular form to a Gantt chart, but the choice should be one or the other, not both.

The first process *Designing a Plan (PL1)* is done only once in a project. Where the project is part of a programme, all the design decisions will probably have been taken at programme level. In a small project it is just a matter of deciding on a planning tool (if any).

Although the other processes within *Planning (PL)* may seem to represent a lot of work, they can be summarised in the list below. It can be seen that this set of steps is needed for the simplest of projects (for example, a shopping expedition!) and may take a correspondingly short time to go through:

- Identify and verify the objectives

- Ascertain whether there are any constraints

- Think about how the work is to be done

- What product(s) must be produced?

- What product(s) will be needed in order to do the work?

- How will the product quality be checked?

- In what sequence must things be done?

- What progress reports will be needed?

- What resources will be needed?

- What assumptions are being made?

- What risks are involved?

- How many grey areas or unknowns are there?

- What tolerances would be reasonable?

Hints and tips

Keep plans relevant. Be aware of the audience for the prepared set of plans and aim to provide an appropriate level of detail.

Time must be allowed for planning because it is a time-consuming exercise. Planning for the next Stage should start towards the end of the current Stage.

It is easier and more accurate to plan short Stages than long ones.

Where the project is part of a programme, programme staff should be involved or referenced during planning to ensure that any questions that affect the programme are resolved. This will help avoid re-work following presentation of the plan.

Involve those with Project Assurance roles in proposing quality checking resources. This should happen in Team Plans as well as Stage Plans.

20.4 Designing a Plan (PL1)

20.4.1 Fundamental principles

A plan is the backbone of every project and is essential for a successful outcome. Good plans cover all aspects of the project, giving everyone involved a common understanding of the work ahead.

Designing a plan will ensure that all aspects are adequately covered. It is important that the plan can be easily assimilated by all involved.

20.4.2 Context

This process includes decisions on the approach to planning for the project and therefore needs to be used early in the project. These decisions must be made before any of the other PL processes can be used.

It may be sensible to have one plan format for presentation in submissions seeking approval, and a more detailed format for day-to-day control purposes.

The strategies for tackling the project and ensuring quality of the products will already have been defined during *Defining Project Approach (SU5)*, and *Planning Quality (IP1)*.

20.4.3 Process description

Choices need to be made for planning tools, estimating methods, levels of plan and monitoring methods to be used for the project. Any recipients of plans and their updates should be identified. There may be a central function that consolidates all plans for senior management, particularly if the project is part of a programme.

Planning tools

One of the first decisions will be to identify any planning-and-control aids to be used by the project. There may be a company standard, or the customer may stipulate the use of a particular set of tools. The choice of planning tool may in part, however, depend on the complexity of the project. If so, the choice may need to be deferred until after some of the other planning processes.

Plan levels

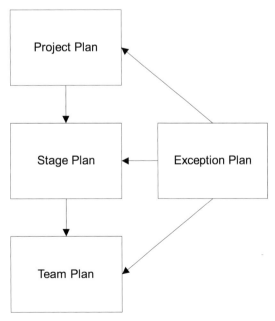

Figure 20–2: Plan levels

According to the size and complexity of the project, the next decision is the number of levels of plan required. The Project Plan is mandatory. The division of the project into stages may already be defined (by common practice or work done previously). The identification and selection of stages is discussed in *Planning a Project (IP2)*. The number of levels of plan will be dictated by the Project Approach, the level of control required and the scale of the project. It may be valid to restrict the number of levels because the additional work involved in maintaining more plans does not justify the extra levels.

The *Plans* and *Stages* components in this manual (see Chapters 5 and 7) describe the PRINCE concept of plan levels. The number of levels chosen for the project should reflect a balance between:

- the different information and control needs of the Project Manager and the Project Board

- the effort of creating extra plans

- the problems involved in ensuring compatibility between different plan levels.

There should be an agreed definition of the contents and level of detail for each level of plan that it has been decided will be required. Examples here would be as follows.

- To what level of detail should the Project Plan go?

- What is the maximum length of time for any activity in a Stage or lower level without further breakdown?

- How is the work on quality to be shown on the various plans?

- Who is to be involved in planning the quality activities in a Stage or Team Plan?

Estimating

The method(s) of estimation must be chosen. Each facet of the project may need its own estimation method. Estimating may be done by:

- using computer tools

- a group of experienced planners

- top-down or bottom-up methods

- discussion with those who will do the work

- any combination of these.

The methods chosen should be evaluated, and comments made in the End Project Report and Lessons Learned Report when the project ends.

The estimating methods to be used in the plan may affect the design, so decisions on the methods to be used should be made as part of plan design.

Allowances

There are two possible allowances that may have to be considered for inclusion within the project's plan structure:

- **a Change Budget**
  The Project Manager and the Project Board must agree how to cater for funding changes to requirements. Producing Exception Plans to ask the Project Board for extra money to cover the implementation of Requests for Change is the basic process, but this can be irritating if it has to be done frequently. If the environment suggests that there will be many changes during the project, it is sensible to discuss with the Project Board whether there should be a change budget. If so, consideration must be given to how this should be handled when producing the plans.

- **Contingency Plans**
  In the Management of Risk, a Contingency Plan is one answer to the question 'What do we do if this risk occurs?'. Where a serious risk exists, the Project Board may require the Project Manager to create a Contingency Plan and add the necessary budget for it – only to be used if the risk occurs.

These are not mandatory and their use depends on each project's circumstances.

20.4.4 Responsibilities

Ultimately, the responsibility for the decisions in designing a plan rests with the Project Board, but in practice the Project Manager would produce recommendations for informal Project Board approval. Local standards may pre-empt some of the decisions. The assurance roles have a responsibility to check the designs.

20.4.5 Information needs

Management information	Usage	Explanation
Project Approach	Input	The approach may impact on the number of Stages and plan levels required
Project Quality Plan	Input	The contents of plans, level of detail and monitoring needs will be affected by the Project Quality Plan
Company Planning standards	Input	These may identify the planning and estimating tools and methods to be used
Project Brief (or PID)	Input	Scope of the work to be planned
Plan Design	Output	A statement of the planning approach, levels of plan, tool set to be used, and major monitoring methods

20.4.6 Key criteria

- What planning, estimating, monitoring and risk assessment methods will be used?
- What tool set should be used to help with planning, estimating, monitoring and risk assessment?
- What level of detail about the products, their creation, quality checks and plan monitoring does the Project Manager require for day-to-day control?
- What level of detail does the Project Board need:
  – before commitment to a plan?
  – to monitor progress against a plan?
- How many levels of plan are suitable for this project?
- To what level of detail does each plan need to go?
- How will any quality checks be shown on the plans?
- How will tolerances be assigned?
- Should there be a change budget?
- What level of productivity for team members should be used?
- How will contingency allowances be handled (if appropriate)?

Hints and tips

A lot of time can be wasted in producing a very good plan to achieve the wrong objective.

The use of planning tools is not obligatory, but it can save a great deal of time if the plan is to be regularly updated and changed. A good tool can also validate that the correct dependencies have been built in and have not been corrupted by any plan updates.

If there is a need to use Team Plans, the Stage Plan would normally act as a summary of the key start and end dates, together with any interfaces between the Team Plans and with the external environment.

The Project Manager should decide what level of efficiency is to be taken for project members when planning their work. No one is 100 per cent efficient. The estimator must know how to treat non-planned time such as telephone calls, ad hoc meetings, sickness.

Watch out for 'double counting' – for example, adding in allowances both when estimating and when scheduling.

The Project Manager should decide in conjunction with the Project Board how to budget for contingency, that is, the allowance for possible estimating shortfalls, delays, overlooked products or activities. This is especially critical in fixed-price work. The amount of contingency budget added should be documented to assist with future estimation, together with how much is actually used.

Small projects may only have one plan after the Initiation Stage Plan and, therefore, only one level of plan. It may be sensible to consider different levels of presentation of the plan for the different levels of readership. Most planning software packages offer such options.

When working with sub-contractor companies, a copy of their plan(s) may form part of the overall plan. A decision will need to be taken on whether sub-contractor plans are shown separately or built into the Project and/or Stage Plans.

Not all projects need a 45-page plan, but equally a half-sheet of paper is likely to be insufficient for most Project Plans.

Where the project is part of a programme, the programme may have developed a common approach to project planning. This may cover standards (for example, level of planning) and tools. These will be the starting point for designing any Project Plans. Any project-specific variations should be highlighted and the agreement of the Programme Executive sought.

20.5 Defining and Analysing Products (PL2)

20.5.1 Fundamental principles

By defining a plan in terms of the products to be delivered, the creation, quality and appropriateness of those products can be managed and controlled more easily. In addition, by defining the required products, everyone involved can see and understand the required outcome.

20.5.2 Context

Once the decisions have been made in *Designing a Plan (PL1)*, this process will be the normal starting point for producing the plan.

20.5.3 Process description

This process is divided into three steps:

- identify the specialist products, plus the management and quality products to be produced

- describe each of them in terms of their quality requirements, and ensure that they are fully understood and agreed by everyone involved

- sequence them in their logical order of creation.

These steps are described in more detail in *Product-based planning* (Chapter 21).

The first step in product-based planning technique is to define the results that are required of the project (the intermediate and end products).

Specialist products

The Project Brief should identify the major products or results that will satisfy the business needs. The planner should develop and refine the list to ensure that it contains a complete and correct specification of both the final products and also the main intermediate ones that have to be developed as stepping stones to the final products.

Management products

Apart from the business products the planner should also list the management products, such as contracts, plans, approvals and reports, that will consume resources and time and that will need to be created at certain points in the plan.

The Risk Log should be examined to see whether extra management products (such as reports) are needed in order to monitor a risk situation.

Quality products

The quality products, such as Product Descriptions and quality control documents should also be listed, particularly in the lower-level plans.

The lists must then be kept up to date throughout the project as changes to the project are agreed.

Product Descriptions

In order to ensure full understanding of every product, a Product Description is written for each one, describing the product in terms of its purpose, content, derivation and required quality attributes. *Appendix A – PRINCE Product Description outlines* gives examples of the description of management products.

Product Flow Diagram

In order to understand the interrelationships between the products, they are put into the required order of creation and any dependencies between them identified.

Product Checklist

This is a useful summary for the Project Board, being a list of the major products to be produced in a stage, plus the expected key dates.

20.5.4 Responsibilities

The Project Manager is responsible for the process. There should be consultation with the Customer, Users and specialists to ensure that all the required products are covered. The results should be vetted by those with assurance responsibilities.

20.5.5 Information needs

Management information	Usage	Explanation
Project Approach	Input	This defines the level of plan required, the tools to be used, estimating techniques and the approach to contingency allowances
Project Quality Plan	Input	This will guide the selection and placement of quality control activities
Product Breakdown Structure	Output	A hierarchical table of all the products required to be created in the plan
Product Descriptions	Output	A description of each product plus its quality criteria
Product Checklist	Output	A draft list of the major products of the plan
Product Flow Diagram	Output	A diagram showing the sequence in which the products should be produced

20.5.6 Key criteria

- Has the plan reached the agreed level of detail?
- Are all quality and management products identified as well as specialist products?
- Are the quality and management products/activities added correctly to the sequence of work?
- Does the plan need any products from external sources?
- Have these been shown correctly in the sequence of work?
- Have known risk factors been identified?
- Does the management of risks require any extra products?
- Have these been shown correctly in the sequence of work?

Hints and tips

A decision point can be associated with one or more intermediate products on which the decision will be based.

The list of products, their required sequence and their descriptions should all be quality-reviewed for accuracy and completeness.

Required quality is a criterion against which the product will be accepted. When working in a Customer/Supplier relationship, this may form the basis of project acceptance.

The definition of the major end-products or results required to satisfy the business needs should be documented within the Project Initiation Document as part of the project objectives.

20.6 Identifying Activities and Dependencies (PL3)

20.6.1 Fundamental principles

Simply identifying products may be insufficient for scheduling and control purposes. The activities implied in the delivery of each of the products need to be identified to give a fuller picture of the plan's workload.

20.6.2 Context

As with the other Planning processes, *Identifying Activities and Dependencies (PL3)* will be performed iteratively. Activities and extra products may be required in response to identified risks, so the Risk Log should be checked.

20.6.3 Process description

This process is divided into three steps:

- identify all activities necessary to deliver the products
- establish the interdependencies between activities
- ensure that dependencies both internal and external to the project are covered.

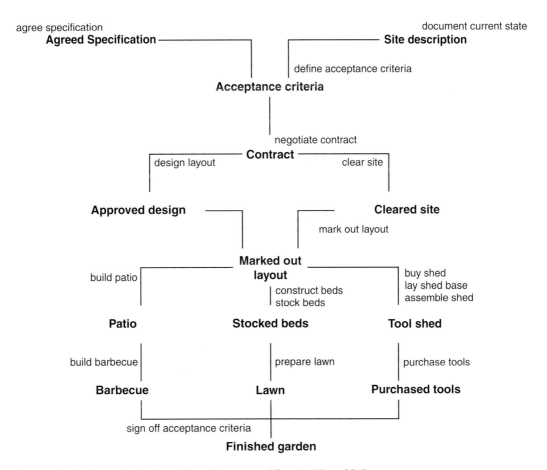

Figure 20–3: Example Product Flow Diagram with activities added

All the activities required to create or change the planned products have to be identified. After a Product Flow Diagram has been created, the activities are most easily identified by using a transformation process. Transformation identifies the activities needed to take one product or set of products and turn it into the next product or set of products in the sequence. There may be only one activity or there may be a group of activities, depending on the level of detail required for the plan.

A very visible means of identifying the activities is to add them to the Product Flow Diagram. Taking the Product Flow Diagram from the example of a project to create a landscaped garden, described in Chapter 21 *Product-based planning*, Figure 20–3 is a simple illustration of adding the activities. It should be remembered that adding activities between products does not necessarily imply their final sequence.

Another way of performing this step is to make out a separate list of the activities, still using the Product Flow Diagram as the source of information. An extra column on the list can be used to store the activity durations when these are calculated in preparation for drawing a network. Figure 20–4 illustrates this type of list.

		Duration
10	Document current state	2
15	Agree specification	4
20	Define acceptance criteria	2
25	Negotiate contract	3
30	Design layout	8
35	Clear site	16
40	Mark out layout	4
45	Build patio	24
50	Construct beds	16
55	Stock beds	16
60	Buy shed	4
65	Lay shed base	8
70	Assemble shed	4
75	Purchase tools	2
80	Build barbecue	4
85	Prepare lawn	16
90	Sign off acceptance criteria	1
95	Present final invoice	1

Figure 20–4: Example list of activities

The list of activities should include management and quality activities as well as the activities needed to develop the specialist products.

The activities are best shown in the order in which they have to be performed. The Product Flow Diagram gives a good indication of the major sequence of activities.

Any constraints should also be identified. There are two types of constraint: internal and external.

An example of an internal constraint is that work on Patio cannot start until Approved design and Marked out layout are finished. Examples of external constraints may be:

- the delivery of a product required by this project from another project

- waiting for a decision from programme management.

Wherever possible, external constraints should be described as a dependency on the availability of an external product. Resource-based constraints (for example, 'Is the resource available to do the work?') are not considered here. They are a question for the scheduling process.

The activities should include any that are required to interact with external parties – for example, obtaining a product from an outside source or converting external products into something that the plan requires.

20.6.4 Responsibilities

The Project Manager is responsible for this process. There should be support from any Team Managers whose team contributes to execution of the plan in question. Help may also be found from any quality assurance or project support staff allocated to the project. The checking of the work is part of the responsibility of the assurance roles.

20.6.5 Information needs

Management information	Usage	Explanation
Product Flow Diagram	Input	The products and their dependencies are the basis of defining the required activities and their dependencies
Product Descriptions	Input	The derivation section of the description may contain information helpful in identifying dependencies
Risk Log	Input	The Risk Log may contribute risk monitoring activities that need to be added to the plan
List of Activities	Output	All the activities required to produce the products
Activity dependencies	Output	Any dependencies between the activities in the above list

20.6.6 Key criteria

- Can any activities be carried out in parallel?
- Can any activities overlap?
- Are any gaps needed between certain activities?

Hints and tips

Guard against an explosion of activities at this stage beyond the detail appropriate to the level of plan.

Keep things simple. If in doubt, don't overlap activities.

20.7 Estimating (PL4)

20.7.1 Fundamental principles

Estimating is not prediction, but it is better than not estimating at all.

20.7.2 Context

Estimating follows identification of the activities and precedes scheduling.

20.7.3 Process description

The objective of this process is to identify the resources and time required to complete each activity. This will include not only people but also all other resources that will be required.

This is an iterative process. Since the type of estimating will vary according to the type of project, the statements here are of a general nature.

A Project Plan will normally require top-down estimating (that is, an estimate for the total project, broken down across the normal stages for a project of this type), whereas a Stage Plan would use bottom-up methods (an estimate for each product, built up into a figure for the whole stage).

The two major steps in a typical estimating process are:

- **Identify resource types required**
  The type of resources required to carry out the activities needs to be identified. Specific skills may be required depending on the nature of the project – that is, type and complexity. Requirements may include non-human resources, such as equipment, travel or money.
  It is important to agree a definition of resource types. For staff this should include:
  – the skills and experience level(s) required
  – their affiliation, so that the commitment required of different parts of the organisation can be identified.

- **Estimate effort required for each activity**
  The estimated effort required, by resource type, can now be added to the activity list. At this point the estimates will be approximate, and therefore provisional.
  The reliability of estimates depends on:
  – how detailed is the understanding of the activity
  – the assumptions made
  – understanding the products (from the Product Descriptions).
  The assumptions that underpin the estimate, the margin of error and the degree of confidence in the estimate should be recorded in the plan. This information will enable the Project Board to set appropriate tolerances. Tolerances are fully described in *Controls* (Chapter 6). If current understanding is insufficient, the earlier planning processes may have to be re-worked.

20.7.4 Responsibilities

The Project Manager is responsible for estimation. It is a difficult job, and wherever possible extra help should be sought. It requires previous experience in the subject matter of the plan as well as training in the job of estimation. This is where expertise from project support can help greatly.

20.7.5 Information needs

Management information	Usage	Explanation
All planning information so far	Input	Products and activities that require estimation
Activity estimates	Output	Estimated activities are passed to the scheduling process

20.7.6 Key criteria

- Is the estimation to be made against known resources or general requirements for skill and experience?

- What level of productivity should be taken for the resources?

- Should allowance be made for different levels of productivity in the resources?

- What supporting infrastructure does the estimate assume is in place? Are these assumptions documented in the plan text?

- Has allowance been made for quality checking products?

Hints and tips

There may be a computerised estimating tool, written text, tables, graphs or formulae available for the type of work identified in the plan. These tools are normally based on information of actual time taken by identical or similar activities to the ones required in the plan. The figures can generally be tailored to some extent to reflect more closely the environment for which the plan in question applies.

Estimation is best performed by a group of two or three people experienced in both the subject matter and estimating. This number tends to balance out any individual over-optimism or pessimism in estimation.

Where possible, estimating should include discussion with the people who will be responsible for doing the work.

In large projects or difficult areas of work, it is prudent to estimate at least twice, either by using two distinct approaches or by allowing two different sets of people to estimate independently.

When resources have been estimated it may become clear that resource constraints cannot be met. If this should happen, the matter should be referred to the Project Board.

More uncertainty should be expected in a Project Plan than in a Stage Plan. A Stage Plan is for a shorter timeframe, in the near future and planned to much greater detail.

Refer to the Lessons Learned Reports from earlier similar projects. Understanding past estimation successes and failures by reading the Lessons Learned Reports of other projects can assist with estimating.

Any assumptions made during the estimation process should be documented under the heading of 'Assumptions' in the plan text. If the assumption refers to a risk, the risk should be documented in the Risk Log.

If contingency has already been added, don't compound it. For example, where contingency is added to an individual's work, the Team Manager should not add more contingency to the Team Plan, nor the Project Manager add more contingency to the Stage Plan.

20.8 Scheduling (PL5)

20.8.1 Fundamental principles

A plan can only show the ultimate feasibility of achieving its objectives when the activities are put together in a schedule which defines when each activity will be carried out.

20.8.2 Context

Scheduling follows estimates of the time for each activity, and is followed by an assessment of the risks inherent in the plan. The schedule may need to be re-visited during the planning process to refine and improve the way in which the plan will be carried out.

20.8.3 Process description

The objectives of scheduling are to:

- match available resources to the identified activities

- schedule work according to the defined sequence and dependencies

- smooth resource usage within the bounds of the identified dependencies and any overall time constraints

- identify surplus resource effort or additional resource effort needed and negotiate with the Project Board to resolve these

- calculate total requirements for human and other resources and produce a cost for these.

There are many different approaches to scheduling. Either the steps can be done manually or a computer-based planning-and-control tool can be used.

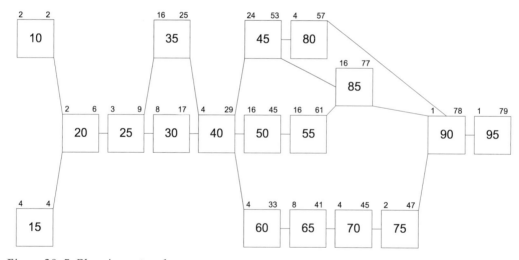

Figure 20–5: Planning network

Typical scheduling steps are:

- **Draw a planning network**
  Take the list of activities and their durations and produce a network of the activities, based on the dependencies, from beginning to end. This provides useful information, such as what the total duration might be, given no resource constraints. Figure 20–5 is a network of the listed activities for a landscaped garden. The activity numbers correspond to the activity list in Figure 20–4.

The number on the left above each box is the duration time for that activity. The number on the right above each box is the Earliest Finish Time for that activity. For example, the Earliest Finish Time for activity 20 is day 6 (activity 15 takes 4 days and activity 20 takes 2 days).

- **Assess resource availability**
  The number of people who will be available to do the work (or the cost of buying in resources) should now be established. Any specific information should also be noted – for example, names, level of experience, percentage availability, dates available from and to, external or internal resource. The project may also require non-human resources; this availability must also be assessed.

- **Produce a draft schedule and assign responsibilities**
  Using the resource availability and the information from the activity network, resources are now allocated to activities. The rule is 'allocate resources in order of ascending float', that is, allocate resources first to activities with zero float (which, by definition, are on the Critical Path). Those activities with the greatest amount of spare time (float) are lowest in priority for resource allocation.
  The result will be a schedule that shows the loading of work on each person and the usage of non-people resources. The duration of each activity can be amended, based on knowledge of the resource effort required and the availability of the appropriate resource type.
  The schedule is often displayed as a Gantt chart. Figure 20–6 illustrates a Gantt chart for the landscaped garden, the activity numbers once more corresponding to the activity list in Figure 20–4.

- **Level resource usage**
  The scheduling of any contingency allowances should be considered and built into the plan.
  The first allocation of resources may result in uneven resource usage, maybe even over-utilisation of some resources at certain times. Responsibilities are reassigned, activities moved about within any 'float' they may have, and activity duration changed from the original estimate to reflect resource constraints. The end result of this step is a final schedule in which all activities have been assigned and resource usage equates to resource availability.

- **Confirm control points**
  The first draft schedule enables the control points identified earlier (in the Product Flow Diagram) to be confirmed by the Project Board. End of Stage activities (for example, drawing up the next Stage Plan, producing an end-of-stage report) should be added to the activity network and a new schedule produced.

- **Calculate resources and costs**
  The resource requirements can now be tabulated, and the cost of the resources and other costs calculated to produce the plan budget. Remember to consult Project Assurance personnel in case they wish to add specific resources to quality checking activities.

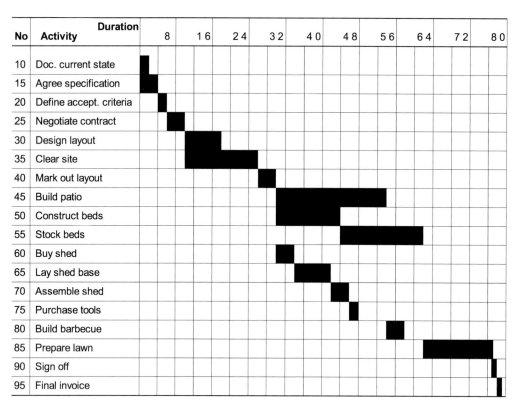

No	Activity	Duration	8	1 6	2 4	3 2	4 0	4 8	5 6	6 4	7 2	8 0
10	Doc. current state											
15	Agree specification											
20	Define accept. criteria											
25	Negotiate contract											
30	Design layout											
35	Clear site											
40	Mark out layout											
45	Build patio											
50	Construct beds											
55	Stock beds											
60	Buy shed											
65	Lay shed base											
70	Assemble shed											
75	Purchase tools											
80	Build barbecue											
85	Prepare lawn											
90	Sign off											
95	Final invoice											

Figure 20–6: Gantt chart example

20.8.4 Responsibilities

The Project Manager is responsible for scheduling. For Team Plans, the Project Manager would involve the person responsible for the work contained in the Plan – for example, a Team Manager.

20.8.5 Information needs

Management information	Usage	Explanation
Activity estimates	Input	When studied with the resource numbers, these give the activity duration
Activity dependencies	Input	These give the required sequence of work in the schedule
Resource availability	Input	The start and end dates of resource availability, plus the amount of time they are available in this period, are required
Schedule	Output	A list of activities and their allocated resources, plus the dates over which the activities will take place

20.8.6 Key criteria

- Have all types of required resource been considered?
- Has the Critical Path been identified?
- Has sufficient monitoring been planned for activities on the Critical Path?
- Have any training requirements been incorporated?
- Has resource availability been realistically assessed?

Hints and tips

At project level, resources need not be identified by name, but the type of skills required to carry out an activity should be identified.

The availability of the resources required (including those required for Quality Reviews) should be checked with the relevant line managers.

Be realistic about the availability of resources. Allowance should be made for holidays and time that people will spend on non-project activities. The average working week is only 4 days after allowing for holidays, training, sickness, etc. Of those 4 days, at least another half-day will be spent on other duties, even by dedicated staff – for example, quality reviewing for other projects, line management, and meetings.

The use of a skills matrix may assist a scheduler when using internal resources. This will allow appropriate people to be pinpointed, as well as giving an overall view of the skills available to the project.

When the availability of resources has been discussed with line managers, any agreement reached with them should be documented immediately.

20.9 Analysing Risks (PL6)

20.9.1 Fundamental principles

Commitment to a course of action without consideration of the risks inherent in that course is courting disaster. Risks should be considered and modifications made to the course of action in order to remove or lessen the impact of those risks.

20.9.2 Context

Once the plan has been produced, it should still be considered a draft until the risks inherent in the plan have been identified, assessed and the plan possibly modified.

20.9.3 Process description

Analysing risks runs parallel to all other planning work. It is an iterative process and the results of analysing risks or making planning assumptions may result in returning to previous steps and repeating the process as necessary.

An overview of the management of risk is given in the *Components* section of this manual (see Chapter 8).

Each resource should be examined for its potential risk content. Is the resource a known quantity? Is the quality of work required and the ability to meet deadlines known? Is the level of commitment known? Will the resource be totally under the control of the Project Manager? Where the answer is 'No', there is a risk involved. Countermeasures would include tighter and more frequent monitoring until confidence in the resource is achieved. It might be better to allocate work that is either easy to do or less critical to the schedule until the skill level has been checked.

Each activity should be checked for risk. Is there any spare time, or does the entire schedule depend on no slippage for the activity? Everything on the Critical Path therefore represents a risk. At the very least the countermeasures should include more frequent monitoring to give early warning of any problem.

The planning information produced so far should be examined for risks. All identified risks should be entered into the Risk Log.

Examples of risk that might be inherent in a plan are:

- a sub-contractor might fail to deliver a needed product on time

- a product to be delivered by a third party might be of poor quality

- a resource may not perform at the required level

- a specific resource, on which the plan is dependent, might be removed from the project

- external events may create a crisis

- the timetable is very tight and depends on the timely delivery of several products, any of which might be delayed.

20.9.4 Responsibilities

The Project Manager is responsible for the analysis and monitoring of risks, with assistance from those with assurance responsibilities. There may be risks outside the control of the Project Manager. These fall within the responsibilities of the Project Board. The Project Manager should discuss any such risks with the Project Board to ensure that the risks are being adequately monitored.

20.9.5 Information needs

Management information	Usage	Explanation
All previous planning information	Input	Basis for the risk analysis
Risk Log	Update	Any new risks should be added to this

20.9.6 Key criteria

- Are there any dependencies on products or other support from external sources that have not been listed as risks?

- When does the cost of risk avoidance or reduction approach the cost of the risk if it occurs?

- Has a range of means of addressing each risk been considered?

- Are the risks so great that it puts the viability of the project in question?

Hints and tips

There are various risk management and analysis methods and tools available to assist with these aspects of the process. Examples are the approach embodied in the CCTA Management of Risk publications, the CCTA Risk Analysis and Management Method (CRAMM), and the European Risk Management Method (RISKMAN).

Allocate to each high risk or critical activity a resource in which management has confidence.

Monitor the schedule and quality of any external product to be delivered on which any activities in the plan are dependent.

Check items such as holidays and training to make sure that they don't have an impact on the schedule.

Consider the actions needed in case of illness of any resource that cannot be replaced. Train other resources as back-up for any critical and scarce skills.

The addition of risk management activities will elongate the schedule and require extra resources. The benefit of the protection against risks is valuable, but remember to allow for the 'cost' of these activities in the plan.

Where the project is part of a programme, any risks identified at programme level should be examined for impact on the project. Where there is an impact, the risk should be added to the project's Risk Log. Careful consideration should be given to whether further project-specific risk analysis is required. Similarly, any project risks should be examined for programme impact.

20.10 Completing a Plan (PL7)

20.10.1 Fundamental principles

A plan is not simply a diagram. It is incomplete without certain supporting narrative sections.

20.10.2 Context

Having completed the schedule and assessment of the risks satisfactorily, the plan, its costs and its supporting text need to be consolidated by the Project Manager for presentation to the Project Board.

20.10.3 Process description

Text needs to be added to explain the Plan, any constraints on it, external dependencies, assumptions made, the risks identified and their required countermeasures. A suggested text for a Project Plan and a Stage Plan is given in *Appendix A – PRINCE Product Description outlines*.

The format of plans presented for approval should be a summary and should show the major products and activities that will occur throughout the plan and describe the resource and cost requirements. Project Board approval will 'freeze' the plan as a Baseline.

The graphical presentation of the plan is normally a Gantt or bar chart. Most computerised planning-and-control packages provide a report in this format. Such packages also provide a report on cost and resource requirements.

The majority of the material for the narrative sections of the plan will evolve as the previous steps in the planning cycle are undertaken. Some of it will already be known because of adherence to local standards.

Tolerance margins for the plan should be agreed with the Project Board. Depending on such factors as size, complexity and risk there must be agreement on what amount of deviation from planned cost and timescale is to be allowed before the plan is considered to be out of control. Tolerances are discussed more fully in *Controls* (see Chapter 6).

The products of the planning cycle should be checked for completeness and reasonableness by people experienced in planning and who know the project subject, prior to presenting them formally to the Project Board for approval.

Amend the Plans as required by the quality check.

The Product Checklist should now have the planned start and end dates added from the Plan.

The Project Plan forms part of the Project Initiation Document and is submitted at the End Stage Assessment of the Initiation Stage. The Plan for the Stage after Initiation is also presented at the Initiation End Stage Assessment.

Subsequent Stage Plans are presented at the End Stage Assessment of the previous stage.

20.10.4 Responsibilities

The Project Manager is responsible for completing each Plan.

20.10.5 Information needs

Management information	Usage	Explanation
Assessed Plan	Input	Basis of the final planning package
Product Checklist	Update	Start and end dates added to the list
Completed Plan for approval	Output	For approval by the Project Board

20.10.6 Key criteria

- When considering a suitable level of tolerance, what level of confidence is there in the plan?

- Has consideration been given to the business risks and constraints when setting tolerance levels?

- Has the format of the Plan's presentation material been agreed with the Project Board?

- Will the planning tool produce acceptable formats and quality for the presentation?

Hints and tips

Keep plans simple. It is a good discipline to try to keep all graphical plans presented to the Project Board to one sheet of paper. In this way the plan is easily prepared, easily read and therefore more likely to be understood. Anything that cannot be displayed in this way should be summarised and the detail included in a lower level of plan. Similarly, do not use complex symbols, or present plans that require education or too much explanation for them to be understood.

It might be worth considering the replacement of the graphical Project Plan with the Product Checklist.

Do not rely on pictures alone. As far as planning is concerned, it is not necessarily true that 'a picture paints a thousand words'. Although a Gantt chart can show what is intended to happen, and then what actually happened, it does not show why it should happen that way, or why something is different from the plan.

The narrative of a plan describes the thought that went into the plan, the assumptions made in preparing the plan, and any risks inherent in the plan. This is particularly important when presenting plans for approval. The readers are then able to accept both the plans and the assumptions and risks behind them, and the planner obtains informed approval and commitment to the plans from senior management.

If the layout of the report produced by a software package is not satisfactory, the data can usually be transferred to a spreadsheet or graphical package, where the required presentation can be constructed.

The Project Manager should discuss the plan informally with the Project Board and any assurance responsibilities appointed by the Project Board before formally presenting it for approval.

The presentation of the plan should be appropriate for the audience. In some circumstances it may be necessary to break down into further detail areas of a plan for the use of teams or individuals.

Be wary of producing an over-complex plan, containing lots of detail that might be better supplied in narrative form. A confusing or too detailed plan may 'switch off' the reader.

It helps if assumptions are consistent across all the projects of a programme.

Techniques

21   Product-based planning

PRINCE provides a product-based framework that can be applied to any project to give a logical sequence to the project's work. The use of this technique is recommended for all levels of plan required in a project. The technique is closely allied to *Defining and Analysing Products (PL2)*.

There are three steps to the product-based planning technique:

- producing a Product Breakdown Structure
- writing Product Descriptions
- producing a Product Flow Diagram.

21.1   Product-based planning example

The explanation of product-based planning is supported by an example. The basis of the example plan is described below.

A landscape gardener is asked to design and construct the rear garden for a local businessman. The area is about half a hectare in size, currently waste land filled with post-building rubbish, brambles, etc. It is bordered by a suitable fence that does not need to be replaced. The businessman says he has some vague ideas about what he wants. These include:

- a large patio
- a brick-built barbecue on the patio
- lots of lawn
- flower beds with lots of colourful shrubs and flowers.

He will get a gardener in to look after the garden when it is finished, so he wants a garden shed to be put in a discreet corner of the garden, filled with the tools that the gardener will need.

All that is known about the businessman is that he has a lot of money, but getting money out of him can be difficult. The landscape gardener decides that he will pin the customer down by getting a written specification, then get agreement to a design. Because of the 'tightwad' reputation, the landscape gardener will ask for part payment in advance for those products requiring heavy expenditure (Stage selection).

The example is done at Project Plan level.

21.2 Producing a Product Breakdown Structure

Breaking down a product into its constituent sub-products helps clarify and identify all necessary work for its creation.

This is the first step in PRINCE product-based planning. The 'product' is the end deliverable of the project and may be a tangible one such as a machine, a document or a piece of software, or it may be intangible, such as a culture change or a different organisational structure. For the purposes of this explanation, these will all be called 'products'.

21.2.1 Identifying products

The objective is to identify the products or outcomes, whether specialist, management or quality, whose creation is the subject of the plan.

All the products of the plan are drawn up in a hierarchical structure, known as a Product Breakdown Structure. At the top of the chart is a single box that summarises the overall product of the plan – for example, a new marketing strategy, a business plan, a new car, a computer system, or a new employment policy. This is then decomposed into three 'boxes', which represent:

- the products whose development is the subject of the plan

- the management 'products'

- quality 'products' that will be created to support the management and control of the plan.

This decomposition into three portions is purely a device to remind the planner to think of the management and quality products.

Each of these boxes is then decomposed into its major parts to form the next level of the structure. Each of these boxes may then be decomposed until an appropriate level of detail for the plan in question is reached. Figure 21–1 shows an example of the typical management products branch of a Product Breakdown Structure. Figure 21–2 shows a hierarchy of the standard quality products. These would be part of a Stage Plan or a Team Plan.

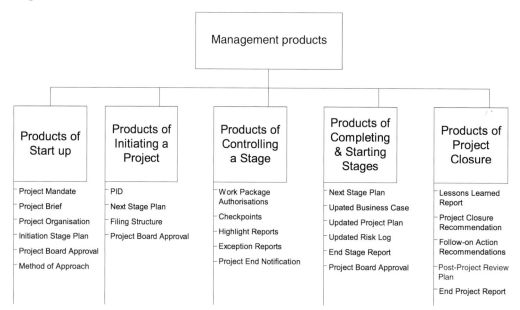

Figure 21–1: Management Product Breakdown Structure

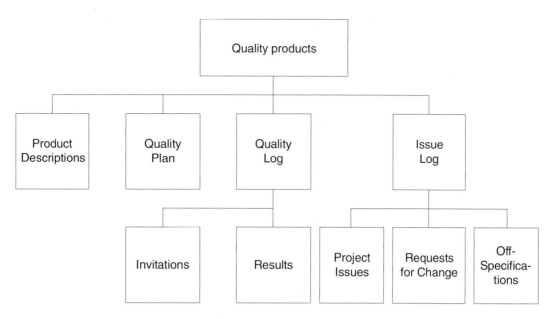

Figure 21–2: Quality Product Breakdown Structure

Higher-level boxes must be completely defined by the lower-level boxes to which they are attached.

In the landscaped garden example, the Product Breakdown Structure for the specialist products might be constructed as shown in Figure 21–3.

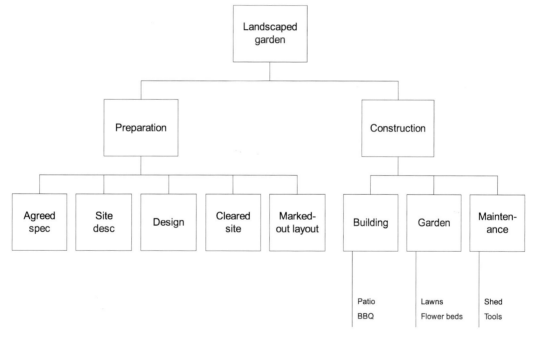

Figure 21–3: Landscaped Garden Example – Specialist Product Breakdown Structure

21.2.2 Key criteria

- What products are required to solve the business need?
- What management products must be generated during the plan to ensure guidance and control?
- What quality products must be delivered for the Customer, audit or quality assurance?
- Does the plan rely on items being delivered from external sources?

- Is responsibility for these clearly identified and agreed?

- How will progress on external products be monitored by this project?

- Are the appropriate Checkpoints in the plan?

- How will the quality of external products be checked?

- Have suitable project staff been appointed to monitor the quality of external products?

- Are the frequency, timing and time allocated sufficient to ensure quality?

Hints and tips

The products in a plan include not only those that will be developed within the plan but any 'products' external to the plan (and possibly outside the project) that are required as input to the work identified in the plan.

If the Product Breakdown Structure is being created manually, a numbering system should be devised that will indicate each product's level in the hierarchy and its parent.

Assistance could be sought from a 'quality specialist' when defining quality, particularly when adherence to recognised standards is part of the Acceptance Criteria.

21.3 Writing Product Descriptions

A clear, complete and unambiguous description of products is a tremendous aid to their successful creation.

A Product Description should be written for a product as soon as possible after the need for the product has been identified. This will be a draft that is liable to be refined and amended as the product becomes better understood and the later planning steps are done. A Product Description should be Baselined when the plan containing its creation is Baselined.

A documented and agreed Product Description ensures that all personnel affected by that product have the same understanding. A description should be written for each significant product to ensure that it is understood, to provide a pointer to the way in which the product is to be presented, and to define the quality expectations for it.

21.3.1 Product Description contents

A Product Description needs to define a number of things about the product. Information is needed about:

- Product Title

- Purpose
  What purpose will this product fulfil? Is it a means to an end, or an end in itself?

- Composition
  What are the components of the product? For example, if the product is a document, this would be a list of the expected chapters or sections. For a low-level component, this section will be a description of the product.

- Derivation
  What are the source products from which this product is derived? Examples are:
  – a design is derived from a specification
  – a product is bought in from a Supplier
  – a product is obtained from another department or team.

- Format and Presentation
  Is there a standard appearance to which the finished product must conform?

- Allocated to
  To whom has the job of creating the product been given?

- Quality Criteria
  To what quality specification must the product be produced, and what quality measurements will be applied by those inspecting the finished product? This might be a simple reference to one or more common standards that are documented elsewhere, or it might be a full explanation of some yardstick to be applied.

- The Type of Quality Check Required
  What kind of test, inspection or review is to be used to check the quality or functionality?

- The Skills Level
  Either identification of the people who are to check the quality, an indication of the skills required to do so, or a pointer to which area(s) should supply the checking resources. Identification of the actual people may be left until planning the stage in which the quality check is to be done.

If there are any relevant checklists covering the product's development, these should also be identified in the Product Description.

Any changes to a Product Description after it is Baselined must pass through change control.

Although responsibility for writing Product Descriptions rests with the Project Manager, it is wise to involve representatives from the area with expertise in the product or products in question. If formal project support is available, this may be a good source of assistance.

21.3.2 Key criteria

- Are the products clearly and unambiguously defined?

- What type of quality check will be needed for the type of product or products to be produced by this plan?

- Are there centrally held standards to which the description can point when it comes to defining the quality criteria?

- Does the User/Customer want any specific standards used?

- Who are the right people to write each Product Description?

- Are suitable checklists available to help check the products?

Hints and tips

Writing a Product Description helps clarify how much work is needed to create the product. This can be a big help in estimation.

Concentrate the writing of Product Descriptions on any products in the project with which the Project Manager is not familiar and those that in past projects have been done badly.

Appendix A – PRINCE Product Description outlines contains outlines of the standard key management and quality products. It should not be necessary for each project to redefine these unless there are changes to them.

Writing good Product Descriptions is not a trivial undertaking. In particular, quality criteria, aimed at determining an acceptable product from an unacceptable one, need careful thought.

It is a good start to get the User or Customer involved in the writing of Product Descriptions, defining quality expectations, and deciding how the product can be checked against these expectations.

Test the setting of quality criteria by asking the question 'How will I know when work on this product is finished as opposed to stopped?'

Listing the composition of a product can often remind the planner of another product that is needed.

Very often the same product types are created in many plans. Standard Product Descriptions can be written, which can be used by many plans.

Are there any standard checklists that can be used?

Be careful not to over-engineer the Product Description. It exists to help and support the production and planning processes and is not an end in itself.

Don't try to replace the requirements specifications with a Product Description.

If the quality criteria for a product are agreed with the Customer, this may assist in the ultimate acceptance of the project.

If Product Descriptions are used as control documents, then additional information, such as estimated and actual dates and effort, may be added.

Identifying who will accept a particular product, and making sure that they agree to the Product Description, can reduce the potential for conflict at later stages of the project.

21.4 Producing a Product Flow Diagram

The Product Flow Diagram is created from the Product Breakdown Structure and precedes the identification of activities in *Identifying Activities and Dependencies (PL3)*.

21.4.1 Creating a Product Flow Diagram

Every planner needs to know the answer to the question, 'What comes next?'. The Product Flow Diagram shows the sequence of development of the products of the plan. It also identifies dependencies on any products outside the scope of the plan.

A Product Flow Diagram needs very few symbols. Time flows in one direction only, either from top to bottom or from left to right. Each product to be developed within the plan is enclosed in a box, and the boxes are connected by arrows showing the sequence in which they are to be created. Any products that should already exist or that come from work outside the scope of the plan should be clearly identified by using a different type of enclosure, for example, an ellipse.

The diagram begins with those products that are available at the start of the plan (perhaps many of these are documents, such as statements of requirements or designs) and ends with the final product of the plan. It is often easiest to fill in the middle of the flow by working back from the final product, asking the question 'Which products should be available in order to create this product?'

Creation of a Product Flow Diagram may reveal new products that are required. These should also be added to the Product Breakdown Structure, and Product Descriptions should be written for them.

Although the Project Manager is responsible for creation of the Product Flow Diagram, it is sensible to use the help of those who are to develop the products contained in the plan. It also enables consistency/validity checking. Figure 21–4 illustrates the Product Flow Diagram for the landscaped garden project.

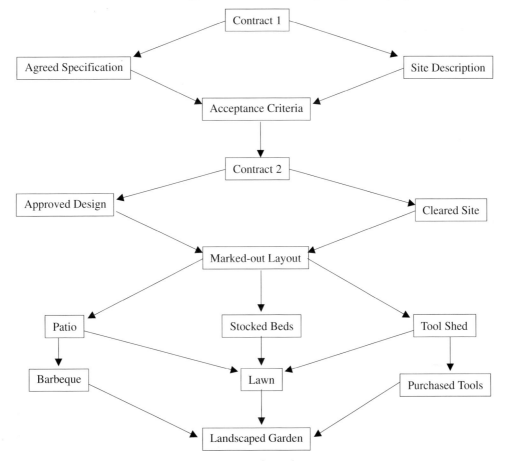

Figure 21–4: Landscaped Garden Example – Product Flow Diagram

253

21.4.2 Key criteria

- On what other products is each product dependent?

- Is any product dependent on a product developed outside the scope of this plan?

- Which products can be developed in parallel?

Hints and tips

At project level, the dependencies can be rather crude – for example, not all elements of major Product 1 need to be done before any elements of major Product 2 can start. To try to break those major products down so that the dependencies can be refined is likely to confuse the diagram. It is better to accept the crude dependencies and resolve them at Stage Plan level.

The easiest way to create a Product Flow Diagram is to put all the specialist products in their required sequence and then add the management and quality products to the correct point in the flow.

Self-adhesive notelets on a whiteboard can be an effective way of developing a Product Flow Diagram, particularly where there is likely to be a lot of modification.

A useful way to get started with the flow of specialist products is to 'top and tail' the diagram – that is, put the final product at the bottom of a sheet of paper and any products that are prerequisite to starting the work at the top (in ellipses). Take each product in the list and match it to every other product to establish if there is any particular dependency between them. Work through all the products in this way. Use this information to connect all the products in their appropriate sequence from such prerequisites as there are to the final product.

If Project Board approvals are listed as management products, their later placement in the sequence will show where the Stage ends should come, if this is not already known.

The Derivation section of a Product Description gives useful information about dependencies.

It is useful to show the source of any products from third parties in the Product Flow Diagram.

The Project Board may find that the Product Flow Diagram and Product Checklist are easy to use to check on plan progress.

22   Change Control approach

A programme or corporate body may have its own change control procedure and forms. This is not a problem as long as its key points are compatible with the approach detailed below.

For those without a mandatory change control procedure, the following will ensure that changes are controlled during the project.

22.1 Change Control steps

All changes are treated as types of Project Issue and are handled through the same change control approach. A Project Issue can be:

- a request to change the specification of requirements (Request for Change)

- a suggestion to improve one or more of the project's products (Request for Change)

- a record of some current or forecast failure to meet a requirement (Off-Specification)

- a question on any project topic.

Whatever its type, every input is logged as a Project Issue in the Issue Log. Suggested content for this log is given in *Appendix A – PRINCE Product Description outlines*. It allocates a unique number and records the author, date and type of Project Issue. The author should indicate the priority of the Issue. A suggested priority rating is:

1   a must; the final product will not work without this change

2   an important change; its absence would be very inconvenient, although a work-around is possible for a while

3   a nice-to-have; but not vital

4   a cosmetic change; of no importance

5   this does not involve a change.

A copy of the Project Issue is returned to the author to acknowledge its receipt and entry into the system.

Any Project Issues that are questions or are based on misunderstandings should be answered directly. A reply is sent to the author, a copy filed, and the Issue Log updated to reflect the action.

An impact analysis is carried out on each remaining Project Issue to identify:

- what would have to change

- what effort would the change need

- what the impact on the Business Case would be

- what the impact on the risks would be.

The priority should be re-evaluated by the Senior User after the impact analysis.

For Off-Specifications, the Project Manager tries to solve the problem within the stage and project tolerance margins. This may mean changes to the plan(s) to include extra activities. Where correction of the Off-Specification is not possible within tolerance levels, the Project Manager follows the exception procedures, *Escalating Project Issues (CS8)* and *Producing an Exception Plan (SB6)*. If the decision of the Project Board is to accept the Off-Specification without any corrective action, this is called a 'Concession'.

The Project Manager decides which Requests for Change, if any, should be implemented within the current Stage Plan constraints. Even for those that the Project Manager is prepared to implement without extra funds or time, there should be discussion with the Senior User and Senior Supplier. This is particularly important in circumstances involving an external Supplier. Without the approval of the Project Board, the Project Manager should not authorise any work that would change a product that has already been approved by the Project Board.

Where the Project Manager does not wish to take the decision personally on whether or not to implement changes, the relevant Project Issues are passed to the Senior User(s). The Senior User can decide to reject Project Issues, put them in 'pending' status, or ask for their implementation. Where implementation is sought, the Senior User canvasses the Executive and Senior Supplier for their agreement to any extra cost and effort required. This may lead to more being rejected or put into 'pending' status. The Project Issues are updated with any change in priority and the Project Board's directives.

The Project Issues are returned to the Project Manager, the Issue Log updated, and an updated copy sent to the author.

Any Project Issues to be implemented at the request of the Project Board may form the basis of an Exception Report, the input to *Escalating Project Issues (CS8)*. According to the project environment, this may be formal or informal. The likely outcome will be a request for the Project Manager to produce an Exception Plan, which will include the extra work, to be submitted via *Producing an Exception Plan (SB6)*.

NOTE: Where the Project Board has delegated decisions on the implementation of changes to some separate change authority, the name of this body should be substituted for that of the Project Board in this technique.

Hints and tips

Evaluating the impact of potential changes can be erroneously taken to mean only the impact on the Customer. Impact analysis must cover the three areas of business, User and Supplier. Before a change goes to the Senior User for consideration, the impact on the Supplier must be known – for example, the cost and effort required, and what products would have to be changed.

Where the project is partially or fully funded by the Supplier, this may change the decision-making authority within the Project Board about changes. It may become more of a joint decision based on the contract terms or including contract modification. Any changes in responsibility and authority should be reflected in the job definitions.

Where the project is part of a programme, is the project in a position to judge the impact on other projects? Does it have the authority to make decisions? There are two potential approaches:

- *screen all changes at programme level to determine where the decision should be made*
- *ensure a programme representative is part of the project's change control authorisation loop.*

23   Quality Review technique

23.1 Fundamental principles

The benefits to be gained from the effective use of Quality Reviews are:

- a structured and organised approach to the examination of subjective quality criteria

- early identification of defects in products and, therefore, a platform for product improvement, with attendant reduction in the costs of the final product during development and in operation

- as products are considered complete once they have successfully passed Quality Review, an objective measurement for management progress control is provided; progress is measured by product delivery

- all vested interests are working together to improve product quality; this helps build the team approach to development

- once a product has gone through the Quality Review procedure, personnel are more willing to commit to that product. As ownership of the product is shared between Quality Review participants, Users, who are represented on the Quality Review team, are much more willing to sign off a reviewed product

- apart from defects on the part of the creator(s), defects may also be caused by deficiencies in standards and methods. Failure to use a standard may indicate that the standard is no longer practical to use. Such events should instigate a review of the suspect standards area and provide a starting point for standards improvements.

23.2 Context

A Quality Review can be invoked at any point in the project, since any document could be subject to a Quality Review if there are subjective elements of quality to be monitored. It has close ties with the following processes:

- *Planning (PL)* for the pre-planning and resourcing of major Quality Reviews.

- *Managing Product Delivery (MP)*, which is the process covering the production of the project's products, and hence where the application of most of the Quality Reviews will take place.

- *Authorising Work Package (CS1)*, which addresses the hand-over of responsibility for product production and will include the requirement for Quality Reviews.

- *Assessing Progress (CS2)*, which deals with progress monitoring and reporting, and which will receive details of completed Quality Reviews.

23.3 What is a Quality Review?

A Quality Review is an involved partnership designed to ensure a product's completeness and adherence to standards by a review procedure. It is a team review of a product, with the emphasis on checking the product for errors (as opposed to, for example, improved design). It has a clear structure, described in this chapter.

23.3.1 The involved partnership

This partnership should involve all those with a vested interest in the product and with any specialist knowledge that can contribute to monitoring quality.

The selection of possible participants in a review should be made during the planning of the relevant stage, guided by the information contained in the Product Description. The most effective Quality Reviews have participants from all areas that can contribute effectively to the quality of the product.

Identification of key products and selection of participants in a review is an important part of the Project Assurance role at Stage planning time.

It is possible to hold a postal review if it is impossible to get the reviewers together.

23.3.2 The deliverable

The deliverable, in the context of a Quality Review, is any product that has been evaluated against mostly subjective criteria involving elements of judgement or opinion. This will typically be a document, such as a plan, a report or a drawing, but could be other products such as models, mock-ups or prototypes.

23.4 Overview of the Quality Review procedure

23.4.1 Objectives

The objectives of a Quality Review are:

- to produce a product that meets business, User and specialist requirements
- to assess the conformity of a product against set criteria
- to provide a platform for product improvement
- to involve all those who have a vested interest in the product
- to spread ownership of the product
- to obtain commitment from all vested interests in the product
- to provide a mechanism for management control.

23.4.2 Steps in the Quality Review procedure

The review procedure has a number of activities, the central element being the review meeting, where all participants gather to identify and agree on any defects in the product.

There are three basic steps in the Quality Review procedure.

- Preparation, consisting of:
  - confirmation of the availability of the nominated reviewers and agreement on dates for the return of comments and the review itself
  - distribution of a copy of the product and its Product Description to reviewers where this is possible, for instance if it is a printed document. Alternatively, making the product available for inspection by the reviewers
  - assessment of the product against the quality criteria
  - entry of the major errors on an Error List
  - annotation of minor errors on the product, where applicable
  - return of the annotated product and Error List to the Producer
  - a plan of the review meeting, and agreement on the agenda.

- Review meeting, consisting of:
  - discussion and clarification of each of the major errors raised by the reviewers
  - agreement of the follow-up appropriate to each error

- documentation of the follow-up actions and responsibilities
- summary of the actions at the end of the meeting
- agreement on the Quality Review outcome, and sign-off of the product, if appropriate.

- Follow-up, consisting of:
  - notification to the Project and/or Team Manager of the Quality Review results
  - a plan of any remedial work required
  - sign-off of the product following successful remedial work.

It is important that Quality Reviews are properly planned, with input from the assurance function. There is therefore an additional Quality Review planning step consisting of:

- identifying the products that will be subject to Quality Review

- planning the timescale for each Quality Review

- identifying the reviewers and adding them to resource plans.

This is carried out as part of the *Planning (PL)* process. The way these basic steps could be applied is as follows.

23.4.3 Responsibilities

There are four specific roles involved in the Quality Review procedure.

The Review Chairperson

This role runs the Quality Review procedure. This is a separate role from that of the Executive who chairs the Project Board.

The role has the following main responsibilities:

- check that the product is ready for review

- ensure that the Quality Review is properly organised

- set the review meeting agenda

- control the Quality Review procedure and chair the Quality Review meeting

- ensure that the Quality Review does not stray from its main aim

- ensure that actions and required results are agreed

- together with the reviewers, determine the Quality Review outcome

- keep the Project and/or Team Manager aware of the status of all Quality Reviews

- provide final review sign-off

- institute Exception procedures via the Project and/or Team Manager where problems with the product cannot be resolved satisfactorily.

Producer

This role represents the creator(s) of the product involved. Typically, it will be filled by the person who has produced the product, or who has led the team responsible. The role has the following responsibilities:

- provide all reviewers with the relevant review products

- prepare for the review meeting

- assess Error Lists prior to the review meeting and use them to assist the Review Chairperson to set the review meeting agenda

- answer questions about the product during the review procedure, explain the implications of any errors, and take agreed errors forward for subsequent action

- agree action to resolve errors

- ensure any agreed actions are carried out

- obtain sign-off from reviewers for changes made to the product

- obtain final sign-off from the Review Chairperson when all changes have been approved by the reviewers.

Reviewers

They have the following responsibilities:

- prepare for the Quality Review

- assess the product against the quality criteria specified in the Product Description

- ensure errors are fully understood by the Producer and are subsequently resolved satisfactorily

- sign off Follow-up Action List items where the reviewers are identified as checkers.

Scribe

The major responsibilities of this role are to:

- take notes of agreed actions during the review meeting

- read back agreed actions at the end of the meeting, and note who is to take corrective action and who is to check the corrections.

In addition to the specific roles involved, there are responsibilities that need to be taken by other people. These are responsibilities that form part of their standard job, but that are particularly relevant to the Quality Review process:

Project Manager

- plan the Quality Reviews in outline

- plan to overcome any identified exception conditions raised as a result of a Quality Review

- act as reviewer where appropriate.

Team Manager

- plan Quality Reviews in detail

- identify any Quality Review resources required from the team (additional to any reviewers chosen by assurance roles)

- monitor Quality Review progress against plan

- report progress to Project Manager.

Note that often the Project Manager will be directly managing the work that is being Quality Reviewed. If this is the case, the responsibilities of Project Manager and Team Manager will be combined.

Project Assurance Roles

- check that the Quality Reviews are being properly constituted

- advise on suitable reviewers for each Quality Review

- check that everyone involved with the Quality Review process is aware of their role and responsibilities, and that adequate training has been given

- ensure that the Quality Review procedure is being properly followed

- check that reviewers are being correctly selected, and that they are being correctly briefed for the work

- check that follow-up actions are being properly monitored

- log and report on corporate standards and advise on improvements and amendments

- act as reviewers where appropriate.

Project support roles

If project support is available to the Project Manager, it can be used to assist the Review Chairperson and Producer in organising a review venue, prepare and distribute the review documentation, act as Scribe and progress-chase the Follow-up Action List until all errors have been corrected and signed off. People in support roles can act as reviewers where appropriate.

The following tables show the detailed job contents for the Quality Review roles for each of the steps.

Preparation

Review Chairperson	Producer	Reviewer	Project Manager/ Team Manager
Check product ready Confirm reviewers available and still appropriate Confirm preparation time Agree agenda Agree presentation format and timing (if any)	Confirm product available Distribute the product and Product Description to reviewers Agree time and location of review meeting Assess Comments/ Error Lists Agree agenda with Chairperson Confirm review details to reviewers prior to the meeting	Consult Product Description of review product Schedule preparation/ review time Review product against Product Description Complete Error List and annotate product Forward Error List and annotated product to Producer Confirm review attendance	Check Quality Review on schedule Ensure Quality Review procedure being followed

Review meeting

Review Chairperson	Producer	Reviewer	Project Manager/ Team Manager
Open review, state objectives, meeting agenda and format Invite general comments (decide if premature closure of meeting is needed) Walk through product as agreed in the agenda Invite Reviewer comments Ensure all Reviewers contribute Agree all errors for Follow-up Action List Agree responsibility for signing off errors Agree Quality Review result Inform Team Manager of Quality Review outcome	Take note of comments and concerns Clarify reviewer comments Agree errors and follow-up action Collect Follow-up Action List and annotated product copies	Raise general comments/remarks Raise specific errors Agree errors and follow-up action	File any Quality Review documen-tation if Quality Review complete Take Exception action if the Quality Review is incomplete

Follow-up of review meeting

Review Chairperson	Producer	Reviewer	Project Manager/ Team Manager
Sign off actions as required Raise Project Issues for any unresolved errors or errors in products other than the one being reviewed Raise Exception if correction schedule exceeded On resolution of all errors, sign off the product and inform Team Manager	Resolve errors Obtain sign-off from reviewers Obtain Follow-up Action List sign-off from Quality Review Chairperson Take Exception action on uncleared errors	Check and sign off errors as they are resolved Assist in error resolution as appropriate	Ensure plans are updated following error resolution File any deliverable sign-off documentation Deal with any exception actions

23.4.4 Quality Review Results

At the end of a Quality Review, the Review Chairperson should obtain a consensus agreement on the result of the review. If any of the reviewers is not prepared to sign off the product, then the product has not met its quality criteria and hence is not ready for use. If the reviewers' comments cannot be resolved for any reason – for example, contention between reviewers – the problem will have to be raised via a Project Issue (see *Change Control*, Chapters 11 and 22).

The result of a Quality Review will normally be one of three:

- the product is error-free and can be approved immediately
- the product can be approved once the identified errors are corrected and signed off
- correction of the errors found will radically alter the product, and it should be reviewed again.

The Review Chairperson may also decide to postpone the review meeting if:

- insufficient reviewers attend to cover the quality issues addressed by the product's quality criteria
- the reviewers who are attending are not qualified to comment on the issues being addressed
- it is clear that the reviewers have not studied the product during the Preparation phase
- it becomes obvious that the product is not fit to be reviewed.

23.4.5 Key criteria

- Have the quality criteria been specified?
- Have the quality criteria been passed to the reviewers, together with the product?
- Have the reviewers fully checked the product prior to the review meeting?
- Have the Error Lists been sent to the Producer or Review Chairperson prior to the review meeting?
- Has the review meeting concentrated on error detection, not error fixing?
- Have the follow-up actions been documented and allocated?
- Have reviewers been asked which changes they wish to sign off?
- Has agreement been reached on the result of the Quality Review?

Hints and tips

Quality Review is there for error/opportunity identification NOT correction. *The temptation to agree solutions for the defects found in a product can be all too inviting. The Quality Review procedure is about identification and agreement of defects. Should resolution become a feature of Quality Review, then the review procedure will lose much of its effectiveness because discussion of solutions takes time and effort away from the key objective of the Quality Review procedure: that is, the identification and agreement of defects in the product, to provide the platform for product improvement. Also, there may be more than one solution to a problem identified and the group of people assembled to review a product may not be the best qualified to select the best solution. Any solutions suggested during the review process should be noted for later consideration.*

There is a need to address the Producer/reviewer psychology.

*The aim of the Quality Review is to identify defects in the product not in the Producer. Reviewers and Producers should approach the review in a constructive 'team' attitude to achieving quality products. If the team approach is not adopted, conflict can arise and be destructive to the Quality Review procedure. It helps if reviewers can refer to **the** product, rather than **your** product.*

There must be management and peer pressure to prepare for the review meeting.

Quality Review is not an ad hoc *gathering of individuals. It is not a first sight of the product for the purpose of problem identification. As in all good meetings, all the participants should attend having checked the product involved and should be prepared to contribute, knowing the agenda and objectives and the role they should perform at the meeting.*

Quality Review participants must prepare for the review by identifying major errors on an Error List, annotating the product where possible with minor errors, and informing review participants of their findings. Not to do so wastes the time of the other reviewers, and devalues the eventual product sign-off since it is more likely that errors will be left undiscovered.

Managers do not attend.

*Care must be taken that managers do not attend a Quality Review in a **people management** role. They do not attend to assess the performance of their staff. This is particularly true of the Producer's manager, it would devalue the meeting and would cause extra stress on the Producer. However, managers may attend in the role of reviewers.*

Checklists should be in existence.

A major means of assessing a product's quality is through the Product Description, which defines the composition, format and quality criteria of a product. Should this not be available, a checklist of the standard criteria for this type of product should be available. Without one or other of these, the reviewers will be left with no guidance as to what the acceptable quality is.

The Chairperson should not act as a reviewer.

It is difficult to both chair the review meeting and review the product involved. Ideally the Review Chairperson should be there just to run the meeting.

Non-attendance of a reviewer.

If a reviewer cannot attend the meeting, the Review Chairperson can decide either to accept an Error List from that reviewer and arrange for its points to be discussed at the meeting, or replace the reviewer. If the number of non-attendees is such as to undermine the effectiveness of the review, either because of the lack of people to form discussions or because of the lack of key skills, it may be necessary to postpone the review meeting. Where reviewers are not prepared for the review or have not submitted Error Lists, it may be appropriate to postpone the review if it is felt that the review might be ineffective.

For inter-project products, there should be cross-project representation at Quality Reviews.

The suggested Scribe role can be taken by the Producer, especially in an informal Quality Review.

Errors in other products.

A Quality Review may turn up an error in a product other than the one being reviewed. This should be recorded as an action item, but closed on its transfer to an appropriate Project Issue.

24 Project filing techniques

This is a suggested filing system to be used by the project.

There are three major types of file in PRINCE:

- Management
- Specialist
- Quality.

It is a project decision whether to include the management and quality products within the Configuration Management method. Even if they are not, a project filing system will be needed.

24.1 Management files

These comprise:

- a Project file
- a Stage file for each Stage.

24.1.1 The Project file

This has the following sections:

Organisation	The project organisation chart and signed job definitions
Plans	The Project Plans. These should include any versions developed, not only the one approved as part of the Project Initiation Document. The various components of each version should be kept (such as Product Breakdown Structures, Product Flow Diagrams) with clear identification of their date, version number and reasoning, such as change of assumptions, scope, stage results or resource availability
	The Project Plan should be updated at least at the end of each Stage
Business Case	Versions of the Business Case, updated at each Stage end or when Exception Plans are created
Risk Log	Updated details of all identified risks, their status and countermeasures
Control	Copies of Project Initiation and Closure documents

24.1.2 Stage files

These have more sections than the Project file.

Organisation	Stage organisation, details of team members. These should reflect all work assignments, achievements and the Project Manager's or Team Manager's assessment of work performance
Plans	Copies of Stage Plans, Team Plans and Exception Plans, updated as available
Control	Copies of Work Package authorisations, Checkpoint Reports, Highlight Reports, Exception Reports, End Stage Assessment plus any Mid-Stage Assessments held
Daily Log	A diary of events, problems, questions, answers, informal discussions with Project Board members, and actions for the Stage
Correspondence	Copies of management correspondence or other papers associated with the Stage

24.2 The Specialist file(s)

This contains all the items under Configuration Management of the project, and is the centre of the Configuration Management activity referred to in Chapter 10, *Configuration Management*.

If an Off-Specification is raised about items under Configuration Management, a copy of the Off-Specification form is filed with the item in this section of the filing.

24.2.1 Specialist correspondence

There may also be a need to create this section of the Specialist file, where correspondence or external documents cannot be specifically related to one item. The section should have its own log of entries, showing cross-references to the items concerned.

24.3 The Quality file

The objective of a Quality file is to permit an audit at any time of the quality work being done and to confirm adherence to quality standards. There is one Quality file that runs through the whole project and is not divided into Stages. It has three major divisions: Product Descriptions, quality checks and Project Issues.

Product Descriptions

The master copy of all Product Descriptions. There should be a Product Description for every major product in the project.

Quality Checks

It is useful to head this section with a log giving a number to each check, the type of check or test (for example, Quality Review), the product and date. This is a quick reference to see or show how many checks have been held in a particular Stage and a guide to where the appropriate documentation can be found.

The subdivision of the quality section will depend on the type(s) of check or test being made. There should be a separate file for the documents relating to each entry in the Quality Log. This file should keep details of the method used, the resources used, the sign-off document where appropriate, details of the tests made, expected and actual results. The filing for Quality Reviews should include:

- invitations
- result notifications
- action lists.

Project Issues

This should have a log, the Issue Log, at the front to facilitate sequential numbering and to record the status and allocation. The subject of Project Issues is covered fully in Chapter 22; *Change Control approach*.

Information

Further information

The following groups of publications provide information that is useful to those implementing or considering implementing PRINCE.

CCTA publications

Details of CCTA publications may be obtained from the CCTA Help Desk, Rosebery Court, St Andrews Business Park, Norwich, NR7 0HS Telephone (01603) 704567.

A CCTA home page is also accessible on the World Wide Web, on: http://www.ccta.gov.uk

Programme and Project Management Library

An Introduction to Programme Management
ISBN: 0 11 330611 3

A Guide to Programme Management
ISBN: 0 11 330600 8

Programme Management Case Studies (Volumes 1 and 2)
ISBN: 0 11 330666 0
ISBN: 0 11 330677 6

Management of Risk Library

An Introduction to the Management of Risk
ISBN: 0 11 330648 2

Management of Programme Risk
ISBN: 0 11 330672 5

Management of Project Risk
ISBN: 0 11 330636 9

An Introduction to Managing Project Risk
ISBN: 0 11 330671 7

Management of Risk Case Studies – Volume 1
ISBN: 0 11 330667 9

Management of Risk Case Studies – Volume 2
ISBN: 0 11 330681 4

Managing Risk to the IS Strategy
ISBN: 0 11 330680 6

IT Infrastructure Library

An Introduction to Business Continuity Management
ISBN: 0 11 330669 5

A Guide to Business Continuity Management
ISBN: 0 11 330675 X

Configuration Management
ISBN: 0 11 330530 3

Other CCTA publications

Post Implementation Review: reviewing IS/IT Projects and Business Change
ISBN: 0 946 683 76 X

Achieving Benefits from Business Change
ISBN: 0 11 330841 8

Standards

BS 4335: 1987 – Glossary of terms used in project network techniques

ISO 8402: 1994 – Quality management and quality assurance vocabulary

ISO 9000–1: 1994 – Quality management and quality assurance standards
        Part 1: Guidelines for selection and use

ISO 9000–2: 1993 – Quality management and quality assurance standards
        Part 2: Generic guidelines for the application of ISO 9001, ISO 9002
        and ISO 9003

ISO 9004: 1994 – Guide to quality management and quality system elements

ISO 10007 – Quality management – Guidelines for configuration management

ISO 10006 – Quality management – Guidelines to quality in project management

ISO/TC176/SC2/WG8N123 – A guide to quality management in project
        management

BSI QMS 32 – A guide to project management

BS 6079 – Guide to project management

Special interest groups

APM Group Ltd
7–8 Queen Square
High Wycombe
Buckinghamshire HP11 2BP
Telephone (01494) 452450

Information Systems Examinations Board (BCS)
1 Sanford Street
Swindon SN1 1HJ
Telephone (01793) 417480

Stichting Exin
Postbus 19147
3501 DC Utrecht
Netherlands
Telephone (00) 30 2344 811

The PRINCE User Group Ltd
The PRINCE User Group Administration
c/o PI Business Services Group Ltd
The Business Exchange
Clayton Road
Hayes
Middlesex UB3 1AN
Telephone 0870 901 5583
Fax 0870 901 6581

Glossary

Acceptance Criteria

A prioritised list of criteria that the final product(s) must meet before the Customer will accept them; a measurable definition of what must be done for the final product to be acceptable to the Customer. They should be defined as part of the Project Brief and agreed between Customer and Supplier no later than the Project Initiation Stage. They should be in the Project Initiation Document.

Baseline

A snapshot; a position or situation that is recorded. Although the position may be updated later, the Baseline remains unchanged and available as a reminder of the original state and as a comparison against the current position.

Business Case

Information that describes the justification for setting up and continuing a PRINCE project. It provides the reasons (and answers the question 'Why?') for the project. It is updated at key points throughout the project.

Change Authority

A group to which the Project Board may delegate responsibility for the consideration of Requests for Change. The Change Authority is given a budget and can approve changes within that budget.

Change Budget

The money allocated to the Change Authority to be spent on authorised Requests for Change.

Change Control

The procedure to ensure that the processing of all Project Issues is controlled, including the submission, analysis and decision making.

Checkpoint

A team-level, time-driven review of progress.

Checkpoint Report

A progress report of the information gathered at a Checkpoint meeting, which is given by a team to the Project Manager and provides reporting data as defined in the Project Initiation Document.

Communication Plan

Part of the Project Initiation Document describing how the project's stakeholders and interested parties will be kept informed during the project.

Concession

An Off-Specification that is accepted by the Project Board without corrective action.

Configuration Management

A discipline, normally supported by software tools, that gives management precise control over its assets (for example, the products of a project), covering planning, identification, control, status accounting and verification of the products.

Contingency Plan

A plan that provides an outline of decisions and measures to be taken if defined circumstances, outside the control of a PRINCE project, should occur.

Corporate Body

Used to describe any company, Government department, corporation or charitable body that is involved in the project. It can be a customer for the end results, supplier of specialist skills or deliverables, assurance or auditing body. The word is used to avoid confusion, particularly between the public and private sectors.

Customer

The person or group who commissioned the work and will benefit from the end results.

Deliverable

An item that the project has to create as part of the requirements. It may be part of the final outcome or an intermediate element on which one or more subsequent deliverables are dependent. According to the type of project, another name for a deliverable is 'product'.

End Project Report

A report given by the Project Manager to the Project Board, that confirms the hand-over of all deliverables and provides an updated Business Case and an assessment of how well the project has done against its Project Initiation Document.

End Stage Assessment

The review by the Project Board and Project Manager of the End Stage Report to decide whether to approve the next Stage Plan (unless the last Stage has now been completed). According to the size and criticality of the project, the review may be formal or informal. The approval to proceed should be documented as an important management product.

End Stage Report

A report given by the Project Manager to the Project Board at the end of each management Stage of the project. This provides information about the project performance during the Stage and the project status at Stage end.

Exception

A situation where it can be forecast that there will be a deviation beyond the tolerance levels agreed between Project Manager and Project Board (or between Project Board and corporate or Programme management).

Exception Plan

A plan that follows an Exception Report. For a Stage Plan Exception, it covers the period from the present to the end of the current stage. If the Exception is at a project level, the Project Plan would be revised.

Exception Report

A report that describes an exception, provides an analysis and options for the way forward, and identifies a recommended option. It is given by the Project Manager to the Project Board.

Executive

The chairperson of the Project Board, representing the Customer.

Follow-on Action Recommendations

A report that can be used as input to the process of creating a Business Case/Project Mandate for any follow-on PRINCE project, and for recording any follow-on instructions covering incomplete products or outstanding issues. It also sets out proposals for Post-Project Review of the project's products.

Highlight Report

Report from the Project Manager to the Project Board on a time-driven frequency on Stage progress.

Issue Log

A log of all Project Issues and Requests for Change raised during the project, showing details of each issue, its evaluation, what decisions about it have been made and its current status.

Lessons Learned Report

A report that describes the lessons learned in undertaking the project and that includes statistics from the quality control of the project's management products. It is approved by the Project Board, and then held centrally for the benefit of future projects.

Off-Specification

Something that should be provided by the project, but currently is not (or is forecast not to be) provided. This might be a missing product or a product not meeting its specification.

Outcome

The result of a project. Useful term where the project result is not an easily definable 'product'.

Post-Project Review

One or more reviews held after project closure to determine if the expected benefits have been obtained.

PRINCE

A method that supports some selected aspects of project management. The acronym stands for **PR**ojects **IN** Controlled Environments.

PRINCE project

A project whose product(s) can be defined at its start sufficiently precisely so as to be measurable against predefined metrics and that is managed according to the PRINCE method.

Process

That which must be done to bring about a particular outcome, in terms of information to be gathered, decisions to be made, and results that must be achieved.

Producer

This role represents the creator(s) of a document that is the subject of a Quality Review. Typically, it will be filled by the person who has produced the product, or who has led the team responsible.

Product

Any input to or output from a project. PRINCE distinguishes between management products (which are produced as part of the management of the project), specialist products (which are those products that make up the final deliverable) and quality products (which are produced for or by the quality process). A product may itself be a collection of other products.

Product Breakdown Structure

A hierarchy of all the products to be produced during a plan.

Product Checklist

A list of the major products of a plan, plus key dates in their delivery.

Product Description

A description of a product's purpose, composition, derivation and quality criteria. It is produced at planning time, as soon as the need for the product is identified.

Product Flow Diagram

A diagram showing the sequence of production and interdependencies of the products listed in a Product Breakdown Structure.

Programme

A portfolio of projects selected, planned and managed in a co-ordinated way.

Project

A temporary organisation that is created for the purpose of delivering one or more business products according to a specified Business Case.

Project Assurance

The Project Board's responsibilities to assure itself that the project is being conducted correctly.

Project Brief

A description of what the project is to do; a refined and extended version of the Project Mandate, which has been agreed by the Project Board and which is input to Project Initiation.

Project Closure Notification

Advice from the Project Board to inform the host location that the project resources can be disbanded and support services, such as space, equipment and access, demobilised.

Project Closure Recommendation

Notification prepared by the Project Manager for the Project Board to send (when the board is satisfied that the project can be closed) to any organisation that has supplied facilities to the project.

Project Initiation Document (PID)

A logical document the purpose of which is to bring together the key information needed to start the project on a sound basis and to convey that information to all concerned with the project.

Project Issue

A term used to cover either a general issue or a Request for Change general issue request raised during a project. Project Issues can be about anything to do with the project. They cover questions, suggestions, Requests for Change and Off-Specifications.

Project Management

The planning, monitoring and control of all aspects of the project and the motivation of all those involved in it to achieve the project objectives on time and to the specified cost, quality and performance.

Project Management Team

A term to represent the entire management structure of Project Board, Project Manager, plus any Team Managers and project assurance roles.

Project Manager

The person given the authority and responsibility to manage the project on a day-to-day basis to deliver the required products within the constraints agreed with the Project Board.

Project Mandate

Information created externally to the project, which forms the terms of reference and is used to start up the PRINCE project.

Project Plan

A high-level plan showing the major products of the project, when they will be delivered, and at what cost. An Initial Project Plan is presented as part of the Project Initiation Document. This is revised as information on actual progress appears. It is a major control document for the Project Board to measure actual progress against expectations.

Project Quality Plan

A plan defining the key quality criteria and quality-control and audit processes to be applied to project management and technical work in the PRINCE project. It will be part of the text in the Project Initiation Document.

Project Records

A collection of all approved management, specialist and quality products and other material, which is necessary to provide an auditable record of the project.

NB. This does **not** include working files.

Project Start-up Notification

Advice to the host location that the project is about to start and requesting any required project support services.

Project Support Office

A group set up to provide certain administrative services to the Project Manager. Often the group provides its services to many projects in parallel.

Quality

The totality of features and characteristics of a product or service that bear on its ability to satisfy stated and implied needs.

Quality Management System

The complete set of quality standards, procedures and responsibilities for a site or organisation.

Quality Review

A Quality Review is an inspection with a specific structure, defined roles and procedure designed to ensure a document's completeness and adherence to standards. The participants are drawn from those with an interest in the document and those with the necessary skills to review its correctness. An example of the checks made by a Quality Review is 'does the document match the Quality Criteria in the Product Description?'

Quality System

See Quality Management System.

Request for Change

A means of proposing a modification to the current specification of a product. It is one type of Project Issue.

Reviewer

A person asked to review a product that is the subject of a Quality Review.

Risk Log

A document that provides identification, estimation, impact evaluation and countermeasures for all risks to the project. It should be created during the start-up of the project and developed during the life of the project.

Senior Supplier

The Project Board role that provides knowledge and experience of the main discipline(s) involved in the production of the project's deliverable(s).

Senior User

A member of the Project Board, accountable for ensuring that User needs are specified correctly and that the solution meets those needs.

Stage

A division of the project for management purposes. The Project Board approves the project to proceed one Stage at a time.

Supplier

The group or groups responsible for the supply of the project's products.

Team Manager

An optional role that may be employed by the Project Manager to manage the work of project team members.

Tolerance

The permissible deviation above and below a plan's estimate of time and cost without escalating the deviation to the next level of management. Separate tolerance figures should be given for time and cost.

User(s)

The person or group who will use the final deliverable(s) of the project.

Work Package

The set of information relevant to the creation of one or more products. It will contain the Product Description(s), details of any constraints on production such as time and cost, interfaces, and confirmation of the agreement between the Project Manager and the person or Team Manager who is to implement the Work Package that the work can be done within the constraints.

Appendices

A   PRINCE Product Description outlines

This Appendix contains Product Description outlines for the standard management and quality products. They lack some of the standard headings and content of a Product Description, such as format and quality method. These may vary from project to project, so no attempt has been made to define what a specific project will need.

Those wishing to turn these outlines into full Product Descriptions will need to add the missing information. This is a good opportunity to compare the given material with the circumstances of a specific project and tailor the text to be a more precise fit. A full description of the contents of a Product Description is given under Section 21.3.1.

A.1   Acceptance Criteria

A.1.1 Purpose

A definition in measurable terms of what must be done for the final product to be acceptable to the Customer and staff who will be affected.

A.1.2 Composition

This will vary according to the type of final product. Suggestions for criteria are:

- target dates
- major functions
- appearance
- personnel level required to use/operate the product
- performance levels
- capacity
- accuracy
- availability
- reliability (mean/maximum time to repair, mean time between failures)
- development cost
- running costs
- security
- ease of use
- timings.

A.1.3 Derivation

Acceptance Criteria are derived from:

- the Senior User
- Customer's quality expectations.

The criteria are either provided by programme management or developed during *Starting up a Project (SU)*.

A.1.4 Quality criteria

- All criteria are measurable.
- Each criterion is individually realistic.
- The criteria as a group are realistic, for example, high quality, early delivery and low cost may not go together.
- Acceptance Criteria form a complete list of criteria to define what will constitute a product acceptable to the Customer.

279

A.2 Business Case

A.2.1 Purpose

To document the justification for the undertaking of a project based on the estimated cost of development and the anticipated business benefits to be gained.

The Business Case is used to say why the forecast effort and time will be worth the expenditure. The ongoing viability of the project will be monitored by the Project Board against the Business Case.

A.2.2 Composition

- reasons
- benefits
- benefits realisation
- cost and timescale
- Investment Appraisal.

A.2.3 Derivation

Information for the Business Case is derived from:

- Project Mandate/Project Brief (reasons)
- Project Plan (costs)
- the Customer.

The existence of a provisional Business Case is checked during *Starting up a Project (SU)*. If the Project Mandate does not contain a Business Case, this would be created. The Business Case is finalised during *Initiating a Project (IP)*.

A.2.4 Quality criteria

- Can the benefits be justified?
- Do the cost and timescale match those in the Project Plan?
- Are the reasons for the project consistent with corporate or programme strategy?

A.3 Checkpoint Report

A.3.1 Purpose

To report, at a frequency defined in the Stage Plan, the status of work for each member of a team.

A.3.2 Composition

- date held
- period covered
- follow-ups from previous reports
- activities during the period
- products completed during the period
- quality work carried out during the period
- actual or potential problems or deviations from plan
- work planned for the next period
- products to be completed during the next period.

A.3.3 Derivation

- verbal reports from team members
- Stage or Team Plan
- previous Checkpoint (Checkpoints are held as part of *Executing a Work Package (MP2)*).

A.3.4 Quality criteria

- every item in the Stage or Team Plan for that period covered
- every team member working to an agreed schedule
- every team member's work covered
- an update on any unresolved problems from the previous report.

A.4 Communication Plan

A.4.1 Purpose

To define all parties with an interest in the project and the means and frequency of communication between them and the project.

A.4.2 Composition

- interested parties (for example, accounts staff, user forum, stakeholders, internal audit, quality assurance)
- information required
- information provider
- frequency of communication
- method of communication.

A.4.3 Derivation

- the Project Board
- the Project Brief
- the Project Quality Plan
- the Project Approach.

A.4.4 Quality criteria

Have all the listed derivation sources been checked?

Is there agreement from all interested parties about the content, frequency and method?

Has a common standard been considered?

Has time to carry out the identified communications been allowed for in Stage Plans?

A.5 End Project Report

A.5.1 Purpose

This report is the Project Manager's report to the Project Board (who may pass it on to corporate or programme management) on how well the project has performed against its Project Initiation Document, including the original planned cost, schedule and tolerances, the revised Business Case and final version of the Project Plan.

A.5.2 Composition

- achievement of the project's objectives
- performance against the planned target time and cost
- the effect on the original Project Plan and Business Case of any changes that were approved
- final statistics on change issues received during the project
- the total impact of approved changes
- statistics for all quality work carried out.
- Post-Project Review date and plan.

A.5.3 Derivation

The End Project Report is derived from:

- updated Project Plan
- Project Initiation Document
- Issue Log.

The End Project Report is produced during *Closing a Project (CP)*.

A.5.4 Quality criteria

- Does the report describe the impact of the approved changes on the Project Initiation Document?
- Does the report cover all the benefits that can be assessed at this time?
- Does the quality work done during the project meet the quality expectations of the Customer?

A.6   End Stage Report

A.6.1 Purpose

The purpose of the End Stage Report is to give a summary of progress to date, the overall project situation, and sufficient information to ask for a Project Board decision on what to do next with the project.

The Project Board uses the information in the End Stage Report to decide what action to take with the project; approve the next Stage, ask for a revised next Stage Plan, amend the project scope, or stop the project.

A.6.2 Composition

- current Stage Plan with all the actuals
- Project Plan outlook
- Business Case review
- risk review
- Project Issue situation
- quality statistics
- Project Manager's report on any events that affected Stage performance.

A.6.3 Derivation

Information for the report is obtained from:

- the Stage Plan and actuals
- the next Stage Plan (if appropriate)
- the updated Project Plan
- the Risk Log
- the embryo Lessons Learned Report
- data from the Quality Log
- completed Work Package data.

The End Stage Report is an output from *Managing Stage Boundaries (SB)*.

A.6.4 Quality criteria

- Does the report clearly show Stage performance against the plan?
- Are any abnormal situations described, together with their impact?
- Do any appointed Project Assurance roles disagree with the report?

A.7   Exception Report

A.7.1 Purpose

An Exception Report is produced when costs and/or timescales for an approved Stage Plan are forecast to exceed the tolerance levels set. It is sent by the Project Manager in order to appraise the Project Board of the adverse situation.

An Exception Report will normally result in the Project Board asking the Project Manager to produce an Exception Plan.

A.7.2 Composition

- a description of the cause of a deviation from the Stage Plan
- consequences of the deviation
- the available options
- the effect of each option on the Business Case, risks, project and Stage tolerances
- the Project Manager's recommendations.

A.7.3 Derivation

The information for an Exception Report may come from:

- current Stage Plan and actuals
- Issue Log
- Risk Log
- Checkpoints
- Project Board advice of an external event that affects the project.

An Exception Report is output from *Escalating Project Issues (CS8)*.

A.7.4 Quality criteria

- The current Stage Plan must accurately show the status of budget and schedule.
- The reason(s) for the deviation must be stated.
- The Exception Plan must have both technical and resource plans.

A.8 Follow-on Action Recommendations

A.8.1 Purpose

To pass details of unfinished work or potential product modifications to the group charged with future support of the final product in its operational life.

A.8.2 Composition

- date of the recommendations

- Requests for Change that were considered to have merit but were not implemented during the project

- Off-Specifications recording missing products or products that do not meet the original requirements

- risks identified during the project, which may affect the product in its operational life

- any identified hand-over or training needs

- any other activities needed to take the product to the next stage of its life.

A.8.3 Derivation

- Issue Log

- Risk Log.

A.8.4 Quality criteria

- There must be an entry for every open Project Issue.

- The relevant Project Issues should have been closed with an entry to signify that they have been transferred to these recommendations.

- Any available useful documentation or evidence should accompany the recommendations.

A.9   Highlight Report

A.9.1 Purpose

To provide the Project Board with a summary of the Stage status at intervals defined by them.

The Project Board uses the report to monitor stage and project progress. The Project Manager also uses it to advise the Project Board of any potential problems or areas where the Project Board could help.

A.9.2 Composition

- date
- period covered
- budget status
- schedule status
- products completed during the period
- actual or potential problems
- products to be completed during the next period
- Project Issue status
- budget and schedule impact of the changes.

A.9.3 Derivation

Information for the Highlight Reports is derived from:

- Checkpoints
- Issue Log
- Stage Plan
- Risk Log.

Highlight Reports are output from *Reporting Highlights (CS6)*.

A.9.4 Quality criteria

- accurate reflection of Checkpoint information
- accurate summary of the Issue Log
- accurate summary of Plan status
- highlights any potential problem areas.

A.10 Issue Log

A.10.1 Purpose

The purpose of the Issue Log is to:

- allocate a unique number to each Project Issue
- record the type of Project Issue
- be a summary of the Project Issues, their analysis and status.

A.10.2 Composition

- Project Issue number
- Project Issue type (Request for Change, Off-Specification, or a general issue such as a question or a statement of concern)
- author
- date identified
- date of last update
- description
- status.

A.10.3 Derivation

Project Issues may be raised by anyone associated with the project at any time.

A.10.4 Quality criteria

- Does the status indicate whether action has been taken?
- Are the Project Issues uniquely identified, including to which product they refer?
- Is access to the Issue Log controlled?
- Is the Issue Log kept in a safe place?

A.11 Lessons Learned Report

A.11.1 Purpose

The purpose of the Lessons Learned Report is to pass on any lessons that can be usefully applied to other projects.

The data in the report should be used by a corporate group, such as quality assurance, who are responsible for the Quality Management System, in order to refine, change and improve the standards. Statistics on how much effort was needed for products can help improve future estimating.

A.11.2 Composition

What management and quality processes:

- went well
- went badly
- were lacking.

A description of any abnormal events causing deviations.

An assessment of technical methods and tools used.

An analysis of Project Issues and their results.

Recommendations for future enhancement or modification of the project management method.

Useful measurements on how much effort was required to create the various products.

Statistics on how effective Quality Reviews and other tests were in error trapping (for example, how many errors were found after products had passed a Quality Review or test).

A.11.3 Derivation

Information for the report is derived from:

- observation and experience of the processes
- the Quality Log
- completed Work Packages
- Stage Plans with actuals.

The Lessons Learned Report is updated at the end of each Stage as part of *Reporting Stage End (SB5)* and completed in *Evaluating a Project (CP3)*.

A.11.4 Quality criteria

- Every management control has been examined.
- Input to the report is being done, minimally, at the end of each stage.
- Every specialist technique is included.
- Statistics of the success of Quality Reviews and other types of test used are included.
- Details of the effort taken for each product are given.

A.12 Off-Specification

A.12.1 Purpose

To document any situation where a product is failing, or is forecast to fail, to meet its specification.

A.12.2 Composition

- date
- Issue Log number
- class
- status
- description of the fault
- impact of the fault
- priority assessment
- decision
- allocation details, if applicable
- date allocated
- date completed.

A.12.3 Derivation

An Off-Specification can be raised by anyone associated with the project at any time. It would be gathered in as part of *Capturing Project Issues (CS3)*. The Project Manager may also decide that a Project Issue is an Off-Specification during *Examining Project Issues (CS4)*.

A.12.4 Quality criteria

- Logged in the Issue Log.
- Accurate description of the problem.

A.13 Post-Project Review

A.13.1 Purpose

The purpose of the Post-Project Review is to find out:

- whether the expected benefits of the product have been realised

- whether the product has caused any problems in use.

Each expected benefit is assessed for the level of its achievement so far, or any additional time needed for the benefit to materialise.

Use of the product may have brought unexpected side effects, either beneficial or adverse. These are documented with explanations of why they were not foreseen.

Recommendations are made to realise or improve benefits, or counter problems.

A.13.2 Composition

- achievement of expected benefits

- unexpected benefits

- unexpected problems

- User reaction.

A.13.3 Derivation

The expected benefits should have been defined in the Project Brief and expanded in the Project Initiation Document.

General comments should be obtained about how the Users feel about the product. The type of observation will depend on the type of product produced by the project, but examples might be its ease of use, performance, reliability, the contribution it makes to their work, and its suitability for the work environment.

The Post-Project Review is planned as part of *Identifying Follow-on Actions (CP2)*, but the product itself is produced after the project has finished.

A.13.4 Quality criteria

Covers all benefits mentioned in the Project Brief and Business Case.

Describes each achievement in a tangible, measurable form.

Makes recommendations in any case where a benefit is not being fully met, a problem has been identified, or a potential extra benefit could be obtained.

Is conducted as soon as the benefits and problems can be measured.

A.14 Product Checklist

A.14.1 Purpose

To list the products to be produced within a Stage Plan, together with key status dates.

Used by the Project Board to monitor progress.

A.14.2 Composition

Plan identification.

Product names (and reference numbers if appropriate).

Planned and actual dates for:

- draft ready
- quality check
- approval.

A.14.3 Derivation

Extracted from the Stage Plan. Produced as an output from *Completing a Plan (PL7)*.

A.14.4 Quality criteria

Do the details and dates match those in the Stage Plan?

A.15 Project Approach

A.15.1 Purpose

To define the type of solution to be developed by the project and/or the method of delivering that solution. It should also identify any environment into which the solution must fit.

A.15.2 Composition

- Description of approach
- Type of solution, for example:
  - bespoke
  - contracted out
  - current product modified
  - design from scratch
  - use company staff
  - hire in contract staff
  - buy a ready-made solution
- Reasons for the approach (for example, part of programme approach).

A.15.3 Derivation

- Project Brief
- Design Authority (if part of a Programme)
- marketplace – that is, what is available.

A.15.4 Quality criteria

It must conform to the strategy that relates to the product's operational environment.

It must be achievable within all known time and cost constraints for the project.

It must be achievable with known technology.

A.16 Project Brief

A.16.1 Purpose

To provide a full and firm foundation for the initiation of the project.

The contents are extended and refined into the Project Initiation Document, which is the working document for managing and directing the project.

The Project Brief is a key document in its own right. It is the basis of the Project Initiation Document, which gives the direction and scope of the project and forms the 'contract' between the Project Management Team and corporate or programme management. Any significant change to the material contained in the Project Brief will thus need to be referred to corporate or programme management.

A.16.2 Composition

The following is a suggested list of contents, which should be tailored to the requirements and environment of each project.

- Background
- Project Definition, explaining what the project needs to achieve. It will contain:
  - project objectives
  - project scope
  - outline project deliverables and/or desired outcomes
  - any exclusions
  - constraints
  - interfaces
- Outline Business Case
  - a description of how this project supports business strategy, plans or programmes
  - the reason for selection of this solution
- Customer's quality expectations
- Acceptance Criteria
- Any known risks.

If earlier work has been done, the Project Brief may refer to the document(s) containing useful information, such as:

- Outline Project Plan,

rather than include copies of them.

A.16.3 Derivation

The Project Brief is developed from the Project Mandate supplied at the start of the project, produced by *Starting up a Project (SU)*, and accepted via *Authorising Initiation (DP1)*.

If the project is part of a Programme, the Programme should provide the Project Brief. In such circumstances it will not have to be derived from a Project Mandate.

If no Project Mandate is provided, the Project Manager has to generate the Project Brief from scratch in discussions with the Customer and Users.

A.16.4 Quality criteria

- Does the Project Brief accurately reflect the Project Mandate?
- Does it form a firm basis on which to initiate a project (*Initiating a Project (IP)*)?
- Does it indicate how the Customer will assess the acceptability of the finished product(s)?

A.17 Project Initiation Document

A.17.1 Purpose

To define the project, to form the basis for its management and the assessment of overall success.

There are two primary uses of the document:

- to ensure that the project has a sound basis before asking the Project Board to make any major commitment to the project

- to act as a base document against which the Project Board and Project Manager can assess progress, change management issues, and ongoing viability questions.

A.17.2 Composition

The following are the base elements of information needed to correctly direct and manage a project. They cover the following fundamental questions about the project:

- **what** a project is aiming to achieve

- **why** it is important to achieve it

- **who** is going to be involved in managing the process and what are their responsibilities

- **how** and **when** it is all going to happen.

The information will be held in various ways, and the following contents should not be read as a list of contents for one document but should rather be seen as the information needed in order to make the initiation decisions.

- **Background,** explaining the context of the project, and how we have arrived at the current position of requiring a project.

- **Project Definition**, explaining what the project needs to achieve. Under this heading will be:
  - project objectives
  - defined method of approach
  - project scope
  - project deliverables and/or desired outcomes
  - exclusions
  - constraints
  - interfaces

- **Assumptions**

- **Initial Business Case,** explaining why the project is being undertaken

- **Project Organisation Structure,** explaining who will be on the Project Management Team

- **Communication Plan** (see the separate Communication Plan Product outline)

- **Project Quality Plan**
  (See the separate Project Quality Plan Product outline)

- **Initial Project Plan**, explaining how and when the activities of the project will occur (for details of the Project Plan content, see the separate Product outline)

- **Project Controls,** laying down how control is to be exercised within the project, and the reporting and monitoring mechanisms that will support this

- **Exception process**

- **Initial Risk Log,** documenting the results of the risk analysis and risk management activities

- **Contingency Plans,** explaining how it is intended to deal with the consequences of any risks that materialise

- **Project Filing Structure,** laying down how the various elements of information and deliverables produced by the project are to be filed and retrieved.

A.17.3 Derivation

- Supplier's project management standards

- Customer's specified control requirements

- Much of the information should come from the Project Mandate, enhanced in the Project Brief. The Project Initiation Document will be completed during the Initiation Stage. Parts of it, such as the Project Plan and Business Case, may be updated and refined by each pass through *Managing Stage Boundaries (SB)* and will finally be archived as part of *Closing a Project (CP)*.

A.17.4 Quality criteria

- Does the document correctly represent the project?

- Does it show a viable, achievable project that is in line with corporate strategy, or overall programme needs?

- Is the project organisation structure complete, with names and titles?

- Have all the roles been considered?

- Does it clearly show a control, reporting and direction regime that is implementable, and appropriate to the scale, business risk and business importance of the project?

- Is the project organisation structure backed up by agreed and signed job definitions?

- Are the relationships and lines of authority clear?

- Does the project organisation structure need to say to whom the Project Board reports?

- Do the controls cover the needs of the Project Board, Project Manager and Team Managers?

- Do the controls satisfy any delegated assurance requirements?

- Is it clear who will administer each control?

A.18 Project Issue

A.18.1 Purpose

A generic term for any matter that has to be brought to the attention of the project, and requires an answer. After receiving a unique reference number, Project Issues are evaluated in terms of impact on the product, effort and cost. The Project Manager may make a decision on what action to take, or the Project Issue may be referred to the Project Board. A Project Issue may be a:

- Request for Change
- Off-Specification
- question
- statement of concern.

A.18.2 Composition

- author
- date
- Project Issue number
- description of the Project Issue
- priority
- impact analysis
- decision
- signature of decision-maker(s)
- date of decision.

A.18.3 Derivation

Anyone may submit a Project Issue. Typical sources are Users and specialists working on the project. *Capturing Project Issues (CS3)* deals with collating Project Issues. They are then examined during *Examining Project Issues (CS4)*.

A.18.4 Quality criteria

- Is the problem/requirement clear?
- Have all the implications been thought out?
- Has the Project Issue been correctly logged?

A.19 Project Mandate

A.19.1 Purpose

The information in the Mandate is used to trigger *Starting up a Project (SU)*. It should contain sufficient information to identify at least the prospective Executive of the Project Board and indicate the subject matter of the project.

It will be used to create the Project Brief.

A.19.2 Composition

The actual composition of a Project Mandate will vary according to the type and size of project and also the environment in which the mandate is generated. The project may be a completely new piece of work that has just arisen, it may be the outcome of an earlier investigation, or it may be part of a larger programme.

The following list contains suggested contents, which should be tailored to suit the specific project.

- authority responsible
- background
- project objectives
- scope
- constraints
- interfaces
- quality expectations
- outline Business Case (reasons)
- reference to any associated documents or products
- an indication of who are to be the project Executive and Project Manager
- the Customer(s), User(s) and any other known interested parties.

If the Project Mandate is based on earlier work, there may be other useful information such as an estimate of the project size and duration and a view of the risks faced by the project.

A.19.3 Derivation

A Project Mandate may come from anywhere, but it should come from a level of management that can authorise the cost and resource usage. It is input to *Starting up a Project (SU)*.

A.19.4 Quality criteria

- Is the level of authority commensurate with the anticipated size, risk and cost of the project?
- Is there sufficient detail to allow the appointment of an appropriate Executive and Project Manager?
- Are all the known interested parties identified?
- Does the mandate describe what is required?

A.20 Project Plan

A.20.1 Purpose

The Project Plan is a mandatory plan that provides a statement of how and when a project's objectives are to be achieved, by showing the major products, activities and resources required on the project.

It provides the Business Case with planned project costs, and it identifies the management stages and other major control points.

It is used by the Project Board as a Baseline against which to monitor project progress and cost Stage by Stage.

A.20.2 Composition

This product forms part of the Project Initiation Document and will contain the following.

- Plan description, giving a brief description of what the plan covers

- Project prerequisites, containing any fundamental aspects that must be in place at the start of the project and that must remain in place for the project to succeed

- External dependencies

- Planning assumptions

- Project Plan, covering:
    - project-level Gantt or bar chart with identified management stages
    - project-level Product Breakdown Structure
    - project-level Product Flow Diagrams
    - project-level Product Descriptions
    - project-level activity network
    - project financial budget
    - project-level table of resource requirements
    - requested/assigned specific resources.

A.20.3 Derivation

- Refined from the outline Project Plan in the Project Brief during *Planning a Project (IP2)*.

- Modified during *Updating a Project Plan (SB2)*.

A.20.4 Quality criteria

- Is the plan achievable?

- Does it support the rest of the Project Initiation Document?

A.21 Project Quality Plan

A.21.1 Purpose

The Project Quality Plan is part of the Project Initiation Document.

The purpose is to define how the Supplier intends to deliver products that meet the Customer's quality expectations and the Supplier's quality standards.

A.21.2 Composition

- quality responsibilities
- reference to any standards that need to be met
- key product quality criteria
- the quality-control and audit processes to be applied to project management
- quality-control and audit process requirements for specialist work
- change management procedures
- Configuration Management plan (see *Configuration Management* Chapter 10, for an explanation of the term)
- any tools to be used to ensure quality.

A.21.3 Derivation

The Project Quality Plan is derived from:

- Customer's quality expectations
- corporate or programme Quality Management System (QMS).

It is produced as an output from *Planning Quality (IP1)*.

A.21.4 Quality criteria

- Does the plan clearly define ways in which the Customer's quality expectations will be met?
- Are the defined ways sufficient to achieve the required quality?
- Are responsibilities for quality defined up to a level that is independent of the project and Project Manager?
- Does the plan conform to the corporate quality policy?

A.22 Quality Log

A.22.1 Purpose

- to issue a unique reference for each quality check planned
- to act as a pointer to the quality check documentation for a product
- to act as a summary of the number and type of quality checks held.

The log summarises all the quality checks that are planned/have taken place, and provides information for the End Stage Reports and End Project Reports as well as the Lessons Learned Report.

A.22.2 Composition

For each entry in the log, the following should be recorded:

- reference number
- product
- method of quality checking
- staff responsible, name, role
- planned date
- actual date
- result
- number of action items
- target sign-off date
- actual sign-off date.

A.22.3 Derivation

The first entries are made when a quality check or test is entered on a Stage Plan. The remaining information comes from the actual performance of the check. The sign-off date is when all corrective action items have been signed off.

An initial, blank Quality Log is created during *Setting up Project Files (IP5)*.

A.22.4 Quality criteria

- Is there a procedure in place that will ensure that every quality check is entered on the log?
- Has responsibility for the log been allocated?

A.23 Request for Change

A.23.1 Purpose

To request a modification to a product or an acceptance criterion as currently specified.

A.23.2 Composition

- date
- Issue Log number
- class
- status
- description of the proposed change
- impact of the change
- priority assessment
- decision
- allocation details, if applicable
- date allocated
- date completed.

A.23.3 Derivation

A Request for Change can be derived by anyone connected with the project. A Request for Change can be submitted as such and gathered in by *Capturing Project Issues (CS3)*, or a Project Issue can be defined as a Request for Change by the Project Manager as part of *Examining Project Issues (CS4)*.

A.23.4 Quality criteria

- source clearly identified
- logged in the Issue Log
- accurate description of the requested change
- benefit of making the change clearly expressed and, where possible, in measurable terms.

A.24 Risk Log

A.24.1 Purpose

The purpose of the Risk Log is to:

- allocate a unique number to each risk
- record the type of risk
- be a summary of the risks, their analysis and status.

A.24.2 Composition

- risk number allocated
- risk type (business, project, Stage)
- author
- date identified
- date of last update
- description
- likelihood of occurrence
- severity of effect
- countermeasure(s)
- owner
- status.

A.24.3 Derivation

Business risks may have been identified in the Project Brief and should be sought during Project Initiation. There should be a check for any new business risks every time the Risk Log is reviewed, minimally at each End Stage Assessment. The Project Board has the responsibility to constantly check external events for business risks.

Project risks are sought during Project Initiation when the Project Plan is being created. Some project risks may have been identified in work that led up to the Project Mandate. Project risks should be reviewed every time the Risk Log is reviewed, minimally at each End Stage Assessment.

Risks to a Stage Plan should be examined as part of the production of that plan. They should be reviewed each time that the Stage Plan is updated.

The Risk Log is created during *Preparing a Project Brief (SU4)*.

A.24.4 Quality criteria

- Does the status indicate whether action has been taken or is in a contingency plan?
- Are the risks uniquely identified, including to which project they refer?
- Is access to the Risk Log controlled?
- Is the Risk Log kept in a safe place?
- Are activities to review the Risk Log in the Stage Plans?

A.25 Stage Plan (or Exception Plan)

A.25.1 Purpose

- used as the basis for project management control throughout the Stage

- identifies all the products that the Stage must produce

- provides a statement of how and when a Stage's objectives are to be achieved, by showing the deliverables, activities and resources required

- identifies the Stage's control and reporting points and frequencies

- provides a Baseline against which Stage progress will be measured

- records the Stage tolerances

- specifies the quality controls for the stage and identifies the resources needed for them.

A.25.2 Composition

This product will contain the following:

- Plan description, covering:
  - a brief description of what the plan covers
  - a brief description of the planned approach

- Quality Plan
  - the quality control methods to be used for each major product
  - the resources to be used in each quality test or check

- Plan prerequisites
  containing any fundamental aspects which must be in place at the start of the stage, and which must remain in place for the plan to succeed

- External dependencies

- Tolerances (time and budget)

- How will the plan be monitored and controlled?

- Reporting

- Planning assumptions

- Graphical plan, covering:
  - diagram showing identified resources, activities, start and end dates (usually a Gantt or bar chart)
  - Product Breakdown Structure
  - Product Flow Diagram
  - activity network
  - financial budget
  - table of resource requirements
  - risk assessment.

- Product Descriptions for the major products.

An Exception Plan or any other detailed Plan will have the same format as a Stage Plan.

A.25.3 Derivation

- refined from the Project Plan during *Planning a Stage (SB1)*

- based on resource availability

- updated during *Assessing Progress (CS2)*

- may be modified during *Reviewing Stage Status (SB5)* and *Taking Corrective Action (CS7)*

A.25.4 Quality criteria

- Is the plan achievable?

- Do all Team Managers involved in the plan's operation believe that their portion is achievable?

- Does the Stage Plan support the Project Plan?

- Does it take into account any constraints of time, resources and budget?

- Has it been taken down to the level of detail necessary to ensure that any deviations will be recognised in time to react appropriately – for example, within the S tage tolerances, and within the activity 'floats'?

- Has the Stage Plan been developed according to the planning standard?

- Does the Stage Plan contain activities and resource effort to review the Issue Log?

A.26 Work Package

A.26.1 Purpose

A Work Package is a set of information about one or more required products collated by the Project Manager to formally pass responsibility for work or delivery to a Team Manager or team member.

A.26.2 Composition

This product will vary in content – and, indeed, in degree of formality – depending on circumstances.

Where the work is being conducted by a team working directly under the Project Manager, the Work Package may be a verbal instruction, although there are good reasons for putting it in writing, such as avoidance of misunderstanding and providing a link to performance assessment. Where the work is being carried out by a Supplier under a contract and the Project Manager is part of the Customer organisation, there is a need for a formal written instruction in line with standards laid down in that contract.

Although the content may vary greatly according to the relationship between the Project Manager and the recipient of the Work Package, it should cover:

- date
- team or person authorised
- Work Package description
- Product Description(s)
- techniques/processes/procedures to be used
- interfaces to be satisfied by the work
- interfaces to be maintained during the work
- quality checking method to be used
- Stage Plan extract
- joint agreement on effort, cost, start and end dates
- sign-off requirements
- work return arrangements
- how completion is to be advised
- any constraints to be observed
- independent quality-checking arrangements
- reporting arrangements.

There should be space on the Work Package to record its authorisation and acceptance of the return of the completed Work Package. This can be enhanced to include an assessment of the work and go towards performance appraisal.

A.26.3 Derivation

There could be many Work Packages authorised during each Stage of a project. A Work Package is created by the Project Manager from the Stage Plan. *Authorising Work Package (CS1)* covers the issue of Work Packages. After the initial start of a Stage, subsequent Work Packages will be triggered after *Reviewing Stage Status (CS5)*. Changes to the Stage Plan brought about when performing *Taking Corrective Action (CS7)* may also trigger the authorisation of new Work Packages.

A.26.4 Quality criteria

- Is the required Work Package clearly defined and understood by the assigned resource?

- Is there a Product Description for the required product(s), with clearly identified and acceptable quality criteria?

- Does the Product Description match up with the other Work Package documentation?

- Are standards for the work agreed?

- Are the defined standards in line with those applied to similar products?

- Have all necessary interfaces been defined?

- Do the reporting arrangements include the provision for exception reporting?

- Is there agreement between the Project Manager and the recipient on exactly what is to be done?

- Is there agreement on the constraints, including effort, cost and targets?

- Are the dates and effort in line with those shown in the Stage Plan?

- Are reporting arrangements defined?

- Is any requirement for independent attendance at, and participation in, quality checking defined?

B   PRINCE and ISO 9001:1994

ISO 9001 is the international standard for quality systems, issued under the authority of the International Organisation for Standardisation (ISO). It applies to quality assurance in design/development, production, installation and servicing.

There are equivalent British and European quality standards that are currently identical in wording to the international standard, although this may change in the future. The equivalence is:

International	British	European
ISO 9001	BS EN ISO 9001	EN ISO 9001
ISO 9002	BS EN ISO 9002	EN ISO 9002
ISO 9003	BS EN ISO 9003	EN ISO 9003

Quality applies to two areas of production: the product itself and the processes that give rise to the product. The international standards vocabulary (ISO 8402) defines quality as:

The totality of features and characteristics of a product or service which bear on its ability to satisfy stated or implied needs.

Widely used informal interpretations of this definition are:

- **'quality of a product'** is its suitability for the purpose for which it is intended. Products include both services and tangible items

- **'quality of a process'** is its ability to deliver its products in a trouble-free way.

The quality standard ISO 9001 can be used by a company when:

- setting up a quality assurance function

- examining the quality assurance system of a Supplier.

PRINCE is not – and was not designed to be – a comprehensive quality system. However, three of its constituents contribute to a significant part of such a system. These are:

- **quality controls,** which are clearly-defined technical and management procedures

- **Product-based planning** and the **Product Descriptions,** which define the product quality criteria

- the **PRINCE organisation**.

ISO 9001 prescribes what should be done within a quality system, but does not say how it should be done. For a quality system to conform to ISO 9001, it must satisfy each of the 20 clauses and associated sub-clauses of the standard relevant to the environment in which the quality system operates.

This Appendix looks at the requirements of the quality standard. Each part of ISO 9001 is briefly defined, followed by how PRINCE can contribute to meeting each requirement. The requirements are presented with the same numbering system and in the same order as they appear in ISO 9001.

B.1   Management responsibility (4.1)

B.1.1   Quality policy

Requirement

The Supplier's management with executive responsibility shall define and document its policy with respect to quality.

PRINCE approach

The corporate or programme quality policy should include the use of PRINCE as the standard project management method.

B.1.2   Organisation

Responsibility and authority

Requirement

The responsibility, authority and interrelation of all personnel who manage, perform and verify work affecting quality must be defined and documented – particularly, personnel who need the organisational freedom and authority to:

- initiate action to prevent product, process and quality system non-conformity

- identify and record product, process and quality system problems

- initiate, recommend or provide solutions

- verify the implementation of solutions

- control further processing, delivery or installation of a non-conforming product until the satisfactory condition has been corrected.

PRINCE approach

This would normally be a responsibility of a quality assurance function that sits above all projects.

Within a project, this requirement is fully satisfied. The organisation roles contain responsibilities/authority for quality. Part of *Starting up a Project (SU)* is the allocation of these roles to individuals.

The Quality Review technique clearly defines the responsibilities listed above for a quality check of an individual product.

Resources

Requirement

The Supplier shall identify resource requirements and provide adequate resources, including the assignment of trained personnel, for management, performance or work and verification activities, including quality audits.

PRINCE approach

Within the context of projects, the verification aspect of this requirement is addressed. The PRINCE Stage Quality Plan contains details of each quality check, as well as who will attend and perform which role.

Any specific responsibilities within a project for corrective actions would be defined in the job descriptions.

Management representative

Requirement

The Supplier shall appoint a management representative, who shall ensure that the requirements of the standard are implemented and maintained.

PRINCE approach

This is intended for a higher level than individual project control. Within a project, this responsibility can be allocated to one of the Project Board roles.

Management Review

Requirement

There should be a regular review of the Quality System to ensure its continuing suitability and effectiveness.

PRINCE approach

The update of the Lessons Learned Report throughout the project goes some way to meeting the requirement of a regular review, but it should really be a corporate-wide quality assurance function to fully meet the requirement.

The logging and filing of quality checking documentation provides the records for Customer inspection. The assurance responsibilities of the Project Board can be tailored to ensure that any review of the quality records is allocated to one or more Customer representatives.

B.2 Quality System (4.2)

B.2.1 Requirement

The Supplier shall establish and maintain a documented Quality System as a means of ensuring that products conform to specified requirements. This shall include:

- the preparation of documented Quality System procedures
- the effective implementation of the quality system and its documented procedures
- documented quality planning activities.

A Supplier should be able to demonstrate compliance with the Quality System.

B.2.2 PRINCE approach

This requirement is not addressed in full. PRINCE presents a framework of procedures and a model organisation structure that enforces adherence to procedures. The adoption, therefore, of PRINCE contributes a major part of the Quality System.

As part of the quality organisation there may be a separate, independent quality assurance function that oversees implementation of the Quality System by projects.

The Project Initiation Document contains the Project Quality Plan of the project. The Project Mandate and Project Brief look for a statement of the Customer's quality expectations.

The project organisation defines the quality responsibilities. In particular, the Project Board roles contain responsibilities for assurance. A Project Board may wish to delegate certain of their assurance responsibilities to a permanent quality assurance group when the roles are being converted into job descriptions.

Inclusion of quality activities in Stage Plans demonstrates that procedures are being followed. Planning steps recommend that the assurance functions are involved in identifying quality checks and participants at Stage planning time. This allows demonstration of compliance with the Quality System.

The Quality Review output demonstrates that services conform to specification.

The Quality Log and filing of the quality check documents provides an audit trail of the quality work carried out, again demonstrating compliance.

B.3 Contract review (4.3)

B.3.1 Requirement

The Supplier shall establish and maintain documented procedures for contract review. Each tender, order or contract shall be reviewed by the Supplier to ensure that:

- the requirements are adequately defined and documented
- any differences between the contract or order requirements and those in the tender are resolved
- the Supplier is capable of meeting the contract or order requirements.

A procedure for control of amendments to contract should be defined and documented, and records of contract reviews should be maintained.

B.3.2 PRINCE approach

This requirement is partially satisfied. Where there is no formal contract, the acceptance of the Project Initiation Document by the Project Board is a confirmation of the Supplier's ability to carry out the Customer's requirements.

The monitoring and review of changing requirements is controlled in PRINCE by the Project Issue procedure. In the case of exceptions or deviations, the Project Board has the authority to either commit further resources to maintain the Supplier's ability to deliver or reduce the scope of the project. The involvement of the Senior User and anyone to whom any of that role's assurance responsibilities are delegated ensures liaison with the purchaser's (Customer's) organisation.

B.4 Design control (4.4)

B.4.1 General

Requirement

The Supplier shall establish and maintain documented procedures to control and verify the design of the product in order to ensure that the specified requirements are met.

PRINCE approach

All the requirements of this clause are addressed in the following sub-paragraphs.

B.4.2 Design and development planning

Requirement

The Supplier shall prepare plans for each design and development activity that define responsibility for their implementation. These activities shall be assigned to qualified personnel with adequate resources. Plans shall be updated as the design evolves.

PRINCE approach

This requirement is mostly satisfied. PRINCE defines the management organisation and responsibilities in the Project Initiation Document.

Each Work Package authorised by the Project Manager identifies the responsibility for that work. Each Stage and Team Plan identifies the responsibility for each activity.

The Stage or Team Plans show the assignment of personnel to activities. They also specify the necessary equipment and facilities.

PRINCE procedures and role descriptions would require addition to embrace relevant staff qualifications.

The updating of plans is carried out on a regular basis in the process *Controlling a Stage (CS)* and also occurs during *Managing Stage Boundaries (SB)*.

B.4.3 Organisational and technical interfaces

Requirement

Organisational and technical interfaces between different groups that input into the design process shall be defined and the necessary information documented, transmitted and regularly reviewed.

PRINCE approach

This requirement is fully satisfied. The interfaces between groups and the job descriptions for the various PRINCE roles are defined and documented in the Project Initiation Document.

The interfaces are reviewed at the following meetings:

- Project Initiation
- Stage Assessments
- Project Closure.

B.4.4 Design input

Requirement

Design input requirements relating to the product, including applicable statutory and regulatory requirements, shall be identified, documented and reviewed by the Supplier for adequacy. Incomplete, ambiguous or conflicting requirements shall be resolved with those responsible for imposing these requirements.

PRINCE approach

This requirement is fully satisfied. The Product Description for design input requirements would state its content, form and quality criteria. Any problems would be raised at its Quality Review, which representatives of the Customer and Supplier would attend. Any changes to the design requirements document would be controlled under change control and Configuration Management.

B.4.5 Design output

Requirement

Design output shall be documented and expressed in terms that can be verified and validated against input requirements. Design output shall:

- meet the design input requirements
- contain or make reference to acceptance criteria
- identify those characteristics of the design that are crucial to the safe and proper functioning of the product.

PRINCE approach

This requirement is partially satisfied.

Quality criteria within Product Descriptions allow the:

- definition of the need for products to conform to legislative requirements and meet the design requirements

- inclusion of acceptance criteria to meet the above list.

B.4.6 Design review

Requirement

At appropriate stages of design, formal documented reviews of the design results shall be planned and conducted. Records of the reviews shall be maintained.

PRINCE approach

The requirement is satisfied. The Quality Review technique allows the assembly of the appropriate personnel to carry out a formal review to check that the design output meets the requirements and to document the findings.

B.4.7 Design verification

Requirement

At appropriate stages of design, verification shall be performed to ensure that the output meets the design stage input requirement by means of appropriate control measures.

PRINCE approach

This requirement is satisfied as part of the Quality Review procedures; unless the design passes its quality check, it is not accepted under configuration control.

B.4.8 Design validation

Requirement

Design validation shall be performed to ensure that products conform to defined User needs and/or requirements. It follows successful design verification and is normally performed under defined operating conditions.

PRINCE approach

This requirement is fully satisfied. The assurance responsibilities of the Senior User ensure that the validation requirements for products are defined and met. In Project Closure, the Project Manager has to provide confirmation of the acceptance of the product by the User, with evidence of successful validation.

B.4.9 Design changes

Requirement

All design changes and notifications shall be identified, documented, reviewed and approved by authorised personnel before their implementation.

PRINCE approach

This requirement is fully satisfied. The Project Issue and Configuration Management procedures ensure that all the design documents are subject to change control, and thus any changes are subject to review and approval.

B.5   Document and data control (4.5)

B.5.1 Requirement

The Supplier shall establish and maintain procedures to control all documents and data that relate to the requirements of ISO 9001. The documents and data shall be reviewed and approved for adequacy by authorised personnel prior to issue. The current revision status of documents shall be established to preclude the use of invalid and/or obsolete documents. Versions of documents are to be available where needed and obsolete copies promptly withdrawn. Changes to documents shall be reviewed by the same functions that performed the original review and approval, unless specifically designated otherwise.

B.5.2 PRINCE approach

This requirement is fully satisfied by product control within the project. The Project Issue technique covers the review of any changes, but product control or Configuration Management procedures are required to handle the issue of copies and the withdrawal of obsolete ones.

A Configuration Management method is needed to meet this quality requirement. Because there are so many automated and manual implementations of Configuration Management, this is regarded as being outside the scope of the project management method. The Configuration Management method to be used is defined in the Project Initiation Document.

B.6   Purchasing (4.6)

B.6.1 Requirement

The Supplier shall establish and maintain documented procedures to ensure that purchased products conform to specified requirements.

B.6.2 PRINCE approach

Product Descriptions would include the quality criteria for purchased products, just as they would for internal products. Purchased products would be required to pass the same quality inspections as internal products. The checking requirements would be part of authorisation of the Work Package.

This would also be a prime target for whoever carries out the assurance responsibilities defined for the Senior Supplier.

B.7   Control of Customer-supplied product (4.7)

B.7.1 Requirement

The Supplier shall establish and maintain documented procedures for the control of verification, storage and maintenance of purchaser-supplied products.

B.7.2 PRINCE Approach

Only the verification part of this requirement is addressed.

Design reviews and testing requirements for Customer-supplied products are defined as part of authorisation of the Work Package.

B.8   Product identification and traceability (4.8)

B.8.1 Requirement

Where appropriate, the Supplier shall establish and maintain documented procedures for identifying the product by suitable means from receipt and during all stages of production, delivery and installation. Where traceability is specified, there should be documented procedures to enable the identification of individual products or batches.

B.8.2 PRINCE approach

This requirement is fully satisfied through:

- Product Breakdown Structures, Product Flow Diagrams and Product Descriptions that state the types of product to be produced, how they are derived and how they may be identified

- Configuration Management procedures that identify individual items and their relationship with other items

- Change control procedures that ensure that any changes to requirements are properly authorised and reflected throughout all relevant products.

B.9 Process control (4.9)

B.9.1 Requirement

The Supplier shall identify and plan the production, installation and servicing processes that directly affect quality and shall ensure that these processes are carried out under controlled conditions. Controlled conditions shall include:

- documented procedures

- use of suitable maintained equipment and compliance with standards, etc.

- monitoring and control of process and product characteristics

- the approval of processes and equipment

- stipulating the criteria for workmanship.

B.9.2 PRINCE approach

Within a PRINCE project this requirement is partially satisfied. Product Descriptions must include:

- references to procedures, standards or working practices – that is, documented work instructions, and to special processes

- quality criteria – that is, criteria for workmanship.

B.10 Inspection and testing (4.10)

B.10.1 General

Requirement

The Supplier shall establish and maintain documented procedures for inspection and testing activities in order to verify that the specified requirements for the product are met.

PRINCE approach

The requirements of this clause are addressed in the following sub-paragraphs.

B.10.2 Receiving inspection and testing

Requirement

The Supplier shall ensure that an incoming product is not used or processed until it has been inspected or otherwise verified as conforming to specified requirements. In case of urgency, the product may be used without such inspection, provided that it has been positively identified in case it needs to be recalled and replaced.

PRINCE approach

Where a product is being received as part of a PRINCE project, then this requirement is satisfied. When the need for the incoming product has been identified, a Product Description is written that must specify the verification and testing required.

B.10.3 In-process inspection and testing

Requirement

The Supplier shall:

- inspect, test and identify products as required by the quality plan and/or documented procedures

- hold products until the required inspection and tests have been completed.

PRINCE approach

This requirement is fully satisfied. Required tests, inspections and associated procedures are specified with the Product Descriptions. The quality plan is incorporated into the Stage and Team Plans.

PRINCE recommends the Quality Review as one mechanism for checking test results. The objective of a Quality Review is to establish conformance to requirements, the results being recorded in the Follow-up Action List.

Non-conforming products are identified:

- through outstanding errors following a Quality Review

- as Off-Specifications by the Project Issue procedure.

B.10.4 Final inspection and testing

Requirement

The Supplier shall carry out all final inspection and testing in accordance with the quality plan and/or documented procedures. The quality plan and/or documented procedures shall require that all specified reviews and tests are carried out, that the results meet specified requirements, and that the associated data and documentation is available and authorised, all before the product is released to a Customer.

PRINCE approach

This requirement is partially satisfied.

The documented procedures and techniques of PRINCE, the Project Quality Plan and the Stage Quality Plans fully meet the requirement for final testing, including Customer acceptance testing. The quality records provide evidence that all checks have been carried out as specified in the quality plans.

B.11 Control of inspection, measuring and test equipment (4.11)

B.11.1 Requirement

The Supplier shall control, establish and maintain documented procedures to calibrate and maintain inspection, measuring and test equipment.

B.11.2 PRINCE approach

This requirement is not addressed, being very specific to each project.

B.12 Inspection and test status (4.12)

B.12.1 Requirement

The inspection and test status of a product shall be identified by suitable means that indicate its conformance or non-conformance with regard to inspections and tests performed. The identification of inspection and test status shall be maintained throughout production and installation.

B.12.2 PRINCE approach

This requirement is fully satisfied.

The Quality Log shows the inspection status of products. Product status is also maintained by Configuration Management.

B.13 Control of non-conforming products (4.13)

B.13.1 Requirement

The Supplier shall establish and maintain documented procedures to ensure that products not conforming to specified requirements are prevented from unintended use or installation. Controls shall provide for the identification, review and disposition of non-conforming products and for those concerned to be notified.

B.13.2 PRINCE approach

This requirement is fully satisfied.

Non-conforming products are managed under the Project Issue procedure as Off-Specifications. The decision is documented as part of the procedure, ensuring that:

- the product is identified
- the problem is evaluated
- a properly authorised decision on disposition is made
- all relevant parties are notified.

In Configuration Management, the configuration status account traces products that are affected by non-conformance.

B.14 Corrective and preventive action (4.14)

B.14.1 Requirement

The Supplier shall establish and maintain documented procedures for implementing corrective and preventive action, including:

- effective handling of customer complaints
- investigating the cause of non-conformities relating to products and quality systems
- determining the corrective action needed, and ensuring it is taken
- analysing processes, work operations, concessions, quality records, service reports and Customer complaints to try to prevent future non-conformities
- initiating preventive action and applying controls to ensure it is effective, including a management review
- implementing and recording any changes needed to documented procedures.

B.14.2 PRINCE approach

This requirement is partially addressed.

The Lessons Learned Report is gradually built up through the stages, looking at procedures that are working badly as well as those that are working well. Where possible, corrective actions are built into future Stage Plans and procedures. When the final Lessons Learned Report is presented to the Project Board at Project Closure, it is passed on to any central quality-assurance function that is empowered to take global corrective action.

B.15 Handling, storage, packaging and delivery (4.15)

B.15.1 Requirement

The Supplier shall establish and maintain documented procedures for the handling, storage, packaging and delivery of products.

B.15.2 PRINCE approach

This requirement is only partially addressed. If a Configuration Management method is in use, this will define procedures for the storage, reproduction and delivery of products.

B.16 Quality records (4.16)

B.16.1 Requirement

The Supplier shall establish and maintain documented procedures for the identification, collection, indexing, filing, storage, maintenance and disposition of quality records.

Quality records shall be maintained to demonstrate conformance to specified requirements and the effective operation of the Quality System.

All quality records must be legible, must easily be retrievable, and must be stored in such a way as to prevent deterioration or loss. Retention times should be stated and, where required, the records should be made available to the Customer.

B.16.2 PRINCE approach

The retention of quality checking documentation plus the maintenance of a Quality Log fulfil this requirement.

The feedback of progress information from the teams provides a channel for obtaining the necessary information. According to the type of project, there may be a need for other types of quality checking. PRINCE does not attempt to define these, but its planning and control structure gives a platform on which extra types of check can be built. These can be compared with the feedback and audit trail from Quality Reviews to ensure that they provide the same information. The basic need is to document any checks and keep this documentation.

The Lessons Learned Report is a vehicle to record whether the Quality System was effective or not.

B.17 Internal quality audits (4.17)

B.17.1 Requirement

The Supplier shall establish and maintain documented procedures for planning and implementing internal quality audits to verify whether quality activities and related results comply with planned arrangements and to determine the effectiveness of the Quality System.

B.17.2 PRINCE approach

This requirement is not directly addressed, but PRINCE does contain the necessary structure for it.

Internal audit responsibilities in line with this requirement can be allocated to personnel as part of the organisation structure. Such a role can monitor the quality checks in use in the project to ascertain:

- that they are being used as planned

- whether or not they are effective.

B.18 Training (4.18)

B.18.1 Requirement

The Supplier shall establish and maintain documented procedures for the identification of training needs and provide for the training of all personnel performing activities affecting quality. Appropriate records shall be maintained.

B.18.2 PRINCE approach

This requirement is not addressed.

The PRINCE framework of role descriptions, its requirement for job descriptions and the detailed Product Descriptions do, however, assist the Supplier in identifying training needs.

B.19 Servicing (4.19)

B.19.1 Requirement

Where servicing is a specified requirement, the Supplier shall establish and maintain documented procedures for performing, verifying and reporting that servicing meets the specified requirements.

B.19.2 PRINCE approach

As this activity comes within service delivery, it is not directly addressed by PRINCE, which assumes a finite project life.

B.20 Statistical techniques (4.20)

B.20.1 Requirement

The Supplier shall identify the need for statistical techniques for establishing, controlling and verifying the acceptability of process capability and product characteristics, and shall establish and maintain documented procedures to implement and control their application.

B.20.2 PRINCE approach

This requirement is not directly addressed, but data suitable for statistical analysis is produced in the Lessons Learned Report.

The option to tune and use assurance roles can assist in the monitoring and inspection requirements.

C Project Management Team roles

C.1 Project Board

The Project Board is appointed by corporate or programme management to provide overall direction and management of the project. The Project Board is accountable for the success of the project and has responsibility and authority for the project within the remit (the Project Mandate) set by corporate or programme management.

The Project Board is the project's 'voice' to the outside world and is responsible for any publicity or other dissemination of information about the project.

C.1.1 Specific responsibilities

The Project Board approves all major plans and authorises any major deviation from agreed Stage Plans. It is the authority that signs off the completion of each Stage as well as authorises the start of the next Stage. It ensures that required resources are committed and arbitrates on any conflicts within the project or negotiates a solution to any problems between the project and external bodies. In addition, it approves the appointment and responsibilities of the Project Manager and any delegation of its Project Assurance responsibilities.

The Project Board has the following responsibilities. It is a general list and will need tailoring for a specific project.

- At the beginning of the project:
  - assurance that the Project Initiation Document complies with relevant Customer standards and policies, plus any associated contract with the Supplier
  - agreement with the Project Manager on that person's responsibilities and objectives
  - confirmation with corporate or programme management of project tolerances
  - specification of external constraints on the project, such as quality assurance
  - approval of an accurate and satisfactory Project Initiation Document
  - delegation of any Project Assurance roles
  - commitment of project resources required by the next Stage Plan.

- As the project progresses:
  - provision of overall guidance and direction to the project, ensuring it remains within any specified constraints
  - review of each completed Stage and approval of progress to the next
  - review and approval of Stage Plans and any Exception Plans
  - 'ownership' of one or more of the identified project risks, as allocated at plan approval time – that is, the responsibility to monitor the risk and advise the Project Manager of any change in its status and to take action, if appropriate, to ameliorate the risk
  - approval of changes
  - compliance with corporate or programme management directives.

- At the end of the project:
  - assurance that all products have been delivered satisfactorily
  - assurance that all Acceptance Criteria have been met
  - approval of the End Project Report
  - approval of the Lessons Learned Report and the passage of this to the appropriate standards group to ensure action
  - decisions on the recommendations for follow-on actions and the passage of these to the appropriate authorities
  - arrangements, where appropriate, for a Post-Project Review
  - project closure notification to corporate or programme management.

The Project Board owns *Directing a Project (DP)*.

The Project Board is ultimately responsible for assurance that the project remains on course to deliver the desired outcome of the required quality to meet the Business Case defined in the Project Initiation Document. According to the size, complexity and risk of the project, the Project Board may decide to delegate some of this project assurance responsibility. Later in this Appendix 'Project Assurance' is defined in more detail.

One Project Board responsibility that should receive careful consideration is that of approving and funding changes. Chapter 11 on *Change Control* should be read before finalising this responsibility of approving and funding changes.

Responsibilities of specific members of the Project Board are described in the respective sections below.

C.2   Executive

The Executive is ultimately responsible for the project, supported by the Senior User and Senior Supplier. The Executive has to ensure that the project gives value for money, ensuring a cost-conscious approach to the project, balancing the demands of business, User and Supplier.

Throughout the project, the Executive 'owns' the Business Case.

C.2.1 Specific responsibilities

- ensure that a tolerance is set for the project in the Project Brief
- authorise Customer expenditure and set Stage tolerances
- approve the End Project Report and Lessons Learned Report
- brief corporate or programme management about project progress
- organise and chair Project Board Meetings
- recommend future action on the project to corporate or programme management if the project tolerance is exceeded
- approve the sending of the Project Closure Notification to corporate or programme management.

The Executive is responsible for overall business assurance of the project – that is, that it remains on target to deliver products that will achieve the expected business benefits, and the project will be completed within its agreed tolerances for budget and schedule. Business assurance covers:

- validation and monitoring of the Business Case against external events and against project progress
- keeping the project in line with Customer strategies
- monitoring project finance on behalf of the Customer
- monitoring the business risks to ensure that these are kept under control
- monitoring any Supplier and contractor payments
- monitoring changes to the Project Plan to see whether there is any impact on the needs of the business or the project Business Case
- assessing the impact of potential changes on the Business Case and Project Plan
- constraining User and Supplier excesses

- informing the project of any changes caused by a programme of which the project is part (this responsibility may be transferred if there is other Programme representation on the Project Management Team)

- monitoring stage and project progress against the agreed tolerances.

If the project warrants it, the Executive may delegate some responsibility for the above business assurance functions.

C.3   Senior User

The Senior User is responsible for the specification of the needs of all those who will use the final product(s), for User liaison with the project team, and for monitoring that the solution will meet those needs within the constraints of the Business Case in terms of quality, functionality and ease of use.

The role represents the interests of all those who will use the final product(s) of the project, those for whom the product will achieve an objective, or those who will use the product to deliver benefits. The Senior User role commits User resources and monitors products against requirements. This role may require more than one person to cover all the User interests. For the sake of effectiveness the role should not be split between too many people.

C.3.1   Specific responsibilities

- ensure the desired outcome of the project is specified

- make sure that progress towards the outcome required by the Users remains consistent from the User perspective

- promote and maintain focus on the desired project outcome

- ensure that any User resources required for the project are made available

- approve Product Descriptions for those products that act as inputs or outputs (interim or final) from the Supplier function or will affect them directly, and that the products are signed off once completed

- prioritise and contribute User opinions on Project Board decisions on whether to implement recommendations on proposed changes

- resolve User requirements and priority conflicts

- provide the User view on Follow-up Action Recommendations

- brief and advise User management on all matters concerning the project.

The assurance responsibilities of the Senior User are that:

- specification of the User's needs is accurate, complete and unambiguous

- development of the solution at all Stages is monitored to ensure that it will meet the User's needs and is progressing towards that target

- impact of potential changes is evaluated from the User point of view

- risks to the Users are constantly monitored

- testing of the product at all Stages has the appropriate User representation

- quality control procedures are used correctly to ensure products meet User requirements

- User liaison is functioning effectively.

Where the project's size, complexity or importance warrants it, the Senior User may delegate the responsibility and authority for some of the assurance responsibilities to a User assurance role.

C.4 Senior Supplier

Represents the interests of those designing, developing, facilitating, procuring, implementing (and possibly operating and maintaining) the project products. The Senior Supplier is accountable for the quality of products delivered by the Supplier(s). The Senior Supplier role must have the authority to commit or acquire Supplier resources required.

It should be noted that in some environments the Customer may share design authority or have a major say in it.

If necessary, more than one person may be required to represent the Suppliers.

C.4.1 Specific responsibilities

- Agree objectives for Supplier activities

- make sure that progress towards the outcome remains consistent from the Supplier perspective

- promote and maintain focus on the desired project outcome from the point of view of Supplier management

- ensure that the Supplier resources required for the project are made available

- approve Product Descriptions for Supplier products

- contribute Supplier opinions on Project Board decisions on whether to implement recommendations on proposed changes

- resolve Supplier requirements and priority conflicts

- arbitrate on, and ensure resolution of, any Supplier priority or resource conflicts

- brief non-technical management on Supplier aspects of the project.

The Senior Supplier is responsible for the specialist integrity of the project. The Supplier assurance role responsibilities are to:

- advise on the selection of development strategy, design and methods

- ensure that any Supplier and operating standards defined for the project are met and used to good effect

- monitor potential changes and their impact on the correctness, completeness and integrity of products against their Product Description from a Supplier perspective

- monitor any risks in the production aspects of the project

- ensure quality control procedures are used correctly, so that products adhere to requirements.

If warranted, some of this assurance responsibility may be delegated to separate Supplier assurance personnel. Depending on the particular Customer/Supplier environment of a project, the Customer may also wish to appoint people to specialist assurance roles.

C.5 Project Manager

The Project Manager has the authority to run the project on a day-to-day basis on behalf of the Project Board within the constraints laid down by the board. In a Customer/Supplier environment the Project Manager will normally come from the Customer organisation, but there will be projects where the Project Manager comes from the Supplier. A typical example would be an in-house project, where the Customer and Supplier belong to the same organisation. In the latter case, the Customer may appoint a 'Project Director' or 'Controller' to be its day-to-day liaison with the Project Manager.

The Project Manager's prime responsibility is to ensure that the project produces the required products, to the required standard of quality and within the specified constraints of time and cost. The Project Manager is also responsible for the project producing a result that is capable of achieving the benefits defined in the Business Case.

C.5.1 Specific responsibilities

- manage the production of the required products

- direct and motivate the project team

- plan and monitor the project

- agree any delegation and use of project assurance roles required by the Project Board

- produce the Project Initiation Document

- prepare Project, Stage and, if necessary, Exception Plans in conjunction with Team Managers and appointed project assurance roles, and agree them with the Project Board

- manage business and project risks, including the development of contingency plans

- liaise with programme management if the project is part of a programme

- liaise with programme management or related projects to ensure that work is neither overlooked nor duplicated

- take responsibility for overall progress and use of resources, and initiate corrective action where necessary

- be responsible for change control and any required Configuration Management

- report to the Project Board through Highlight Reports and Stage Assessments

- liaise with the Project Board or its appointed Project Assurance roles to assure the overall direction and integrity of the project

- agree technical and quality strategy with appropriate members of the Project Board

- prepare the Lessons Learned Report

- prepare any Follow-on Action Recommendations required

- prepare the End Project Report

- identify and obtain any support and advice required for the management, planning and control of the project

- be responsible for project administration

- liaise with any Suppliers or account managers.

C.6 Team Manager

The use of this role is optional. The Project Manager may find that it is beneficial to delegate the authority and responsibility for planning the creation of certain products and managing a team of specialists to produce those products. There are many reasons why it may be decided to employ this role. Some of these are the size of the project, the particular specialist skills or knowledge needed for certain products, geographical location of some team members, and the preferences of the Project Board.

The Team Manager's prime responsibility is to ensure production of those products defined by the Project Manager to an appropriate quality, in a timescale and at a cost acceptable to the Project Board. The Team Manager reports to and takes direction from the Project Manager.

The use of this role should be discussed by the Project Manager with the Project Board and, if the role is required, planned at Project Initiation time.

C.6.1 Specific responsibilities

- prepare plans for the team's work and agree these with the Project Manager
- receive authorisation from the Project Manager to create products (via a Work Package)
- manage the team
- direct, motivate, plan and monitor the team's work
- take responsibility for the progress of the team's work and use of team resources, and initiate corrective action where necessary within the constraints laid down by the Project Manager
- advise the Project Manager of any deviations from plan, recommend corrective action, and help prepare any appropriate Exception Plans
- pass back to the Project Manager products that have been completed and approved in line with the agreed Work Package requirements
- ensure all Project Issues are properly reported to the person maintaining the Issue Log
- ensure the evaluation of Project Issues that arise within the team's work and recommend action to the Project Manager
- liaise with any Project Assurance roles
- attend any Stage Assessments as directed by the Project Manager
- arrange and lead team Checkpoints
- ensure that quality controls of the team's work are planned and performed correctly
- maintain, or ensure the maintenance of, team files
- identify and advise the Project Manager of any risks associated with a Work Package
- ensure that all indentified risks are entered on the Risk Log
- manage specific risks as directed by the Project Manager.

C.7   Project Assurance

The Project Board members do not work full time on the project; therefore they place a great deal of reliance on the Project Manager. Although they receive regular reports from the Project Manager, there may always be the questions at the back of their minds, 'Are things really going as well as we are being told?', 'Are any problems being hidden from us?', 'Is the solution going to be what we want?', 'Are we suddenly going to find that the project is over budget or late?' There are other questions. The Supplier may have a quality assurance function charged with the responsibility to check that all projects are adhering to the Quality System.

All of these points mean that there is a need in the project organisation for an independent monitoring of all aspects of the project's performance and products. This is the Project Assurance function.

To cater for a small project, PRINCE starts by identifying these project assurance functions as part of the role of each Project Board member. According to the needs and desires of the Project Board, any of these assurance responsibilities can be delegated, as long as the recipients are independent of the Project Manager and the rest of the Project Management Team. Any appointed assurance jobs assure the project on behalf of one or more members of the Project Board.

It is not mandatory that all assurance roles are delegated. Each of the assurance roles that is delegated may be assigned to one individual or shared. The Project Board decides when an assurance role needs to be delegated. It may be for the entire project or only part of it. The person or persons filling an assurance role may be changed during the project at the request of the Project Board. Any use of assurance roles needs to be planned at Initiation Stage; otherwise, resource usage and costs for assurance could easily get out of control.

There is no stipulation on how many assurance roles there must be. Each Project Board role has assurance responsibilities. Again, each project should determine what support, if any, each Project Board role needs in order to achieve this assurance.

For example, the Supplier's work standards may be certificated under ISO 9001. A requirement of the certification is that there will be some form of quality assurance function, which is required to monitor the Supplier's work. Some of the Senior Supplier's assurance responsibilities may be delegated to this function. Note that they would only be delegated, the Project Board member retains accountability. Any delegation should be documented. The quality assurance could include verification by an external party that the Project Board is performing its functions correctly.

Assurance covers all interests of a project, including Business, User and Supplier.

Project assurance has to be independent of the Project Manager; therefore the Project Board cannot delegate any of its assurance responsibilities to the Project Manager.

C.7.1 Specific responsibilities

The implementation of the assurance responsibilities needs to answer the question 'What is to be assured?' A list of possibilities would include:

- maintenance of thorough liaison throughout the project between the Supplier and the Customer
- User needs and expectations are being met or managed
- risks are being controlled
- adherence to the Business Case
- constant reassessment of the value-for-money solution
- fit with the overall programme or company strategy
- the right people are being involved
- an acceptable solution is being developed
- the project remains viable
- the scope of the project is not 'creeping upwards' unnoticed
- focus on the business need is maintained
- internal and external communications are working
- applicable standards are being used
- any legislative constraints are being observed
- the needs of specialist interests (for example, security) are being observed
- adherence to quality assurance standards.

It is not enough to believe that standards will be obeyed. It is not enough to ensure that a project is well set up and justified at the outset. All the aspects listed above need to be checked throughout the project as part of ensuring that it remains consistent with, and continues to meet, a business need and that no change to the external environment affects the validity of the project.

C.8   Project Support

The provision of any Project Support on a formal basis is optional. It is driven by the needs of the individual project and Project Manager. Project Support could be in the form of advice on project management tools, guidance, administrative services such as filing, and the collection of actuals, to one or more related projects. Where set up as an official body, project support can act as a repository for lessons learned, and a central source of expertise in specialist support tools.

One support function that must be considered is that of Configuration Management. Depending on the project size and environment, there may be a need to formalise this, and it quickly becomes a task with which the Project Manager cannot cope without support. See Chapter 10 on *Configuration Management* for details of the work.

C.8.1   Specific responsibilities

The following is a suggested list of tasks:

Administration

- administer change control
- set up and maintain project files
- establish document control procedures
- compile, copy and distribute all project management products
- collect actuals data and forecasts
- update plans
- administer the Quality Review process
- administer Project Board meetings
- assist with the compilation of reports.

Advice

- specialist knowledge (for example, estimating, risk management)
- specialist tool expertise (for example, planning and control tools, risk analysis)
- specialist techniques
- standards.

Project Support Office (PSO)

The concept of a Project Support Office is one of a central pool of skilled resources to provide the roles of project support, such as clerical support, Configuration Librarians and possibly PRINCE consultants to individual projects. The overall objectives of a Project Support Office are to:

- support managers in project administration
- ensure correct and efficient use of PRINCE standards across all projects.

A Project Support Office is not essential, but can be useful:

- where resource shortages, either in numbers or skills, make it difficult to supply people to perform project administration for each current project

- where there are a number of small projects of a diverse nature that individually require only limited support from project support

- where there is a large programme, requiring co-ordination of individual projects.

A Project Support Office provides continuity of standards across all projects. The office can be the centre of expertise in the PRINCE method, any software packages used (such as planning and control software), Configuration Management and the Quality Review technique. Often, a member of the Project Support Office can handle aspects of the Project Support role for several projects. Typically, the Project Support Office role includes some or all of the following:

- operating a central filing system for several projects

- liasing with individual Project and Team Managers

- being a centre of expertise for estimating techniques

- providing expertise in the planning and control software used

- advising on the preparation of plans

- updating plans with actuals

- producing management reports

- producing multi-project reports

- keeping a historical database of how long specific activities take

- keeping track of the actual use of contingency

- analysing productivity

- providing PRINCE expertise and advice

- advising on cost/benefit analysis

- co-ordination of standards

- acting as Quality Review scribe (and even Chairperson)

D   PRINCE 2 Healthcheck

It can be very useful for an organisation to check on the correct use of PRINCE in its projects. The following set of questions forms a good basis for any such 'Healthcheck'. The questions can be the basis of a table or spreadsheet, with entries in extra columns to indicate whether and how well each element of the method is being used.

Start Up

- Was there a Project Mandate?
- Was the Project Board designed/appointed before Initiation was authorised?
- Was a Project Brief produced?
- Is the Project Brief to PRINCE 2 standards?
- Are quality expectations set?
- Has the Project Approach been defined?
- Was an Initiation Stage Plan produced?
- Was the Initiation Stage Plan approved?

Initiation

- Was the Initiation Stage formally authorised?
- Were the 'Authorising Initiation' agenda items covered?
- Is there a Project Initiation Document (PID)?
- Is the PID produced to PRINCE 2 standards?
- Are the project objectives stated?
- Have project constraints been identified?
- Is project tolerance defined?
- Are any project interdependencies stated?
- Is the project scope stated?
- Are reporting procedures, contents and freqency defined?
- Is there a Communication Plan covering both inward and outward communication needs?
- Does the PID contain the Project Plan?
- Is there a Business Case in PID?
- Are the reasons for the project given?
- Is there an Investment Appraisal or Cost/Benefit Analysis?
- Was the PID Quality Reviewed?
- Did the Project Board formally approve the PID?
- Was the Project Board committed to the process?
- Was Initiation done before work on specialist products began?
- Was there an Initiation End Stage Assessment *Authorising a Project (DP2)*?
- Was the next Stage Plan presented at the Initiation End Stage Assessment?
- Were issues affecting the PID managed effectively?
- Was formal approval to proceed to the next Stage given?

Organisation

- Is there a Project Board?

- Are any limits to the authority of the Project Board documented?

- Is it clear to whom the Project Board reports?

- Which member of the Project Board reports to senior management?

- Does the Senior User adequately represent all user areas?

- Are Project Board members contributing fully to all Mid-Stage Assessments and End Stage Assessments?

- Are Project Board members carrying out their other project duties?

- Is there a Project Manager (PM)?

- Have assurance roles been agreed?

- Has any role for Project Support been clarified?

- Does each person have a job description?

- Has each person agreed/signed their job description?

- Was the organisation agreed by the end of *Starting up a Project (SU)*?

- Is the documented version of the organisation correct?

- Is the role of the Supplier(s) clearly defined?

- Have any changes to the management team been recorded?

- Has the Project Board received training for its roles?

- Is the Team Manager role used effectively?

- Are job descriptions agreed with any late appointments?

Business Case

- Is there a Business Case?

- Are the reasons for the project clearly defined and valid?

- Is there an Investment Appraisal?

- Are figures based on defined items that can be measured?

- Is the Business Case passed down from pre-project work?

- If so, have the figures been checked out?

- Are costs based on the Project Plan or some other figures?

- Are benefits stated in terms that can be measured in the Post-Project Review?

- Have 'before' measurements been taken in order to assist comparisons in the Post-Project Review?

- Is the Business Case updated and reviewed for each End Stage Assessment?

- Who measures the impact of changes on the Business Case?

- Is the impact of changes on the Business Case assessed?

- If the project is part of a programme, is the programme's Business Case fully reflected in the project?

Risk

- Is there a Risk Log?

- Is it being kept up-to-date?

- Are risks to each plan identified, analysed and acted upon?
- Are business risks identified?
- Is a formal procedure for the mangement of risk in use?
- Is risk assessment part of each End Stage Assessment?
- Were the major risks entered in the PID?
- Have risk 'owners' been identified?
- Are risks monitored on a sufficiently regular basis?
- Is risk assessment part of each major change request assessment?
- Were risk likelihood and impact assessed?
- Have proactive risk actions been taken where necessary?
- Were any needed contingency plans prepared?
- Were all obvious risks covered?
- Were the risks and countermeasures discussed with the Project Board?
- Were appropriate countermeasures taken?
- Were risks reassessed when plans were changed?

Project Plan

- Is there a Project Plan?
- Does the Project Plan comply with PRINCE 2 requirements?
- Are planning assumptions stated?
- Does the Project Plan show the stage divisions?
- Has each risk to the plan been added to the Risk Log?
- If an end date was imposed, is it realistic?
- Was the Project Plan quality reviewed?
- Were the assurance roles involved in the review?
- Was the product-based planning technique used?
- Is there a Checklist of key products?
- Are there Product Descriptions for each major product?
- Are the Product Descriptions to the standard PRINCE format?
- Are Product Descriptions being reviewed before the start of building those products?

Stage Plan

- Is there a Stage Plan for each management Stage?
- Do Stage Plans comply with the PRINCE 2 standard?
- Is Stage tolerance defined?
- Are Stage controls identified and suitable?
- Are planning assumptions stated?
- Are Stage Plan risks identified and included in the Risk Log?
- Are Stage Plans consistent with the Project Plan?
- Is next Stage planning carried out correctly in each Stage?

- Is the quality of Stage Plans reviewed?
- Was the current Stage Plan approved?
- Is product-based planning used in Stage planning?
- Is there a Product Checklist for each Stage?
- Are there Product Descriptions for each product on the Checklist?
- Are the Product Descriptions to standard?
- Are Product Descriptions reviewed prior to the start of the build process?
- Were Team Managers/team members involved in planning?
- Did the assurance roles review the draft Stage Plan?
- Did assurance add quality checks to the draft Stage Plan?
- Did assurance add names to these quality checks?
- Is time and effort allowed for Project Management activities?
- Is time allowed for the analysis of Project Issues?
- Has a reasonable rate of staff effectiveness been chosen?
- Is the method of quality checking identified for each product?

Control
- Are checkpoints held at the frequency stated in the plan?
- What actual progress information is captured?
- Are actuals used to update the Stage Plan regularly?
- Is the update frequency commensurate with the plan size?
- Is there a record of Work Package authorisation and return?
- Are estimates collected to complete any further information?
- Are product Checklists kept up-to-date?
- Are Checkpoint Reports produced?
- Are Highlight Reports produced when stated in the plan?
- Are Highlight Reports produced to the agreed standard?
- Is the Stage Plan regularly checked against tolerances?
- Are Exception Reports used when tolerances are threatened?
- Were any required Exception Plans produced?
- Were Mid-Stage Assessments held to approve any Exception Plans?
- Do Stages complete within the agreed tolerance levels?
- Are End Stage Assessments carried out at the end of each Stage?
- Is there an End Stage Report (ESR) for each stage?
- Is the End Stage Report to standard?
- Is End Stage Assessment documentation circulated prior to the meeting?
- Is the End Stage Report accepted at the End Stage Assessment?
- Are unfinished products included in the next Stage Plan?
- Does the Project Board sign off Stages and give approval to proceed?

- Do relevant project members attend End Stage Assessments?
- Are End Stage Assessment actions recorded?

Quality

- Has the Customer specified quality expectations?
- Is there a Project Quality Plan?
- Will the Project Quality Plan achieve the Customer's expectations?
- Does the Project Quality Plan point at specific quality procedures?
- Are quality responsibilities defined in the Project Quality Plan?
- Are there Stage Quality Plans?
- Are individuals and quality methods identified in the Stage Quality Plans?
- Is there a Quality Log?
- Is the Quality Log up-to-date?
- Do the teams maintain one central Quality Log?
- Does the Project Manager get sufficient feedback to ensure quality is OK?
- Are assurance roles sufficiently involved in quality checking?
- Do the Quality File and Quality Log match?
- Is any external quality assurance function happy with its involvement?

Quality Reviews

- Has training in Quality Reviews been given to attendees?
- Have the Chairperson and reviewers been identified at stage or team planning time?
- Are products sent out before Quality Review meetings?
- Are Product Descriptions and blank error lists sent with the products?
- Are products reviewed against their Product Descriptions?
- Are products reviewed by the means stated in the Product Description?
- Is enough time planned for preparation, review and follow-up?
- Are error lists completed prior to Quality Reviews?
- Is there a Quality Review agenda for each Quality Review?
- Do reviewers unable to attend Quality Reviews send error lists?
- Do Quality Reviews generate Follow-up Action Lists?
- Are corrections signed-off by the reviewers?
- Are product authors always present?
- Are second reviews carried out if needed?
- Is there a review result for each review?

Change Control

- Is there a documented procedure for Change Control?
- Is that procedure the same as stated in the Project Plan?
- Are Project Issues recorded?
- Is there an Issue Log?

- Are Project Issues assessed regularly?
- Is the impact of Issues on the Business Case assessed?
- Is the impact of Project Issues on the Risk Log assessed?
- Are all Project Issues actioned?
- Is the status of Project Issues monitored?
- If the impact of a Project Issue exceeds tolerance, is it escalated to the Project Board?
- Are plans updated to incorporate agreed changes?
- Is a distinction made between Off-Specification and Request for Change?

Configuration Management

- Is there a formal Configuration Management method in use?
- Are products controlled once submitted to Configuration Management?
- Are products uniquely identified?
- Are relationships between products identified?
- Are products identified as complete?
- Do products have version identifiers?
- Are product records up-to-date?
- Is the accuracy of the product records checked regularly?
- Are all old versions preserved?
- Is it easy to retrieve old versions?
- Are the Configuration Management records in line with the supports requirements?
- Is the Configuration Librarian role well-defined, allocated and agreed?
- Are new records created during product-based planning?

Project Filing

- Is there a recognisable filing system?
- Is its structure documented and available?
- Does it cover management, quality and specialist products?
- Does it cater for multiple versions – for example, of plans?
- Does the filing system provide an audit trail?
- Is it easy to find things in the filing system?
- Is the filing kept up-to-date?
- Is filing responsibility clearly defined in a job description?

Index

Index

Page references shown in italics are definitions listed in the Glossary; page references shown in bold are Product Outlines.

Dear customer...

We would like to hear from you with any comments or suggestions that you have on how we can develop new products for the PRINCE2 method. We would be grateful if you take a few minutes to complete this questionnaire and send it back to us. A FREE disk containing PRINCE2 templates will be sent to all respondents.

1 First name ....

Last name ....

Name of Organisation ....

Organisation Address....................................

....

Your Occupation ....

2 What is the nature of your organisation?

☐ Consultancy/Training
☐ IT/Computing/Software
☐ Government Department/Local Authority
☐ Academic/Further Education
☐ Manufacturing
☐ Health
☐ Banking/Insurance
☐ Utilities
☐ Retail
☐ Other

3 Overall how do you rate Managing Successful Projects with **PRINCE2**?

☐ Excellent
☐ Very Good
☐ Good
☐ Fair
☐ Below Average
☐ Poor

4 What do you like most about this book?

....

5 What do you like least about this book?

....

6 How do you use this book (problem solver, tutorial, reference...)?

....

....

7 Where did you buy this book?

8 How did you hear about the **PRINCE2** Method?

☐ Training course
☐ Through work
☐ Word of mouth
☐ From CCTA
☐ On the Internet
☐ Other

9 From where else do you get information about **PRINCE2** Method?

....

10 Is there anything that we could publish to aid you in your use of **PRINCE2**?

....

....

11 What types of projects do you work on?

....

....

12 Additional comments?

....

....

....

Best Practice Customer Service Desk
CCTA
Rosebery Court
St Andrews Business Park
Norwich
NR7 0HS

Thank you for completing this questionnaire. Your free disk is on its way.